S0-BBC-323

The Food Pharmacy Guide to Good Eating

JEAN CARPER

THE FOOD PHARMACY GUIDE TO GOOD EATING

With More Than 200 Totally Healthy Recipes

BANTAM BOOKS
NEW YORK • TORONTO • LONDON • SYDNEY • AUCKLAND

THE FOOD PHARMACY GUIDE TO GOOD EATING

A Bantam Book / May 1991

Library of Congress Cataloging-in-Publication Data

Carper, Jean.
The food pharmacy guide to good eating : with more than 200 totally healthy recipes / Jean Carper.
p. cm.
Includes index.
ISBN 0-553-07285-4
1. Diet therapy. 2. Vegetarian cookery. 3. Nutrition.
4. Health. I. Title.
RM217.C37 1991
615.8′54—dc20 90-19470
CIP

Published simultaneously in the United States and Canada

Bantam Books are published by Bantam Books, a division of Bantam Doubleday Dell Publishing Group, Inc. Its trademark, consisting of the words "Bantam Books" and the portrayal of a rooster, is Registered in U.S. Patent and Trademark Office and in other countries. Marca Registrada. Bantam Books, 666 Fifth Avenue, New York, New York 10103.

PRINTED IN THE UNITED STATES OF AMERICA

BVG 0 9 8 7 6 5 4 3 2 1

Contents

List of Recipes

Appetizers, Starters, and Snacks

Soups

Salads, Relishes, and Chutneys

Vegetables and Legumes

Pizza, Pasta, and Grains

Seafood, Poultry, and Meat Main Dishes

Desserts

Breads, Muffins, Biscuits, and Crackers

Beverages

Sauces and Dressings

Acknowledgments

First, I am grateful to the physicians and researchers who have the wisdom, curiosity, and skill to pursue the investigations on which this book is based and for their willingness to share their exciting new findings with me. Next, I must thank the testers and tasters of the recipes in this book, the people who so graciously gave recipes and suggestions for improving the recipes. Foremost is Maxine Rapoport, coauthor of four cookbooks with Nina Graybill, including the best-selling *Pasta Salad Cookbook,* who generously shared her impeccable recipe-writing sense as well as many of her own recipes. Other food professionals I depended on for a number of recipes are Kenneth Juran, executive chef, Park Hyatt Hotel in Washington, D.C., and his executive sous chef, Gerard Thompson; Carol Mason, chef and cooking instructor in Washington, D.C.; Steven Raichlen, a national food writer based in Miami; and Howard Solganik, food consultant, newspaper columnist, and TV chef in Dayton, Ohio.

Then there are the many tasters who graciously consented to try the dishes I put before them. Many thanks to Pat Altobello, Lisa Berger, Ashley Barnes, Laurel Barnes, Evan Berlack, Phyllis Bonanno, Jim Boring, David Burnham, Suzanne Bywaters, Natella Carper, Robert Carper, Judy Carper, Aaron Carper, Ashley Carper, Michael Carper, Melissa Carper, Lauren Carper, Jennifer Carper, Terry Carper, Patti Carper, Daniel Carper, David Carper, Douglas Carper, Chauncey Ching, Teddie Ching, Rolf Clark, Joan Claybrook, Mary Crisp, Kathleen Drew, Susan Dweck, Jamie Fenwick, John Foldes, Daryl Glenny, Manny Goldstein, Mariana Gosnell, Nina Graybill, Ray Heverling, Jill Hickson, Scott Hickson, George Jacobs, Cynthia Johnson, Clyde and Connie Kauffman, Patricia Krause, Joan Levin, Bill Mead, Jenny Mead, Joanne Omang, Richard Pollock, David Rall, Gloria Rall, Daniel Rapoport, Leora Rosen, Norman Rosenthal, Jerilyn Ross, Jim Rutledge, Ray Shibley, Novera Herbert Spector, Judy Stevens, Ben Stevens, Lynn Stevens, Bart Stevens, Jane Stevens, Jerry

Stilkind, David Taylor, Isabel Taylor, Katie Taylor, Michael Whalen, and Lilyan Wilder.

Some of the above also gave me their favorite recipes for the book, as did many others whose names are mentioned with the recipes. I wish to thank them—and in particular, Nina Graybill, Phyllis Richman, and Lee Koromvokis.

For comments on the entire manuscript, thanks to my friend Thea Flaum.

As always I wish to express my affection and respect for my agent, Raphael Sagalyn, and my editor, Michelle Rapkin. Also my appreciation to Lisa Di Mona of the Sagalyn Literary Agency.

And a special thanks to Lynn Hill of Hill Nutrition Associates for her expert guidance.

Foreword

I do not pretend to be an expert on food, recipes, or medicine. But I do know something about powerful trends that transform society and individuals. And Jean Carper is the nation's foremost chronicler of a monumental shift toward the use of food as potent modern-day medicine that vitally affects all our lives.

In her ground-breaking book, *The Food Pharmacy,* she reported on astonishing discoveries by leading scientists of the powers of common foods to treat and prevent disease and the biological principles explaining food's medicinal properties. She told how respected professors at prestigious medical schools are prescribing onions to control cholesterol, chili peppers to fight emphysema, carrots to prevent cancer, cranberries to ward off infections, garlic to thin the blood, beans to regulate diabetes, fish to lower blood pressure, and yogurt to boost immunity. She gave the complete therapeutic possibilities of fifty-five common foods—apples through yogurt—as suggested by folklore and confirmed by current scientific studies.

In this book she carries the concept further by offering prescriptive recipes against disease, in the tradition of pharmacopoeias of the past. Thus she merges old traditions with new truths, bringing the use of food to treat and prevent disease into mainstream practice.

Of course using food as medicine is ancient. The pharmacopoeias of ancient Egypt, Babylonia, Greece, and China, as well as those of the Middle Ages, were based on food. Only in this century has society become almost exclusively dependent on manufactured pills to cure our miseries. But now that pharmaceutical model is breaking down as a panacea for today's plague of chronic diseases such as cancer, arthritis, and heart disease, and the ancient wisdom about food's medicinal powers, newly confirmed by twentieth-century scientific research, is increasingly infiltrating mainstream medicine.

Compelling new scientific evidence is thrusting us into a new age in which food is becoming a very credible medicine.

It's not surprising to see food reemerge as a therapeutic agent at this time. Nor is it coincidental that the new trend parallels another major health thrust: preventive medicine. The two are made for each other, for food is the perfect preventive medicine. Food as medicine dovetails perfectly with our continual modern-day battle against chronic disease, which is most effectively coped with by prevention, not treatment.

For a civilization wracked with chronic disease, the traditional pharmaceutical model for the most part is bankrupt. What pill does one dispense to try to forestall cancer, for example? Or arthritis? Diabetes? Thrombosis? Flooding the populace with potent drugs to try to ward off maladies that develop over many years, strike erratically, and are of uncertain origin and course would subject millions to untold hazard and expense without clear-cut knowledge of risk or benefit. Generally prophylactic drugs are too risky and are too expensive and time-consuming to develop to use as scattershot medicine to try to protect individuals from diseases that may never occur.

But food's medicinal powers mesh perfectly with the new imperative of preventive medicine. For they provide not single large jolts of curative medicine but a regular, steady regimen of low levels of nontoxic therapeutic chemicals over a lifetime. Such minute infusions of natural drugs, many scientists believe, provide cells with a shield of protection against everyday assaults, lessening the body's susceptibility to full-fledged illness in later years.

What also makes food a superior preventive medicine—and the antithesis of the current pharmaceutical model—is its potential for fighting many diseases at once. Conventional pharmacology demands one drug to combat a single disease factor. Claiming a drug can alleviate numerous disparate illnesses is a hallmark of quackery. But a single food indeed may trigger far-reaching mechanisms that help ward off seemingly unconnected diseases.

Researchers, for example, believe that fish—or certain constituents of oils in fish called omega-3 fatty acids—affect underlying biological processes that can help thwart cancer growth, high blood pressure, blood clots, psoriasis, rheumatoid arthritis, and migraine headaches. Dutch scientists have reported in the *New England Journal of Medicine* that eating only an ounce of fish a day—two or three servings a week—could cut your risk of fatal heart attack in half. Additionally, several foods, such as garlic, have been found in both animal and human studies to bolster the immune system, showing a potential for battling both a range of acute infections and chronic diseases at once.

Using food as medicine also removes some of the worry generated by modern drugs with their often frightening side effects. Food implicitly has passed a 5,000-year toxicity test, although it sometimes does possess natural toxicants as well as modern man-made ones such as pesticides, which we should do our best to eliminate. Nevertheless, food is rarely harmful even in outrageously high doses and seldom triggers life-threatening druglike reactions except in rare cases of serious allergic reactions. Everybody is already "on" food; it is hardly an unfamiliar new substance.

So why not, as some pioneering doctors suggest, simply find out how to use common food in more targeted scientific fashion? Dr. David Jenkins, a professor at the University of Toronto and leading expert on diet and blood sugar, envisions the day that foods will be prescribed to combat many specific diseases. He is already utilizing food not to cure diabetics but to regulate their blood sugar and insulin, in efforts to reduce complications. As quoted in *The Food Pharmacy,* he says: "Actually all we are doing is taking the sort of thinking understood by pharmacists for centuries and applying it to food. I mean food is a [combination therapy] drug we take every day. We should find out its pharmacological effects and direct them to our individual needs and benefits, just as we do drugs."

The economics are right, too. In a nation burdened by the overwhelming expense of chronic diseases, relief cannot come too soon. And it's a bargain to get both instant nourishment and long-term medication in one dose. In the April 15, 1988, issue of the *Journal of the American Medical Association,* two physicians compared the cost-effectiveness of treating high blood cholesterol with food, such as oat bran cereal, with treatment with a pharmaceutical drug. Both, they said, can slash cholesterol by about 20 percent. But, after calculating the cost of the two medications, the University of Maryland doctors suggested that oat bran "may be preferable as public health policy." Their reason: a lifesaving year's supply of cereal costs $249 compared with $1,412 for the common cholesterol-lowering drug cholestyramine.

Surely some of the impetus to accept food as medicine comes from a new emphasis on natural healthful foods, as well as influences from Far Eastern cultures and new scientific discoveries. But it is also intriguing that low-cost food is making a comeback as medicine at a time when we are increasingly fed up with the extravagance of our health care system.

Thus food, not drugs, is the therapeutic model in a new age of preventive medicine.

In this book Jean Carper tells you how to become a part of that trend by learning to use foods as drugs in the everlasting pursuit of staying well.

John Naisbitt, author of *Megatrends*
and coauthor with Patricia Aburdene of *Megatrends 2000*

Introduction

Medicines in Your Food

Food is definitely a drug. Every time you put food in your mouth you experience hidden pharmacological and biological reactions. Indeed, it can be a wonder drug. Food can cause your cholesterol to drop, your blood pressure to fall, your blood sugar to remain steady, your pain to disappear, your blood to resist clots.

Food can act as an anti-inflammatory agent, cancer-blocker, antidepressant, tranquilizer, diuretic, anticoagulant, painkiller, vasodilator or vasoconstrictor, antibiotic, antiviral agent.

More critically, food—because it is the most frequently consumed drug—can keep cells in continual pharmaceutical supply with armies of powerful compounds that resist assaults by malicious invaders intent on precipitating both acute and chronic diseases.

Certain foods can put more killer cells in your blood to ward off infections and cancer. Food can set certain enzymes in action to neutralize cancer-causing agents that otherwise could force their way into cell nuclei, damaging the DNA and setting the stage for cancer development. Certain foods can tell your liver's production of cholesterol to slow down, triggering mechanisms that deplete cholesterol in the bloodstream, lessening chances of dangerous plaque buildup and consequent heart attack. Certain foods can kill bacteria outright in the body or flush them away so they don't induce infections.

Foods can help ward off nausea, gas pains, headaches, arthritis, heart attack and stroke, cancer of many types, hemorrhoids, colds and influenza, diabetes, ulcers, bone diseases, dizziness, depression, gallstones, arthritis, psoriasis, constipation, and virtually any other malady you can think of.

In my book *The Food Pharmacy,* published in 1988, I explored the scientific evidence to date supporting those myriad ways foods can act as medicines. Since then research on food's pharmacological agents has exploded.

The National Cancer Institute has developed a vast new $20 million program to study the natural phytochemicals found in microscopic amounts in fruits and vegetables that experts believe inhibit cancer. At the top of the Institute's list are garlic and onions, citrus fruits, the cruciferous family, which includes cabbage, and the parsley family, which includes carrots. By 1995 Dr. Herbert Pierson, director of the Cancer Institute's program, plans to have test results from both laboratory and human studies on the cancer-preventive potential of twenty common foods.

As Dr. Pierson says, "The future is prevention, and looking for preventive agents in foods is more cost-effective than looking for new drugs." He agrees that both the government and science now "look at food as a preventive medicine of the future."

Scientists in the academic community have stepped up their research on all facets of food pharmacology. What was once a faintly questionable pursuit has now become not only respectable but prestigious, attracting leading scholars and investigators from around the world. Appearing at international conferences to discuss the merits of eating fish and using fish-oil capsules to stop the spread of breast cancer are professors of medicine at Harvard. Investigating the molecular reasons onions, grapes, and broccoli may thwart cancer are professors of medicine at the University of California. Trying to decipher the biochemical and genetic interactions that make legumes a secret weapon against cancer consumes the energies of professors of medicine at New York University. And similar pursuits by men and women of similar stature are going on at Cornell, the University of Minnesota, the University of Florida, the University of Texas, Tufts, Ohio State University, the University of Utah, the Massachusetts Institute of Technology, George Washington University, and practically any other major university you can mention.

The U.S. Department of Agriculture has teams of researchers, spread throughout the country, who constantly probe the secrets of the food pharmacy, coming up with startling new discoveries. Some examples: cinnamon stimulates insulin, vitamin E improves immunity, and fruit and nuts improve brain functioning and protect aging bones. From the numerous publications I receive, the data bases I consult, and the materials sent to me, often by researchers, it appears to me that the amount of research on food's pharmacological properties has surged at least 500 percent since I first undertook to investigate the subject in 1985.

On the following pages you will find the latest findings on the multiple ways foods can promote your health as well as information on important directions of research and new discoveries of underlying disease-fighting mechanisms that may explain how a specific food or a group of foods exerts its therapeutic benefits.

Additionally, you will find much practical advice on using the food pharmacy. After publication of *The Food Pharmacy* I was peppered with questions on radio and television and from the print media and from friends concerning practical ways to exploit food's pharmacological treasures. Is it better to eat foods raw? How can I get so much garlic into my diet? How can I eat more raw onions—one of the best ways to boost good-type HDL cholesterol? Do you have any good recipes for collard greens and kale—two super cancer-inhibiting (but unpopular) vegetables?

The Food Pharmacy Guide to Good Eating is designed to answer such questions and to meet the need for practical advice and recipes based on eating for pharmacological effects. I have selected more than 200 recipes. They come from the collections of friends and relatives as well as from cooking professionals, including chefs, food consultants, cooking instructors, and restaurant and food critics. A few recipes come from my favorite cookbooks. Many come from my own recipe files, including adaptations of recipes I have loved.

With each recipe you'll find not just the conventional prologue—what to expect from the recipe gastronomically—but also what to expect pharmacologically. Since a headnote to a recipe cannot include everything, you will also find throughout the recipe section new food pharmacy facts and advice from both scientists and culinary experts.

All of the recipes are generally low in total fat and consequently calories. If there is added fat, it almost always is highly unsaturated, usually monounsaturated vegetable fats. You will find very little saturated fat in these recipes, for I think the evidence is persuasive beyond a doubt that such dairy and meat fats in overabundance cause general havoc in the body, possibly promoting a wide range of diseases, primarily heart disease. The oil I prefer is olive oil, for good reason. (See Mediterranean Lifesaver: Olive Oil, page 32.) This does not mean you should not use other oils occasionally; my choice, as a close second, is canola oil. Flaxseed oil also appears spectacular but at this writing is of limited availability. Soybean, sesame, and walnut oils are okay sometimes. I shy away from corn, safflower, and sunflower oils, fearing their high concentrations of so-called omega-6 polyunsaturated fatty acids. (See Wonder Medicines from the Sea, page 27.)

Seafood is used liberally in the recipes. Poultry, especially white meat, is also a favorite. Red meat is used more sparingly; it is usually higher in fat, which not only raises cholesterol but appears to have other deleterious effects on the blood and cells.

You will find a few recipes that call for whole eggs. If you want to use egg substitute, that is up to you. It should make little difference in the recipe's outcome. Be aware, though, that eggs have less cholesterol than previously thought and some egg substitutes have added vegetable oils, often corn oil.

How much salt you use is also an individual decision. The evidence of salt's harm to a general population is equivocal. However, for many people with high blood pressure, excessive salt does not seem advisable, and there is considerable evidence that sodium elevates blood pressure in those genetically predisposed to it. Additionally, some new evidence is coming out from animal studies suggesting that salt may be detrimental by precipitating strokes and premature death even when it does not boost blood pressure.

Of course, since pungent foods appear to be so health-promoting, the recipes contain lots of onions, garlic, peppers, and spices. Many recipes come from other cultures—Asian, Mediterranean, Mideastern—known for their healthful cuisines. More than a few recipes naturally have a southwestern or Mexican flavor. You will also find the frequent use of curry spices, which pep up the breathing apparatus as well as the taste buds. And most of all, you will find a multitude of ways to prepare vegetables and fruits, which are surely the brightest and most numerous stars in the food pharmacy.

Important: No single food, or foods of one type, should be eaten at the exclusion of others for the purpose of preventing or treating a specific disease or maintaining health, except on the advice of your own physician, whom you should consult before starting any medical treatment or diet. The information in this book is not medical advice and is not given as medical advice. Various types of food provide known and unknown substances vital to health; thus, varying your diet is an essential part of maintaining and achieving better health.

PART ONE

Exciting New Discoveries You Need to Know About

On the Frontier with Antioxidants

Imagine that your body is slowly rotting and rusting from being exposed to oxygen. Now imagine that scientists in their labs, aware of this problem, are discovering specific bullets—many in common foods—that can disarm oxygen's damaging effects and presumably slow down the deterioration.

This is not your imagination. It is actually happening. The investigation of the detrimental health effects of oxygen reactions and the benefits of oxygen antagonists called *antioxidants* is one of the biggest scientific stories currently unfolding. It gets extravagant play in scientific journals; however, news of the discoveries rarely reaches the public. Yet such findings are of enormous consequence in our lives, particularly in choosing what we eat. For our diet, unwittingly or by intention, supplies some of the ammunition to disarm these oxygen-chemical reactions that ultimately disable and kill us.

Consider the cholesterol problem, for example. Here's a new way some researchers see it. High cholesterol may not be particularly harmful unless it undergoes extensive chemical transformation. That happens when molecules of bad-type LDL cholesterol circulating in the blood collide and chemically react with oxygen free radicals—unstable molecules created by normal metabolic processes or from outside factors like cigarette smoke, radiation, or environmental chemicals. This reaction, called *lipid peroxidation,* turns the cholesterol molecules rancid or toxic.

The theory holds that receptors jutting from cell surfaces then snag these toxic cholesterol molecules in misguided efforts to dispose of them, and suck them into cells. Eventually these cells become cholesterol-stuffed and are transformed into "foam cells" that amass against artery walls, building up fat deposits that clog arteries.

Now, what if something intervened in that plaque-depositing process so it didn't happen? What if you could even prevent the oxygen from chemically altering the cholesterol molecule in the first place so that the cholesterol did not turn toxic?

As scientists understand more about how atherosclerosis occurs—and that is not yet entirely clear—they will be able to devise new intervention strategies to interrupt the process. Lowering cholesterol so there's less of it to turn toxic is one way of saving yourself from heart disease and stroke. Another seems to be blocking the chain of events that renders cholesterol dangerous.

A possibility: call in the antioxidants. Certain compounds can help block the oxygen reaction (lipid peroxidation) that turns cholesterol toxic. Surprisingly, one of the most potent antioxidants that may help retard that arterial clogging and stiffening known as atherosclerosis turns out to be vitamin C, according to several studies, including a remarkable one by Dr. Balz Frei, a biochemist at the University of California at Berkeley.

Essentially, in laboratory tests, Dr. Frei, to his and his colleagues' astonishment, found that vitamin C completely eradicated the oxygen free radicals in blood plasma that attack LDL cholesterol molecules, turning them rancid and destructive. "Of all the antioxidants we tested, only ascorbic acid destroyed 100 percent of the radicals and totally protected the lipids [cholesterol] from oxidative harm," says Dr. Frei. As soon as vitamin C is exhausted, free radical damage to fats in the blood starts immediately, even if other antioxidants, including vitamin E, are present, he says. This makes vitamin C "much more important than anyone ever dreamed," says Dr. Frei.

The way Dr. Frei explains it, the LDL cholesterol globules exist in blood plasma, the water part of the blood, where they are vulnerable to chemical attack by the oxygen free radicals. But if enough vitamin C is present, it traps all the radicals before they can even corrupt the fatty globules. Thus the chemically altered cholesterol is not ushered into the cell membranes where it can carry on its destruction, eventually resulting in clogged arteries and heart attacks and strokes.

Vitamin C works only in the water part of the blood, Dr. Frei points out. Once a fat molecule is corrupted by free radicals and taken into the membrane of fatty cells, it is out of reach of vitamin C antioxidant capabilities. At that point fat-soluble antioxidants, such as vitamin E, must take over, doing what they can to clean up the mess by continuing to fight off the free radicals. (Dr. Frei's studies, however, show that vitamin E does not offer a perfect defense against free radicals circulating in the lipids or fat. He found that, unlike vitamin C, vitamin E wiped out only 70 percent of the radicals.)

Thus, clearly, if this theory is correct, vitamin C stands at the vanguard, in premier position to zap cardiovascular disease at the instant of its genesis.

The antioxidant muscle that both vitamin C and vitamin E can exert has been demonstrated dramatically in studies on the arteries of primates by Dr. Anthony J. Verlangieri, director of the Atherosclerosis Research Laboratories at the University of Mississippi. For six years Dr. Verlangieri observed the effects of doses of vitamins C and E on monkeys fed lard and cholesterol to give them heart disease. He found that too little vitamin C and E allowed the linings of arteries to deteriorate and become inflamed and embedded with plaque. In fact he documented that moderately high doses of both vitamins C and E slowed the progression of artery damage (atherosclerosis), and thus heart disease, by an astonishing 50 percent. Further, the vitamins caused a healing or regression of the arterial damage amounting to about 30 percent. Thus both antioxidant vitamins separately prevented and reversed heart disease in the test animal closest to humans.

Dr. Frei is convinced that modest doses of vitamin C—easily obtained from food—are crucial in curtailing arterial damage leading to heart attacks and strokes. He says that a mere 160 to 250 milligrams per day is enough to keep body tissues saturated with maximum pools of vitamin C needed to mount a 100 percent defense against the artery-destroying free radicals used in his experiments. That is two-and-a-half times the recommended dietary allowance (RDA) for nonsmokers and smokers, respectively. Smokers need the most because their bodies are constantly assaulted by floods of free radicals in cigarette smoke, says Dr. Frei.

Vitamin C is just one example of the potential power of antioxidants in food. Countless other antioxidants exist, usually in plants, and work in quite different ways to vanquish free radicals. Two other premier food antioxidants are vitamin E, concentrated in grains, seeds, and vegetable oils, and beta-carotene, a member of the carotenoid family found in deep orange fruits and vegetables and green leafy vegetables.

Vitamin E is also crucial in protecting cell membranes, says Dr. Joseph McCord, an antioxidant researcher and a leading authority on the subject at the University of South Alabama. Different antioxidants perform their execution of free radicals in various ways. Vitamin E is particularly useful because it defends the membranes of cells from becoming attacked by out-of-control free radicals. Without such defense free radicals literally tear apart cell membranes; the cell leaks its vital fluids and dies.

One of the most catastrophic events in the body is a chain reaction of oxidizing cell membranes. Dr. McCord explains how this happens. Suppose you inhale ozone from polluted air or cigarette smoke, both of which contain oxygen free radicals. If one free radical oxidizes one lipid (fat) molecule, it sets off a monumental chain reaction in which oxygen reacts with lipids, and so on indefinitely until something squelches it. Says McCord: "From this single oxidation event, a chain reaction might go on for, let's say, 2,000 molecules. But if vitamin E happens to intercept one of those chains, the reaction will stop right where it is. So if a membrane has lots of vitamin E, the chain might last for only 200 molecules. Vitamin E is like a little fire extinguisher in a cell's membrane."

Beta-carotene's antioxidant capabilities are altogether different. Beta-carotene is a pigment in dark orange fruits and vegetables and green leafy vegetables and is considered a major reason such fruits and vegetables are consistently linked to lower rates of certain cancers, notably lung cancer. Beta-carotene, among other things, can seek out and quench a particular type of free radical called *singlet oxygen.* Such singlet oxygen molecules are linked to sunlight-sensitive diseases like skin cancer.

Numerous other cousins of beta-carotene in the large carotenoid family are also antioxidants, with exotic names like lycopene and leutin. Lycopene is a red pigment found in strawberries and tomatoes, both linked to lower rates of cancer. Tomatoes are also high in leutin.

Many prominent food antioxidants being studied are of a family of plant compounds called *polyphenols;* these include quercetin, ellagic acid, caffeic acid, and ferulic acid. For example, Dr. Terrance Leighton, a professor of biochemistry and molecular biology at the University of California at Berkeley, has tested quercetin and found it "a very effective antioxidant and one of the most potent anticancer agents ever discovered." Quercetin, says Dr. Leighton, is one of the few food substances that promises to block cancer both at the earliest stage—when a single cell's genetic material is altered—and during the crucial promotional phase, when the single cell proliferates into a tumor, a period that in humans takes ten to twenty years or more.

Quercetin is most highly concentrated in yellow and red onions and shallots, but, oddly, there is none in white onions or in garlic, a close cousin of onions, Dr. Leighton has found. "It's rather amazing how much quercetin onions have; quercetin can account for up to 10 percent of an onion's dry weight," he says. "There's enough in a couple or three ounces of onions to give a pretty substantial dose." Next highest in quercetin are red grapes, then broccoli and yellow Italian (crookneck) squash.

Onion eaters have been found to have lower rates of cancer, notably stomach cancer, than non–onion eaters. Quercetin, in animals, also protects arteries and discourages blood clots. And the compound, according to lab tests, kills bacteria, inhibits viruses, and is an anti-inflammatory and anti-allergenic agent.

U.S. Department of Agriculture researchers are investigating ellagic acid, found primarily in strawberries, blackberries, raspberries, blueberries, cranberries, grapes, apples, and various nuts, including Brazil nuts and cashews. Dr. Gary Stoner, director of experimental pathology, at the Medical College of Ohio in Toledo, says ellagic acid helps block four different types of cancer-causing agents, including the mold aflatoxin and nitrosamines, a class of virulent cancer-producing compounds.

A team of researchers at Emory University School of Medicine is exploring the disease-fighting potential of glutathione, another antioxidant concentrated in green leafy vegetables, namely broccoli, parsley, and spinach. In laboratory tests glutathione can inactivate at least thirty cancer-causing agents that may damage cells, according to Dr. Dean P. Jones, associate professor of biochemistry at Emory.

Although free radicals have most extensively been investigated for their part in triggering heart disease and cancer, they have also been implicated in about sixty different diseases, including autoimmune diseases like arthritis (free radicals promote inflammation), Parkinson's disease, and cataracts.

New knowledge about the immense powers of food antioxidants in fighting disease is just emerging. But scientists think these chemicals possess an important secret as to why certain foods—notably fruits and vegetables, legumes, grains, and nuts—promote health and help ward off disease.

FOODS HIGHEST IN ANTIOXIDANT VITAMIN C
(MILLIGRAMS OF VITAMIN C PER 3½ OUNCES)

Red and green bell peppers	128
Broccoli	113
Brussels sprouts	102
Cauliflower	78
Strawberries	59
Spinach	51
Oranges	50
Cabbage	47
Grapefruit	38
Cantaloupe	33

FOODS HIGHEST IN ANTIOXIDANT VITAMIN E
(MILLIGRAMS OF VITAMIN E PER 3½ OUNCES)

Vitamin E is fat-soluble and thus concentrated in vegetable oils, nuts, and seeds, as well as legumes and brans that are fairly high in oils. Vitamin E does not occur in animal foods.

Food	Vitamin E (mg)
Nuts and Seeds:	
Sunflower seeds	52
Walnuts	22
Almonds	21
Filberts, hazelnuts	21
Cashews	11
Peanuts, roasted	11
Brazil nuts	7
Pecans	2
Brans and Legumes:	
Wheat germ	28
Soybeans, dried	20
Rice bran	15
Lima beans, dried	8
Wheat bran	8
Corn	6
Oils	
Wheat germ	250
Soybean	92
Corn	82
Sunflower	63
Safflower	38
Sesame	28
Peanut	24
Coconut	4

The Vegetarian Advantage

> *Recommendation:* Eat fruits and vegetables with abandon—at least five servings a day. Vegetarians definitely have a health advantage. But you don't have to give up meat entirely to reap the disease-fighting rewards of fruits and vegetables. Nonvegetarians, too, can help save themselves by upping their consumption of fruits and vegetables.

Nothing looks surer in the food pharmacy than the powers of fruits and vegetables to help ward off disease and prolong life. Evidence is piling up at a fast pace, confirming that fruits and vegetables are full of exotic health-promoting compounds that boost bodily defenses against disease in all kinds of ways. Undeniably vegetarians and even meat eaters who eat lots of plant foods have an impressive health advantage.

Amazingly, the first of many studies showing that vegetarians have a health edge was done in the fifth century B.C., some 2,500 years ago. According to the biblical account, Daniel implored the guard of King Nebuchadnezzar, ruler of ancient Babylon, to perform an experiment: " 'Submit us to this test for ten days. Give us only vegetables to eat and water to drink; then compare our looks with those of the young men who have lived on the food assigned by the king. . . .'

"The guard listened to what they said and tested them. . . . At the end of ten days they looked healthier and were better nourished than all the young men who had lived on the food assigned them by the king. So the guard took away the assignment of food and the wine they were to drink, and gave them only the vegetables." (Daniel 1:11–16.)

This ancient finding is echoed constantly by current research. Advice to eat more fruits and vegetables is insistent from leading physicians, investigators, and public bodies. After a massive survey of the medical evidence linking diet and disease, the National Academy of Sciences/National Research Council in 1989 issued a 747-page report, *Diet and Health,* assessing hundreds of studies. The case for fruits and vegetables was overwhelming, leading the council to a prime recommendation: "Every day eat five or more servings of a combination of vegetables and fruits, especially green and yellow vegetables and citrus fruits."

Unquestionably fruits and vegetables are full of potent chemicals with known and unknown effects on health. Scientific teams throughout the world are probing the vegetable kingdom in search of their unique compounds and combination of compounds that promote health and fight specific diseases. For example, the National Cancer Institute regularly funds such research and has developed a $20 million five-year program to analyze the cancer-fighting properties in twenty common foods, including garlic, onions, and citrus fruits. Laboratory tests in both human cell cultures and animals have demonstrated powerful abilities of chemicals from these and other fruits and vegetables to put the brakes on cancer.

Numerous dietary studies also show that eating fruits and vegetables may dramatically reduce your chances of contracting an array of health problems, including cancer, heart disease, diabetes, high blood pressure, high blood cholesterol, gallstones, kidney stones, degenerative eye diseases, and diverticular disease of the colon. To be sure, vegetarians have the best health odds, but research shows you don't have to swear off all meat to derive monumental vegetable benefits. Simply raising your intake of fruits and vegetables, studies show, may help offset some of the damage inflicted by a meat diet.

New Reasons to Eat More Fruits and Vegetables

Vegetarians Live Longer. Since 1958 doctors at Loma Linda University in California have been studying the diet–disease connection in a group of 34,000 Seventh-day Adventists, half of whom are vegetarians and also rarely smoke or drink alcohol. When the researchers account for all such factors, they still find that vegetarians within the group live about three years longer than the nonvegetarians.

More dramatic, the longevity odds soar when compared with those for typical Americans, according to Dr. Jan W. Kuzma, professor of vital statistics at Loma Linda. Dr. Kuzma finds that a thirty-five-year-old male Seventh-day Adventist, who eats a vegetarian or near-vegetarian diet, can expect to live to be eighty-two, nine years longer than a typical California white male, who is expected to reach age seventy-three. Dr. Kuzma predicts others who eat similar diets (and don't drink or smoke) could also stretch their life spans.

Vegetables Fight Cancer and Heart Disease. Seventh-day Adventists, according to the study, also are only 85 percent as likely to die of cancer and 65 to 75 percent as apt to die of coronary heart disease as other Americans. Within the group of Seventh-day Adventists, vegetarians again win out. They have lower rates of all cancers (except brain tumors and lymphomas) and of cardiovascular disease. Researchers have even identified specific plant foods that appear to protect against certain cancers and heart disease.

"Consumption of legumes and dried fruits seems markedly protective in cancer of the pancreas," says Dr. Gary Fraser, professor of epidemiology and medicine at Loma Linda's School of Medicine and head of the research project. Beta-carotene seems to help ward off colon cancer, which means carrots and green leafy vegetables such as spinach, says Dr. Fraser. Meat, beef in particular, may be a hazard for colon cancer, he notes. There was some suggestion that eating meat also predisposed to bladder cancer. On lung cancer: "We found strong protection from fruit consumption." The same was true for stomach cancer.

Extremely fascinating is the food link to cardiovascular disease revealed in the study. "When we accounted for every other factor, such as age and sex," Dr. Fraser says, "one food stands out as protective against heart disease—nuts." Those who ate nuts four times a week were about half as likely to have a fatal or nonfatal heart attack as once-a-week nut eaters. The question now, says Dr. Fraser, is what kind of nuts? "Are all nuts equal?"

He speculates the type of fat in nuts might account for the lower risk. Although nuts are high in fat—deriving 70 percent of their calories from fat—the fat is unique, he says, usually quite high in monounsaturated-type fat, the same type that dominates olive oil, known to benefit blood cholesterol and blood pressure. To find out which nuts most benefit the heart, Dr. Fraser's team plans to feed men different types of nuts and then check their blood pressure, blood fats, blood-clotting mechanisms, and other such factors.

Immune Superiority. Vegetarians have a more active immune system, according to a 1989 study at the German Cancer Research Center in Heidelberg. When researchers compared the blood of male vegetarians and meat eaters, they found that the white cells of vegetarians were twice as deadly against tumor cells as those of meat eaters. In other words, it took half the vegetarian white blood cells to kill tumor cells. Vegetarians did not have *more* white blood cells, but apparently more ferocious ones. One theory: their white blood cells may harbor more natural killer cells, or the natural killer cells may be more powerful. Vegetarians also had more carotene coursing in their veins, a vegetable substance also found (in high doses) to boost immune functioning. This new finding may be one reason vegetarians and heavy vegetable eaters have lower cancer odds.

Fruits Block Meat-Induced Cancer. So powerful are foods of the plant kingdom, it appears, they can even help counteract some of the damage inflicted by a high-meat diet. A dramatic example comes from a National Cancer Institute study that showed meat eaters who ate lots of fruits and vegetables were less likely to develop pancreatic cancer than meat eaters who skimped on fruits and vegetables.

A research team headed by Roni T. Falk recently linked the diet and life-style of people living in a region of southern Louisiana with one of the highest rates of pancreatic cancer in the nation. The area is heavily populated by Cajuns, descendants of French settlers whose diets are high in pork, mainly bacon, ham, sausage, cold cuts, and unprocessed fresh pork, usually eaten along with rice.

Indeed Cajuns who ate the most pork products and rice were more apt to develop pancreatic cancer. Those who ate a serving of pork once a day were about 70 percent more likely to have the cancer than those who ate pork less than twice a week. On the other hand, those who ate fruit or fruit juice (bananas, oranges, strawberries, canned fruits, orange juice, and apples) twice a day were only 40 percent as likely to develop the cancer as those eating fruits less than once a day. All well and good.

But what most surprised researchers was the fact that eating fruit seemed to wipe out the risk of eating too much pork. In other words, if you ate both a lot of fruit and a lot of pork you were no more at risk of pancreatic cancer than skimpy pork eaters. Why? Apparently something in the fruit counteracted the danger of eating pork. One possibility is vitamin C, highly concentrated in fruit. Further analysis did find that the amount of vitamin C intake in foods seemed to protect against cancer to the same degree as the fruit.

And there was a dose response—the more fruit consumed, the lower the cancer risk. A possible explanation for this is that vitamin C is known to help prevent formation of nitrosamines, cancer-causing agents that can arise from nitrite put into cured pork products.

In dozens of other studies it has been shown that people who eat the most vegetables and fruits have lower odds of various cancers, in particular lung, colon, stomach, throat, breast, and pancreatic cancer. For example, a couple of dozen studies find that people who eat the most foods high in carotenoids, like carrots and spinach, have about half the chances of developing lung cancer—even if they are ex-smokers.

Exactly how the plant kingdom protects against disease is unclear. Scientists are now trying to sort that out. But there is little question that your best bet for a long life and less disease is to eat more fruits and vegetables of all types.

New Fiber Mysteries

> *Recommendation:* If you're a typical American, you need to eat two or three times as much fiber as you are now eating. That means lots more fruits, vegetables, legumes, grains, and nuts.

Yes, you should eat foods full of fiber.

That's what health experts have been saying over and over until they are hoarse—and they are unquestionably right. But, amazingly, nobody really knows why fiber works or if in fact it does work.

Fiber, seemingly one of the most boring subjects, is actually one of the most exciting and most mysterious. Just when scientists think they have it figured out, some new finding throws them a curve. Fiber itself comes in maybe a hundred different shapes and sizes and chemical makeups—all of which may have varying physiological effects. Just as mysterious are the many co-travelers in high-fiber foods. In other words, maybe health benefits in high-fiber foods derive not entirely from fiber per se, but partly or wholly from other constituents that tag along with fiber.

Gone are the days when the main fiber fact you needed to know was that there are two types: soluble and insoluble. Soluble fiber, as found in apples and oat bran, supposedly lowered cholesterol. Insoluble fiber, found in grains and cereals, supposedly did not, but protected against bowel problems, including colon cancer.

Now it's been discovered that a food high in insoluble fiber like rice bran also lowers cholesterol. High-soluble-fiber starchy foods, like potatoes, may help fight cancer in strange ways. And in one of the most intriguing discoveries, fiber may relieve gastrointestinal disorders by killing off a parasite that until recently virtually nobody even blamed.

We've come a long way from the original contemplations of Denis Burkitt, the British gastroenterologist who sparked the fiber craze in the late 1970s by noting that Africans who ate a high-fiber diet were spared a multitude of Western maladies of the digestive tract.

New Reasons for Eating More High-Fiber Foods

Here are some fascinating new reasons for eating more high-fiber foods like grains, cereals, legumes, fruits, and vegetables:

The Hidden Parasite. Chronic digestive problems, striking nearly thirty million Americans, are often given the catchall diagnosis of irritable bowel syndrome. It's characterized by abdominal gas, bloating, pain, and alternating diarrhea and constipation.

Some physicians, including Dr. Burkitt, blame too little fiber in the diet for the symptoms. Now there's a surprising new rationale for that. Dr. Leo Galland, a New York internist, claims, as a result of his studies, that about half of patients with digestive complaints may be actually infected with an intestinal parasite, *Giardia lamblia,* commonly picked up from drinking contaminated water. He says antibiotics kill the parasite and cure the intestinal complaints in 90 percent of the cases.

But cellulose, an insoluble fiber in corn and wheat bran, can also destroy the parasite, according to a new discovery by physiologist Gordon J. Leitch at Atlanta's Morehouse School of Medicine. The fiber creates mucus in the gut, entrapping the parasite; it is then swept from the small intestine into the large intestine, where it cannot survive. Dr. Leitch found that gerbils fed a low-fiber diet were about twice as likely to get the parasitic infection as those fed a diet high in cellulose fiber. He says fiber in human colons would do the same thing. It's a novel and unexpected but credible new explanation for some of fiber's long-reputed powers to relieve intestinal distress. The food highest in cellulose: corn bran.

All-Bran Breakthrough. A remarkable study in 1989 by Dr. Jerome J. De Cosse, Memorial–Sloan Kettering Cancer Center, found that eating two ordinary servings (one ounce each) of Kellogg's high-fiber All-Bran cereal a day could shrink precancerous growths in the colon that often erupt into tumors. The fifty-eight patients in the study all had an inherited tendency to develop the small growths, called *polyps,* which are the foundation for tumors. If the polyps are not present, experts believe, colon cancer does not arise.

In the carefully conducted study patients ate either All-Bran or a look-alike low-fiber cereal. The All-Bran eaters took in about twenty-two grams of fiber a day; the low-fiber eaters ate twelve fiber grams, average for Americans.

Six months into the four-year study Dr. De Cosse noticed that the polyps of those eating the high-fiber diet were decreasing in size and number. By three years the shrinkage was at its peak.

Most exciting is how quickly the cereal fiber acted to slow down the progress toward this deadly cancer. That suggests it's not too late even after the initial signs of colon cancer appear to switch to a high-fiber diet, although De Cosse noted that starting early in life is preferable. What in the cereal worked? Maybe it was the fiber, says De Cosse, but it could have been other things, including a sugar called *pentose.*

Barley and Rice Bran Surprise. Barley is rich in soluble fiber, similar to that in oat bran; rice bran is high in insoluble fiber, like that in wheat bran, generally thought to have little impact on cholesterol. Nevertheless, both barley bran and rice bran—the outer coat of the kernels—lower blood cholesterol, according to new studies. In a study at the University of California at Davis, eating three daily ounces of rice bran for six weeks drove cholesterol down an average 8 percent in people with moderately high cholesterol.

At Texas A&M University Dr. Joanne Lupton found that one ounce of barley bran a day for a month also pushed cholesterol down an average 8 percent in men and women with high cholesterol (250 to 300).

How could two such different types of fiber push down cholesterol? Experts suspect in both cases that fiber is not the only or most active cholesterol-lowering agent in either barley or rice bran. "We think what suppresses cholesterol is actually a specific chemical in the oil of rice bran," says Dr. Robin Saunders, a U.S. Department of Agriculture authority. University of Wisconsin researchers say the same thing about barley. In fact they have identified specific chemicals in the oil that can lower cholesterol in animals. Interestingly, the barley oil compound is tocotrienol. It is also a formidable antioxidant.

The Phytate Phenomenon. Dr. Lilian Thompson, nutrition researcher at the University of Toronto, spends much time trying to figure out what makes high-fiber, complex-carbohydrate foods so good for you. She has a theory, too—with facts to back it up—that it's not just fiber but also so-called antinutrients that are plentiful in high-fiber foods, especially one called phytic acid or phytate.

Legumes, for example, are well documented to prevent steep rises in blood sugar, which is especially crucial for diabetics. The credit almost always goes to the soluble fiber in beans. Dr. Thompson says that's a mistake; she contends the active agent is phytate. In an experiment she removed phytate from the beans and left the fiber. The beans no longer had the ability to hold down surges of blood sugar. In fact the phytate-free legumes allowed starch to be digested more quickly, sending blood glucose levels up sharply. When Dr. Thompson restored the phytate, the beans once again kept blood sugar under control. Since the mechanism is thought to be the same for lowering cholesterol, it may be phytate, not soluble fiber in beans, that brings cholesterol down.

Phytates, present in oat bran and wheat bran, may also play a role in high-fiber foods' reputed cancer-fighting capabilities. Phytates are antioxidants, squelching cancer-promoting oxygen free radicals. Scientists at the University of Maryland have blocked cancer in animals by giving them phytate.

Agents in wheat bran have also thwarted conversion of compounds to nitrosamines, powerful cancer-causing chemicals. Even the starch in high-complex carbohydrate foods, like potatoes, can react in the intestinal tract to form anticancer agents, according to British tests.

With all this new research swirling around, perhaps it is unfair to prize a high-fiber food purely for its fiber, when other agents coincidentally found in high-fiber foods may also have potent pharmacological activity. Even so, it seems abundantly clear that high-fiber foods, for whatever reason, can help rescue you from disease and prolong your life.

Foods That Fight Strokes

Recommendation: If you are at all concerned about strokes, be sure to eat foods that contain more than 3,500 milligrams of potassium every day. That could cut your risk of stroke by 40 percent.

Amazing as it may seem, experts say that adding any one of the following foods to your daily diet could cut your chances of dying of stroke by 25 to 40 percent:

A quarter of a cantaloupe, half an avocado, a baked potato, a glass of milk, ten dried apricots, a half cup of lima beans, a five-ounce piece of salmon, a half cup of spinach or beet greens, two ounces of almonds or peanuts—or a serving of any other food rich in potassium.

Potassium seems to be a prime regulator of high blood pressure, a major cause of strokes. Adding potassium to the diet can lower blood pressure, studies show. High intakes of potassium can even help counteract the ability of salt or sodium to raise blood pressure in animals. Especially intriguing, researchers say, potassium seems to help immunize blood vessels against damage from high blood pressure, allowing cells of the blood vessel walls to function normally despite high blood pressure. Potassium even acts to thwart strokes that are unrelated to high blood pressure.

Potassium is widely distributed in roots, fruits, tubers, nuts, grains, and seeds—the forage available to our prehistoric ancestors. Early humans thrived on these high-potassium, low-sodium foods. Today we eat less than a quarter of the potassium consumed by prehistoric humans. And we are much worse off for it, says Louis Tobian, Jr., chief of the hypertension section at the University of Minnesota at Minneapolis. He urges practically everybody to "eat more potassium." He is persuaded that potassium helps prevent strokes from blood clots and hemorrhages in people with and without high blood pressure.

In exquisite studies on the brains of animals, Dr. Tobian has documented the hazard of too little potassium. In one experiment he fed rats high amounts of salt to induce high blood pressure. Then he fed some rats a high-potassium diet and others a "normal" potassium diet.

Forty percent of the rats fed the "normal" potassium diet suffered bleeding in the brain—small strokes. None of the rats on the high-potassium diet had any signs of brain hemorrhage. Tobian's theory is that the extra potassium kept artery walls elastic and able to withstand increased pressure, averting arterial rupture and bleeding and thus preventing strokes.

The evidence is impressive that potassium also protects *humans* from strokes. The first major study demonstrating this was among an elderly population in California; it was published in the *New England Journal of Medicine* in 1987. Dr. Kay-Tee Khaw, at the University of Cambridge, and Elizabeth Barrett-Connor, at the University of California at San Diego, studied the diets of 859 men and women over age fifty and their stroke rates over a twelve-year period. Those with the highest potassium diets had no strokes in that time, compared with twenty-four strokes among those eating less potassium. And there seemed to be a dose response. The more potassium, the fewer the strokes.

For example, those eating the least potassium—about 1,950 milligrams per day—were two-and-a-half times more likely to die of stroke than those eating up to 2,600 milligrams per day—which is the average among Americans. But no one died of stroke in the group that took in more than 3,500 milligrams per day.

This meant, to the amazement of researchers, that the stroke death rate fell 40 percent for every daily addition of 400 milligrams of potassium in the diet. (Incidentally, our prehistoric ancestors probably ate between 7,800 and 11,000 milligrams of potassium a day.)

Other studies confirm potassium's stroke-fighting abilities. In a study of 7,591 men of Japanese descent living in Hawaii, high-potassium diets appeared to lower the rate of fatal stroke from blood clots to the same degree as in the California study. A large-scale Norwegian study found about a 25 percent reduction in deadly strokes, primarily "bleeding" strokes from brain hemorrhage, in the highest consumers of potassium.

Japanese researchers who tracked the diets of two groups with decidedly differing intakes of potassium and sodium over a twenty-five-year period found that the population with the highest-potassium/lowest-sodium diets were much less susceptible to strokes. Some of the farmers in the study ate eight to ten apples a day, providing from 1,280 to 1,600 milligrams of potassium—a factor the researchers credited in preventing strokes.

It's probable that fruits and vegetables may harbor other compounds that could fight stroke and high blood pressure. One is vitamin C. A large-scale study in Finland documented "marked high blood pressure" among those with the lowest blood levels of vitamin C and selenium, a trace mineral concentrated in some vegetables, for example, garlic and Brazil nuts, as well as seafood.

Interestingly, a series of studies in Japan also showed that heavy seafood eaters were much less likely to die of strokes. Residents of fishing villages who eat about nine ounces of seafood daily have a 25 to 40 percent lower risk of stroke than farmers who eat only three ounces of fish a day. In Japan most strokes come from hemorrhages, in the U.S. from blood clots. Researchers theorize that the omega-3 fatty acids in seafood may modify blood factors, helping protect against stroke. Seafood is also high in potassium.

A new study by Japanese scientists at Tohoku University School of Medicine found that drinking green tea may reduce vulnerability to strokes. Their four-year study of 5,910 women over age forty found that those who drank at least five cups of green tea per day were only half as likely to have a stroke as those who drank less tea. Interestingly, the tea did not seem to reduce blood pressure, considered a common cause of stroke.

Green tea, like many vegetables and fruits, contains compounds called *phenols*. Tannin is a phenol commonly found in tea. Numerous studies have found that such phenols operate as antioxidants, helping protect cells from a variety of assaults, including possibly those leading to strokes.

Some researchers have speculated that eating more fruits and vegetables simply replaced fat in the diet, especially saturated meat fat, that could promote high blood pressure. But Dr. Frank M. Sacks, Harvard Medical School, who studied vegetarian populations in New England, says otherwise. He believes that the low blood pressure of vegetarians is "so striking" that it is most likely accounted for by active agents in fruits and vegetables that lower blood pressure.

It would be surprising if there were not several unidentified agents in foods that help protect against high blood pressure and its frequent consequence: strokes. While research determines what they are, here are some foods high in potassium, so far the best-proved antagonist of strokes. Each serving has at least 400 milligrams of potassium, providing that daily margin of safety between no stroke and a fatal stroke as shown in

Dr. Khaw's California study. Most are also low-calorie and give the most potassium for the fewest calories.

HIGH-POTASSIUM ANTISTROKE FOODS

Food	*Serving*	*Potassium (mg)*
Blackstrap molasses	1/4 cup	2,400
Potato, baked	1 medium	844
Cantaloupe	1/2 fruit	825
Avocado, Florida	1/2 fruit	742
Beet greens, cooked	1/2 cup	654
Peaches, dried	5 halves	645
Prunes, dried	10 halves	626
Tomato juice	1 cup	536
Tomatoes	1 cup	530
Yogurt, low-fat	1 cup	530
Snapper	3 1/2 ounces	522
Lima beans, dried, cooked	1/2 cup	517
Salmon	3 1/2 ounces	490
Soybeans, dried, cooked	1/2 cup	486
Swiss chard, cooked	1/2 cup	483
Apricots, dried	10 halves	482
Pumpkin seeds	2 ounces	458
Sweet potato, cooked	1/2 cup	455
Banana	1 fruit	451
Acorn squash	1/2 cup	446
Almonds	2 ounces	426
Spinach, cooked	1/2 cup	419
Herring	3 1/2 ounces	419
Milk, skim	1 cup	418
Mackerel	3 1/2 ounces	406
Peanuts	2 ounces	400

The Therapeutic Powers of Spices, Herbs, and Seasonings

The phrase "the spice of life" is not a misnomer. Since early civilization our most potent medicines have been spices and herbs, and there is increasing proof of their pharmacological effects. Here's what modern science knows about the health benefits of some common spices and herbs.

Ginger

The best studied of all spices is ginger. It has a formidable reputation in folklore as a "medicine for the stomach" and has long been proclaimed an antinausea agent, especially for preventing seasickness. And that it does. Several years ago scientists tested the theory in simulated circumstances, and ginger worked—even better than the common antinausea drug Dramamine.

But would it work in the actual tumult of ocean waves? In 1988 researchers at Odense University in Denmark came back with the answer. They accompanied eighty green naval cadets sailing on the high seas. One day out of port the investigators gave one gram of gingerroot (a scant half teaspoon ground) to one group of the rookie sailors and a placebo to another group. Then they checked for symptoms of seasickness every hour for four hours.

Sure enough, gingerroot reduced the severity of seasickness by suppressing vomiting, cold sweating, nausea, and vertigo. The most pronounced effect was control of vomiting—dampening it by 72 percent. Overall they pronounced ginger 38 percent protective against the symptoms of seasickness. The Danish scientists note that the pharmacological component in ginger that combats motion sickness is totally unknown. However, they say it takes effect within twenty-five minutes and lasts for at least four hours.

Curbing motion sickness is not ginger's only pharmacological asset. In animal tests ginger lowers blood cholesterol; in test tubes it is an antibiotic, very effective against salmonella, the bacteria that frequently contaminate eggs and chickens. (Could that account for the Chinese wisdom behind Ginger Chicken?) Ginger is a strong antioxidant, perhaps giving it some anticancer properties. In certain medical circles ginger is best recognized as a blood thinner, or anticoagulant, even in doses present in commercial jars of ginger marmalade.

Japanese scientists recently found that ginger (as well as Japanese ginseng) has antiulcer effects in animals, inhibiting stomach ulceration by more than 90 percent.

Ginger may even help patients with rheumatoid arthritis. It's been used in folk medicine to treat a variety of rheumatic disorders. Recently Dr. Krishna C. Srivastava, also at Denmark's Odense University, found that patients with rheumatoid arthritis got significant relief from rheumatic pain by eating ginger for three months. The dose: five grams (one-sixth of an ounce) per day of fresh gingerroot or between one-half gram and one-and-a-half grams (about a teaspoonful) of ginger powder daily. The ginger eaters also said they could move around better and had less swelling and morning stiffness. Dr. Srivastava found no side effects from the ginger.

Cinnamon

Dr. Richard Anderson, U.S. Department of Agriculture, is an expert on the metabolism of sugar. He suspected that certain foods might stimulate the activity of insulin and help the body process sugar more efficiently—with less insulin. That could be especially important to Type II (adult-onset) diabetics. Eating such foods might reduce their need for insulin, he figured.

When he measured insulin activity in test tubes in the presence of many foods, most had slight or no effect. But three spices and one herb actually tripled insulin activity: cinnamon, cloves, turmeric, and bay leaves. Cinnamon was the most powerful. Dr. Anderson says eating cinnamon, even in small amounts sprinkled on toast, can boost insulin activity. Thus there is pharmacological wisdom behind using cinnamon and cloves in sweets like pumpkin pie.

Rosemary

This leaf has been shown to be a potent antioxidant by Japanese scientists. They have isolated at least four compounds in rosemary that act as antioxidants. In fact two of the rosemary compounds were about four times more active than (and the two others equal to) BHT and BHA, antioxidants used in the food industry to prevent rancidity.

Thyme

In the Middle Ages thyme was used as a stimulant and an antispasmodic and was inhaled as a remedy for melancholia and epilepsy.

Today thyme is used in folk medicine to fight cold symptoms, especially as a cough medicine and expectorant. According to modern scientific tests, the herb decidedly relieves coughing. It also contains in its oil a potent antibiotic called *thymol,* which was detected by a German scientist in 1725. Largely because of the thymol, thyme acts as an expectorant that breaks up phlegm in the respiratory tract so that it can be coughed up. Thyme additionally, tests show, can help relieve muscle spasms, as medieval herbalists claimed.

Turmeric

Yellow-colored turmeric, a primary ingredient in curry powders, appears to have anticancer properties. American scientists recently noted that turmeric contains a compound called *curcumin* that is anticarcinogenic.

Indian scientists at the Cancer Research Institute, Tata Memorial Centre, Bombay, also found that turmeric neutralized certain compounds that are mutagenic—that is, they disrupt the genetic material of cells, which is the first step toward the initiation of cancer. Turmeric worked against dangerous mutagenic agents in cigarette smoke, which led the Indian scientists to speculate that the Indian people who smoke a lot and are exposed to carcinogens in the environment may be somewhat protected from cancer because they eat so much curried food that includes up to a gram or more of turmeric per day.

Anise

Used since ancient days as a licorice-type flavoring, anise was touted as a carminative—to relieve gas pains. Modern research shows anise does have such capabilities—which gives credibility to the longtime European practice of using anise liqueurs to settle upset stomachs.

Basil

Herbalists have long recommended tea brewed from this sweet, popular, spicy green leaf to relieve nausea, gas pains, and dysentery. No question, basil does relieve intestinal gas and inhibits organisms that can cause dysentery.

Fenugreek

Now commonly used in Middle Eastern spice and curry mixtures, fenugreek seeds are an ancient medicinal herb, prescribed in ancient Egypt and India as a cure-all but in particular for tuberculosis, bronchitis, and sore throat. The seed is a carminative, relieving intestinal gas. It is used in the Mideast to treat diabetes, and there is increasing evidence showing that fenugreek seeds do lower blood sugar, as well as blood cholesterol.

Peppermint

Definitely this mint is an aid to digestion, mainly because of its volatile oil, containing various forms of menthol. These compounds stimulate bile flow, promoting digestion. Peppermint stimulates the appetite; it also acts on the sphincter muscle, leading to both belching and heartburn in susceptible persons.

Sage

Adding a little sage to your meals may help ward off gas pains and even might lower a fever.

Additionally, sage and several other spices are known antioxidants that may help protect cells from numerous assaults associated with as many as sixty different diseases. In recent tests spices showing the greatest antioxidant activity against lipid peroxidation were, in order, oils of caraway, sage, cumin, rosemary, thyme, and clove.

Soy Sauce

There is something about soy sauce that may help ward off cancer. That's what researchers at the Food Research Institute at the University of Wisconsin in Madison suggest. They found that animals given soy sauce and then subjected to potent cancer-causing chemicals had fewer tumors than mice deprived of soy sauce.

"We actually went into this to confirm some work by Japanese scientists showing that soy sauce is a mutagen that predisposes cells to turn cancerous. We found just the opposite," says Dr. Michael Pariza, director of the institute. Surprised, the researchers repeated the studies twice, each time witnessing an even greater cancer-fighting effect.

In a study completed in February 1989 they found "a tremendous reduction with one particular batch of soy sauce." The mice not given soy sauce had three-and-a-half times more cancers of the forestomach than mice protected by soy sauce. "There is definitely something in soy sauce that's combating the tumors," says Dr. Pariza. "But we have no idea what it is—whether it's in the fermentation or the soybean itself."

A large-scale study in Japan several years ago did show that daily eaters of soup made from fermented soybean paste, known as *miso,* had lower rates of stomach cancer.

Wonder Medicines from the Sea

Recommendation: Eat seafood, especially fatty fishes like salmon, mackerel, sardines, and tuna, at least twice a week and more often if you can. So far no other single food has been shown to have such broad influence on health and disease.

"Eat more seafood!" is the clarion call from scientists around the world. And for good reason. Eating fish, especially deep-sea, cold-water fish high in omega-3 fatty acids, is one of your best bets for escaping numerous modern maladies, including heart disease, cancer, arthritis, psoriasis, high blood pressure, and strokes. Fish and fish oil may even slow down the spread of already existing cancer.

Here's why:

Once upon a time, eons ago, our cells existed in physiological normalcy, explains Alexander Leaf, chairman of the Department of Preventive Medicine at Harvard Medical School. Then came agriculture and modern technology and Big Macs and Mazola oil. And our cells, overwhelmed by modern fat and starved for the quieting oils of the sea, went into major malfunction.

Because of this recent "fat imbalance," our cells are continually besieged by biochemical assaults, giving rise to a rampage of chronic diseases, such as heart attacks, cancer, high blood pressure, diabetes, strokes, arthritis, and other inflammatory diseases, theorize experts.

Infusing our cells with the oil in seafood may restore that biochemical balance of old and help rid us of our modern plague. In other words, eating more fish may help prevent and relieve the symptoms of an array of diverse diseases.

What makes seafood so pharmacologically attractive is its unique type of fat or oil made up of long chains of molecules called *omega-3 fatty acids.*

These omega-3s, it is thought, help suppress the activity of bodily messengers called *prostaglandins* and leukotrienes that promote all kinds of havoc, including blood clots and inflammation. The omega-3s also have direct effects on the immune system.

Rather quickly after you eat seafood, the omega-3s enter the membranes of your cells, rendering them less stiff and more pliable—more "normal," in evolutionary terms. By regulating the activities of prostaglandins and leukotrienes, fish oil decreases blood platelet stickiness, boosts clot-dissolving mechanisms, and hampers inflammatory damage to artery walls, discouraging blood clot formation, the primary cause of heart attacks and strokes. For sure, fish oil is also an anti-inflammatory agent and probably an anticancer agent, and animal studies show it can stave off heart arrhythmias (irregular heartbeats) that are the most immediate trigger of deadly heart attacks.

New Reasons to Eat More Seafood

The evidence for the benefits of omega-3 and seafood is piling up in medical journals. Here are the new, compelling reasons to eat more seafood and get more omega-3s into your cells:

Combats Heart Disease. Most dramatic is the connection between eating more seafood and having less heart disease. A recent study by Dr. Therese Dolecek, Bowman Gray School of Medicine in Winston-Salem, North Carolina, is a striking example. Her study of 6,000 middle-aged American men discovered that those who ate the amount of omega-3s in a single one-ounce bite of mackerel or a three-ounce portion of bass every day had a 36 percent lower chance of dying of heart disease over a six-year follow-up period.

A large-scale British study reported that eating more fish could intervene to save the lives of men who had already suffered heart attacks. Eating fatty fish but twice a week reduced their odds of a future fatal heart attack by about one third over a two-year period.

Additionally, three major studies at this writing have shown that arteries did not close up as rapidly after angioplasty—a procedure to dilate clogged arteries—in patients fed fish oil. In one study the rate of reblockage was cut in half in men taking fish oil and eating a low-fat diet.

Thwarts Cancer Spread. There's evidence that fish eaters have lower rates of cancer, notably breast cancer. More dramatic: eating more fish and taking fish oil capsules may actually help halt the spread of cancer in those who already have the disease, says Dr. George Blackburn, associate professor of surgery at Harvard Medical School. Fish oil does suppress the promotion of cancer in animals. Also, Rashida Karmali, associate professor of nutrition at Rutgers University, found that fairly low doses of fish oil suppressed increased biological activity signifying developing cancer in women at highest risk of breast cancer.

Consequently Dr. Blackburn has launched a major two-year test to see if fish oil can curb the cancer spread, or metastasis, in a large group of women with breast cancer. The women in one group are instructed to eat more seafood and take low-dose supplements of fish oil for two years after breast cancer surgery. Dr. Blackburn believes the oil from fish will strengthen their immune systems, helping to destroy wandering cancer cells that may escape during surgery, as well as creating other changes hostile to cancer-cell growth. He suspects fish oil may also thwart the spread or metastasis of cancer in those with lung, pancreatic, and colon cancers.

Relieves Inflammatory Diseases. Unquestionably authorities term fish oil an anti-inflammatory agent. In some patients with rheumatoid arthritis symptoms of joint swelling, tenderness, and fatigue have diminished after taking fish oil equal to that in a daily serving of seven ounces of salmon.

Psoriasis, an inflammatory skin disease, also improves in about 30 to 60 percent of people given varying doses of fish oil, according to reports. One double-blind British study found that daily doses of fish oil—equal to that in five ounces of an oily fish like mackerel—significantly alleviated redness, scaling, and especially itching in psoriasis patients.

Fish oil has also improved the blood flow in the hands of some patients with Raynaud's disease. It has lessened the pain and frequency of migraine headaches, lowered blood pressure, and helped victims of bronchial asthma breathe better.

Contrary to popular belief, fish oil does not consistently lower blood cholesterol. It does generally reduce triglycerides, another type of blood fat linked to heart disease. Most authorities believe that fish's ability to fend off heart disease has very little to do with an impact on cholesterol. Far more important is fish oil's ability to "thin" the blood, keeping clots away.

A Delicate Balance. As research marches on, scientists have come to the crucial realization that simply dumping more omega-3 into your cells does not always suppress disease processes. What is critical is the "correct balance" of different types of fatty acids in cells. That's because omega-3 must fight for control over the cells with another type of fatty acid known as omega-6. This omega-6 type fat is concentrated in land-based foods, like corn, safflower, and sunflower oils. Animals like beef cattle fed plant foods also have lots of omega-6 in their fat.

Once inside a cell, the omega-6 and omega-3 molecules seem to battle for biochemical supremacy and control over cell activities. Because American diets usually contain about fifteen times more omega-6 than omega-3, the land-based omega-6s almost always win by virtue of sheer numbers. Thus omega-6s rule the cellular activities of most Americans most of the time.

This is exceedingly detrimental, say the experts, because too much omega-6 tends to incite cellular destruction, leading to numerous disease symptoms. The omega-6 tends to trigger overproduction of overactive prostaglandins and leukotrienes that carry out destructive deeds, promoting events like inflammation and inappropriate blood clotting. Conversely, omega-3s put the brakes on such rampages caused by omega-6s. If cells are short on omega-3, the omega-6s are free to carry out destructive disease-promoting missions with less restraint.

Thus it's important both to cut back on foods with omega-6 and to eat more seafood with omega-3, says Dr. William Lands, professor of biological chemistry at the University of Illinois at Chicago and a pioneer in fish oil research. If you don't, you simply cancel out fish's benefits. For example, Dr. Jay Whelan, a researcher at Cornell University, says that if you eat a big slab of salmon along with a salad doused in corn oil, you wipe out some of the benefits of the fish. (For foods highest in omega-3s, see page 268; for oils highest in omega-6s, see page 37.)

Nobody knows for sure how much omega-3 you must eat to keep fatty acids in the proper balance needed to counter the hazardous effects of omega-6. Dr. Blackburn of Harvard thinks the best balance is equal amounts of each. That means that if you eat 30 percent of your calories in fat, as U.S. health authorities recommend, 5 percent should be from land-based omega-6 and 5 percent from marine-type omega-3. The other 20 percent comes from a combination of saturated animal-type fat and monounsaturated fats, the type concentrated in olive oil.

To meet that quota a person consuming 2,000 calories a day should eat about five ounces of fish every day. If this sounds like a lot, it is still far less than many populations eat, including the Japanese, who typically consume nine ounces of seafood a day.

Generally, to help stave off heart disease, authorities recommend at least two servings of fish a week. But you may need more, depending on the rest of your diet and the current state of your health.

To what extent fish and its oil can cure and treat disease is yet unknown. Certainly it appears potent against heart disease. In the British study only small amounts of fish (twice a week) reduced death risk by one third in the amazingly short period of two years.

But most experts think the more profound benefits of eating omega-3s lie in *preventing*, not necessarily *curing*, disease. Several experts, including Drs. Leaf and Lands, think regular, small bits of fish oil in the diet over the years are likely to thwart the constant assaults that turn into full-blown disease. That's one reason they, along with virtually all other experts, urge people to eat more fish regularly. It promises to be the best dietary insurance against a variety of chronic diseases.

Nonseafood Omega-3

You can also get some omega-3 from plant foods. A few terrestrial edibles contain considerable amounts of omega-3 fatty acids—notably, English walnuts, flaxseed, and a green leafy plant called *purslane* that grows wild in the U.S. and is cultivated and used in cooking in France, Greece, and around the Mediterranean, where heart disease and cancer rates are low. Soybeans also contain omega-3.

Scientists at Cornell, however, find that the short-chain omega-3 in plants is less powerful than the long-chain marine-type omega-3 in suppressing destructive prostaglandin and leukotriene activity in the body. Nevertheless, recent studies at the U.S. Department of Agriculture showed that the body can convert some of the plant-type omega-3 into the long-chain seafood-type omega-3. "Think of it this way: the body can naturally make its own fish oil . . . from soybean oil," said Edward A. Emken, USDA chemist who led the research. In Dr. Emken's tests about 20 to 25 percent of the soybean omega-3 was converted to seafood-type omega-3.

Mediterranean Lifesaver: Olive Oil

Recommendation: Do as many experts do—substitute olive oil for other fats, especially if you're concerned about heart disease. But that doesn't mean exclusively. Other excellent-health choices: canola oil and flaxseed oil. Go easy on corn, safflower, and sunflower oils. Important: restrict all fats, including oils.

It's scant surprise to people who live around the Mediterranean Sea that olive oil is emerging as one of the superstars in fighting disease. After all, numerous studies find that Italians, Greeks, and in particular citizens of Crete, who are said to drink olive oil, have lower death rates from heart disease (about half that of Americans) and cancer. Yet, oddly, they eat as much fat as we do—about 40 percent of calories in fat. The big difference: their fat calories come primarily from olive oil, 77 percent of which is monounsaturated fat.

A decided advantage of monounsaturated-type fat is that it can lower blood cholesterol without lowering the beneficial HDL-type cholesterol. Polyunsaturated fats like corn and safflower oils are unfortunately indiscriminate; they typically lower both good HDL and bad LDL cholesterol. Since Dr. Scott Grundy, a leading cholesterol researcher at the University of Texas Health Science Center at Dallas, made that crucial discovery a few years ago, olive oil has displayed ever more of its fascinating pharmacological tricks.

New Reasons to Eat Olive Oil

Down Goes Blood Pressure. Several studies now confirm early clues that olive oil can lower both systolic (higher number) and diastolic blood pressure. Dr. Stephen Fortmann, Stanford Medical School, analyzed the intake of monounsaturated fats and the blood pressure readings of a group of seventy-six men ages thirty to fifty-five. He discovered that systolic blood pressure fell by three quarters of a point and diastolic by half a point for every gram of monounsaturated fat the men ate. That would mean that three tablespoons of olive oil a day might depress systolic pressure by 9.4 points and diastolic by 6.3 points.

Helping clinch the case is a major analysis of the diets of nearly 5,000 Italians in nine communities, published in the *Journal of the American Medical Association.* As anticipated, those who ate the most olive oil had lower cholesterol. But the big news from the study was that their blood pressure was also lower by three or four points, with the main reduction in systolic blood pressure. Enthusiastic male olive oil eaters, but not women, also showed lower diastolic readings.

Olive oil can even lower blood pressure in people eating a high-fat diet—40 percent of calories from fat. That's what Dutch researchers discovered when they put twenty-three subjects with normal blood pressure on a high-fat diet, most of it coming from olive oil. Their blood pressure fell 2.7 systolic and 4.4 diastolic points. It dropped similarly in those on a low-fat, high-carbohydrate diet.

Blood pressure went up in subjects eating lots of saturated animal fats, as is typical. In the Italian study, for example, eating butter pushed up blood pressure.

Olive Oil Zaps Cholesterol. In reducing cholesterol, a high-fat olive-oil diet outstripped the usual low-fat diet in another study by researchers at the University of Nijmegen in the Netherlands. For thirty-six days half of a group of forty-eight healthy individuals ate a high-fiber, low-fat diet (22 percent of calories from fat). The other half ate a high-fat diet (41 percent of calories from fat), most of it from olive oil. The cholesterol of the low-fat dieters dropped an average seventeen points. But the cholesterol fell twenty points in the olive-oil eaters. Also crucial, the desirable HDL cholesterol, thought to ward off heart disease, sank in the low-fat dieters but not in the olive-oil group.

Blood Sugar Regulator. The large-scale Italian survey also showed that those eating the most olive oil had significantly lower blood glucose. This confirms what Dr. Grundy found in a small study of ten patients with Type II (adult-onset) diabetes. For twenty-eight days they ate a high-carbohydrate, low-fat diet and then switched for twenty-eight days to a diet high in fat (50 percent of calories from fat), most of it from olive oil's monounsaturated fats. On the high-olive-oil-type-fat diet the patients had lower LDL (bad-type) blood cholesterol, higher good-type HDL cholesterol—and lower blood sugar levels, which meant they required less insulin.

An Antioxidant Surprise. One of the most exciting new findings about olive oil is that it has potent antioxidant activity that appears to inhibit that awful process called lipid peroxidation that makes LDL cholesterol in the blood so dangerous. Such oxidation of fats is believed to be the first step in triggering a chain of events causing buildup of plaque on artery walls, subsequent arterial clogging, and heart attacks. Thus olive oil's remarkable antioxidant powers may help explain its abilities to ward off heart disease.

Pioneering research by Dr. Daniel Steinberg and coworkers at the University of California in San Diego shows that LDL cholesterol from animals fed monounsaturated oil is "remarkably resistant" to becoming oxidized. In fact only one third to one fourth as much LDL cholesterol from rabbits fed monounsaturated oil became oxidized as LDL from rabbits fed regular safflower oil, low in monounsaturated fat.

Other research reveals at least two antioxidants in olive oil—oleic and palmitoleic fatty acids. The discovery, made by scientists at London's United Medical School, identified oleic acid as olive oil's most potent antioxidant. Nearly all olive oil's monounsaturated fat is oleic acid. Sure enough, when researchers at the Medical Center of Athens, Greece, recently analyzed the blood of seventy-six boys in Crete, who consume lots of olive oil, they detected extremely high levels of oleic acid circulating in their arteries. Crete is known for its extremely low rate of heart disease. The bottom line: highly monounsaturated fats like olive oil appear to help block LDL cholesterol from becoming capable of destroying arteries.

Olive oil's antioxidant capabilities could also be expected to inhibit development of cancer and numerous other diseases, even aging, promoted by destructive oxygen free radicals. Other oils high in antioxidant oleic acid are canola, peanut, walnut, and avocado. (This is good news for avocado lovers. Most of the fat in an avocado is monounsaturated, and 95 percent of that is made up of antioxidant oleic acid.)

Research on animals turns up even more surprising clues about how olive oil may thwart heart disease. In both rabbits and rats olive oil's protection was not limited to changes in blood and blood cholesterol. Independently the oil induced beneficial changes in the aorta, the heart's main arterial trunk. In rats, for example, olive oil stimulated production in the aorta of a hormonelike substance called *prostacyclin,* one of the "good guys" in squelching disease at the cellular level. Increased prostacyclin lowers blood pressure.

A Final Good Word About Olive Oil. "There's only one fat that's safe to eat—olive oil," contends Dr. Harry Demopolous. But then, you might expect him to say that since he's of Greek heritage and grew up eating olive oil. But he has also spent thirty years studying the ravaging effects of oxygen free radicals and their ability to turn oils rancid. When you eat rancid oils, he says, you infuse your body with destructive free radicals that create chain reactions, breeding more free radicals to attack your cells. Of all the oils, olive oil, because it is so concentrated in monounsaturated fatty acids, is least likely to turn rancid and destructive, he says. On the other hand, most likely to become rancid are oils high in polyunsaturated fatty acids, like corn, safflower, and sunflower.

Still, all this does not mean you should overdose on olive oil. Like other oils, it is 100 percent fat and thus has the same number of calories as other fats, 120 per tablespoon. So overdoing it can add unwanted pounds just as other fats do, leading to other health problems. Best advice is to substitute olive oil for both saturated animal fats, such as lard and butter, and other vegetable oils like corn, safflower, and soybean. And to eat less of all of them.

The Health Scoop on Other Oils

New knowledge about the chemistry of oils and their impact at the cellular level is making judgments about the health consequences of all oils exceedingly complex. Oil's constituents, once they enter cell membranes, exercise unimagined powers over cell functions, discouraging or encouraging disease processes.

New research tries to tease out not just the physiological effects of single types of fatty acids in oils but also their interactions within cells. Such a "balance of power" among fatty acids in cells—the chains of molecules that make up a fat or oil—appears to be a big determinant of whether you are healthy or ill.

Cheers for Canola and Flaxseed Oils. As a result of such research, new oils, notably canola (rapeseed) oil, rice bran oil, and the mighty flaxseed oil—are coming on strong, backed by substantial scientific claims for their health-promoting properties. For example, little-known flaxseed oil is popular with cancer researchers because in addition to other health-boosting qualities it contains anticancer agents, lignans. Other health experts praise flax oil, pressed from flaxseed, because it is nearly 60 percent omega-3 fatty acids, similar to the amazing oily stuff in seafood that scientists think helps protect cells from a multitude of diseases. Flaxseed, at this writing, is found in health food stores. Canola oil is sold in health food stores and in supermarkets—a popular brand is Puritan.

Questions About Peanut and Soy Oils. Both soybean oil and peanut oil seem poised in scientific limbo, with some good points, some bad ones. Soybean oil has some omega-3-type oil, which is a plus, but lots of omega-6s, which is a minus. Peanut oil is high in favored monounsaturated fat but is still controversial. Dr. Grundy doesn't like it because studies found it detrimental to the arteries of monkeys. But other experts, including one who did some of the negative studies, pronounce it okay, pointing out it does not seem to trigger high heart disease among Orientals who use it frequently.

Doubts About Corn, Safflower, and Sunflower Oils. The spotlight of scientific acclaim is definitely dimming on such highly polyunsaturated oils as corn, safflower, and sunflower. As one expert says, "I think we oversold these oils." The shine is off corn oil, especially because in animals it lowers immunity and enhances cancer. Corn oil's most obvious fault is its high concentration of omega-6 fatty acids and absence of omega-3s. Ditto sunflower and safflower oils.

Such a skewed ratio in favor of omega-6 alarms many authorities. Omega-6, they say, incites cellular activities leading to lowered immunity, inflammation, blood clots, deadly heart arrhythmias, cancer, and other disasters, whereas omega-3s cool down disease processes. When omega-6s so outnumber omega-3s within cells, theory goes, the destructive omega-6s have free rein to go on their cellular rampages.

Some authorities believe that, unfortunately, our cells are ruled and doomed by too much omega-6 and that most of it comes from an overconsumption of corn oil and similar oils.

TYPES OF FATTY ACIDS IN OILS (IN PERCENTAGES)

Oil	Saturated	Mono-unsaturated	Polyunsaturated Omega-6	Polyunsaturated Omega-3
Flax	9	18	16	57
Pumpkin seed	9	34	42	15
Canola	6	62	22	10
Soy	15	24	54	7
Walnut	16	28	51	5
Olive (extra virgin)	14	77	8	1
Peanut	18	49	33	
Corn	13	25	61	1
Safflower, regular	10	13	77	
Sesame	13	46	41	
Sunflower, regular	11	20	69	

Source: U.S. Department of Agriculture

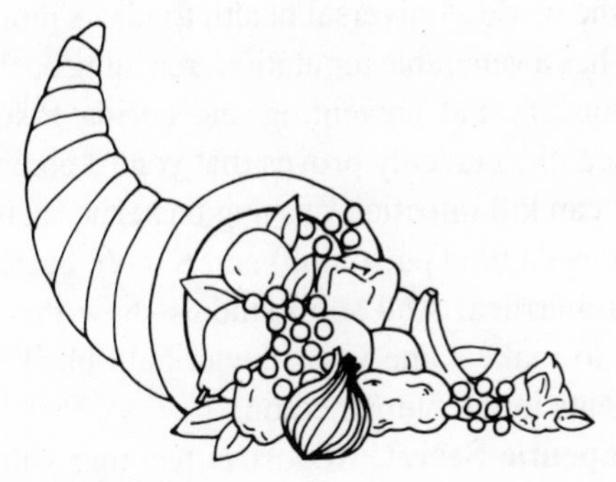

Yogurt: An Ancient Medicine Looks Better Than Ever

Recommendation: Eat yogurt regularly, especially if you are prone to upset stomach, infectious diarrhea, ulcers, vaginal yeast infections, or an "allergy" to milk (lactose intolerance).

The active bacteria in yogurt can often help correct what is wrong in the stomach and colon, may boost immunity, and may have other beneficial long-term effects, even perhaps reducing the risk of colon cancer.

Yogurt, one of the world's universal health foods, is more than just tangy, thickened milk. It has a venerable reputation, reaching back to biblical days, for settling the stomach and preventing and curing gastrointestinal maladies. Modern research decidedly proves that yogurt contains several natural antibiotics that can kill infection-causing bacteria, including salmonella (the cause of salmonella food poisoning) and *E. coli*, bacteria often responsible for traveler's diarrhea. And solid studies show that the acidophilus-type culture used to make some yogurts can help block the activation of cancer-causing agents in the human colon.

Yogurt's Therapeutic Secret. Yogurt is teeming with quadrillions of living bacteria. It is the quantity and type of bacterial cultures and strains in yogurt that create both its distinctive tangy taste and powers against disease. In the U.S. manufacturers must make yogurt by adding two cultures: *Lactobacillus bulgaricus* and *Streptococcus thermopolis;* plus any others of their choice. Occasionally companies add acidophilus culture, one of the most health-promoting.

The bacteria convert milk into yogurt by the process of fermentation. When subjected to a warm temperature, the microbes multiply rapidly, causing the milk protein to coagulate and thicken. The organisms even continue to multiply in the warm environment of the stomach and intestines. During fermentation the bacteria create numerous chemical by-products, such as lactic acid, that also fight disease.

New Reasons to Eat Yogurt

Ulcer Fighter. As modern science discovers strange new causes of age-old diseases, foods, like yogurt, emerge with unexpected powers to cure and prevent such maladies. For example, who a few years ago would have dreamed that stomach and duodenal ulcers may be partly or entirely due to an infection that promotes stomach acid damage—and that if you cure the basic infection, you are more likely to get rid of the ulcer? Yet that's what physicians are finding. They are also finding that yogurt kills the particular bacterium, now called *Helicobacter pylori* (formerly named *Campylobacter pylori*), incriminated in both ulcers and gastritis, an inflammation of the stomach lining.

According to new studies, 95 percent of all people with duodenal ulcers are infected with *H. pylori*. So are almost three quarters of sufferers with stomach ulcers and about half of those with gastritis. Some doctors now prescribe antibiotics to destroy the bacteria, promote healing, and prevent recurrence of the ulcer.

"Yogurt is an antibiotic that can do the same thing," says Dr. Jean-Michel Antoine, an adviser on nutrition and toxicology at the BSN Groupe in Paris. When he and colleagues put the *H. pylori* bacteria in test tubes with yogurt, all the bacteria died in thirty minutes. The question: does yogurt hang around the stomach long enough to zap the ulcer-promoting bacteria? "Yes," says Dr. Antoine. "Experiments show that when you eat two cups of yogurt, about half ordinarily stays in the stomach for forty minutes. Since *H. pylori* pathogens are killed in thirty minutes, that's long enough for the yogurt to destroy the bacteria," he says. The assassin is probably the *L. bulgaricus* culture in yogurt, he adds.

This new research confirms animal studies of several years ago, showing that mice that ate yogurt were less likely to develop ulcers.

Cure for Vaginitis. Score points for another folk remedy. For years yogurt has been used as a folk treatment for vaginitis, a recurring candida, or "yeast" infection. But the medical community was skeptical. Now a controlled study by Dr. Eileen Hilton, an infectious disease specialist at Long

Island Jewish Medical Center in New York, shows that eating yogurt does indeed ward off the vaginal infections.

In fact eating one cup of yogurt a day reduced the incidence of vaginitis threefold in a group of women susceptible to the infection. Whereas the women ordinarily had three vaginitis episodes in a six-month period, they had only one or none when eating plain yogurt. Dr. Hilton called the results "dramatic." She says studies in Europe show the same thing.

However, the therapeutic culture in yogurt that fights vaginitis is *Lactobacillus acidophilus*—a culture that is not required in yogurts made in the U.S. Some companies do add it. The yogurt used in the study that proved so effective is the Colombo brand, sold mostly on the East Coast. Dr. Hilton's analyses found that all varieties of this brand contained acidophilus. Some large manufacturers and many smaller yogurt manufacturers also include *L. acidophilus,* which they may or may not note on the label. If you aren't sure whether yogurt contains the *L. acidophilus* culture, try making your own yogurt using an acidophilus culture, available at health food stores, Dr. Hilton suggests.

Immunity Booster. Exciting new human studies in Italy confirm animal and test-tube studies showing that yogurt can boost immune functioning, meaning that yogurt may have broader powers than suspected in broadly combating disease. Dr. Claudio DeSimone, an immunologist at the University of Rome, has found that eating yogurt boosted blood levels of gamma interferon in a group of volunteers.

Dr. DeSimone first determined that the group had similar levels of gamma interferon, a component of the immune system that rallies killer cells to fight off infections and possible cancer. Half of the group then ate about five cups of yogurt a day for four weeks. Half ate no yogurt. At the end of the test the yogurt eaters had about two-and-a-half times more disease-fighting gamma interferon in their blood.

Although DeSimone used large amounts of yogurt in his study, experts say smaller amounts of yogurt would be expected to stimulate immune functioning to a lesser degree. DeSimone credits *L. bulgaricus* in yogurt for the medical job. This particular culture is required in all U.S. yogurts and is commonly used around the world to make yogurt.

Lactose Intolerance. About 70 percent of the world's population cannot drink milk or use dairy products because they lack the lactose enzyme needed to properly digest milk sugars, or lactose; thus drinking milk inflicts diarrhea, bloating, flatulence, nausea, and abdominal pain, a condition known as *lactose intolerance.* But such people can almost always eat yogurt with no ill effects—a fact pinned down by new research.

Studies at the University of Minnesota by Dr. Dennis Savaino demonstrate that yogurt reduces problems of lactose malabsorption by 50 to 100 percent in most lactose-intolerant people. Once again the active agent is *L. bulgaricus* bacteria that reportedly chew up the offending lactose in the milk. In Dr. Savaino's tests neither buttermilk nor acidophilus milk, both lacking *L. bulgaricus,* was safe to drink for people with lactose intolerance. Nor were many frozen yogurts on the market. Although freezing per se does not destroy the cultures, some manufacturers repasteurize yogurt before freezing, destroying the protective *L. bulgaricus* and other cultures.

New research also suggests that yogurt may help fight dental caries and enhance absorption of calcium in the diet.

No question, modern science is making this age-old medicine look better than at any time in its long history.

Hooray for the Hot Stuff!

Recommendation: Eat some garlic and onion every day. The bulbs contain chemicals that may help ward off numerous ills, including cardiovascular disease, diabetes, infections, and cancer. Also eat more peppers, especially the fiery-hot ones, if you are vulnerable to lung or respiratory problems. All three foods are highly recommended for smokers and ex-smokers.

Listen to your ancestors. Listen to modern science. If there is a single bit of dietary advice that can boost your defenses against disease easily, quickly, and safely, it is: eat more onions, garlic, and peppers!

The ancient reputation of these pungent foods as disease combatants is formidable and gaining credibility daily in scientific circles throughout the world. By finding ways to put garlic, onions, and peppers into your diet, you supply your body with regular infusions of known and unknown compounds that protect cells from regular assaults that can result in numerous diseases, such as infections, cardiovascular disease, and cancer.

Since the beginning of civilization humankind has used garlic, onions, and peppers as natural medicines. The scientific validity behind that practice is becoming clear.

In tests on humans garlic has been found to lower cholesterol; raise good-type HDL cholesterol; lower blood pressure; produce more NK (natural killer) cells in the blood, cells that help fight off infections and tumors; inhibit blood platelet stickiness, reducing the risk of blood clots; destroy infection-causing bacteria and viruses; cure encephalitis; and reduce the risk of certain cancers.

Onions, too, can dramatically boost good-type HDL cholesterol (when raw), lower total cholesterol even in people eating high-fat foods, rev up the blood-clot-dissolving activity, help control blood sugar, kill infection-causing bacteria, act as a decongestant, and reduce cancer odds.

Peppers seem to be God's gift to the lungs. In ancient Chinese traditional medicine hot peppers were the drug of choice for respiratory problems. They contain capsaicin, the stuff that provides their bite and also helps lungs function better, according to Dr. Irwin Ziment, professor of medicine and a pulmonary expert at the University of California at Los Angeles.

New Reasons to Eat Onions, Garlic, and Peppers

Anticancer Bulbs. National Cancer Institute researchers have found that people in Shandong province of China, known for its high stomach cancer rate, have less cancer the more garlic and onions they eat. Chinese who eat at least a daily total of three ounces of garlic, onions, scallions, and leeks are only 40 percent as likely to develop stomach cancer as those who eat only an ounce of the allium vegetables daily. In other words, those who skimped on eating garlic and onions were two-and-a-half times more vulnerable to stomach cancer. One-half cup of raw onions or thirty cloves of garlic each weigh about three ounces.

This is the first well-controlled study documenting the bulbs' anticancer powers in humans, and it confirms studies showing that onion and garlic extracts suppress formation and spread of tumors in animals, according to William Blott, Ph.D., epidemiologist and biostatistician at the National Cancer Institute.

Garlic Improves the Blood. New research is closing in on garlic's mechanisms for favorably modifying the blood, particularly blood-clotting factors that help stave off blood clots—the immediate cause of most heart attacks and strokes.

At Tulane University Dr. Krishna Agrawal, professor of pharmacology, has traced the biochemical pathway by which allicin—one of the odoriferous compounds in raw garlic—stops blood platelets from clumping together to help form blood clots. Infinitesimal amounts of allicin from both raw garlic and synthetic allicin halted a specific enzyme from instructing platelets to stick together. Aspirin also "thins" the blood, but by working on a different enzyme. Like aspirin, garlic's allicin would be expected to be anti-inflammatory, says Dr. Agrawal, confirming folklore practices using garlic to curb inflammation and pain. Since the amounts of allicin needed to block platelet aggregation are so small, Dr. Agrawal says eating raw garlic probably has beneficial effects on the blood. But if you cook garlic, the allicin is destroyed.

However, other research by Drs. Amar Makheja and John M. Bailey, at George Washington University School of Medicine, has identified another onion-garlic chemical called *adenosine* as the primary blocker of platelet clumping in allium vegetables. They found that 46 percent of such antiplatelet activity was due to adenosine. The good news here is that adenosine is not destroyed by cooking. Thus cooked garlic and onions, as well as raw ones, can help "thin" the blood, warding off clots, they say.

German researchers at the University of Heidelberg have found that garlic acts to ward off clots in another way. They gave dried garlic to twenty patients with high cholesterol and other blood fats. After four weeks of garlic eating the patients' blood levels of fibrinogen—an important protein that forms the basis for blood clots—went down. The famous Framingham (Massachusetts) Heart Study has noted that high fibrinogen is a prominent risk factor for heart disease—as dangerous as high blood pressure and high cholesterol. The German tests also found that garlic pushed down blood cholesterol levels by 10 percent and reduced both systolic and diastolic blood pressure.

New Onion Power. Dr. Victor Gurewich, professor of medicine at Tufts School of Medicine, advises all his patients with coronary heart disease or high cholesterol to eat more onions. He has found raw onions boost good HDL-type cholesterol by an average of 30 percent. Even cooked, he finds onions help thin the blood and rev up the fibrinolytic system that wards off blood clots.

Now researchers at the University of California at Berkeley have identified a compound in onions that may be partly responsible for those benefits—plus more. It's quercetin, a powerful antioxidant and anticancer agent. Yellow and red onions and shallots have higher concentrations of quercetin than any other food. White onions, however, have none.

Not only does quercetin possess all the powers of an antioxidant, says researcher Dr. Terrance Leighton, but it has another critical role. It can shut off the growth control switch that allows cancer cells to go berserk and start wildly reproducing. Dr. Leighton explains that a principal way cancer cells escape ordinary controls and grow abnormally is by activating a substance called *protein kinase C*. But quercetin blocks this activation, squelching release of protein kinase C.

Thus, with quercetin in your system, your cells are much less likely to be turned on to cancer. Incidentally, eating a high-animal-fat diet helps switch on the devastating protein kinase C switch. Dr. Leighton speculates this may be one reason people eating lots of animal fat tend toward certain cancers, especially of the colon. But the procancer activity of fatty meat may be blunted by the presence of quercetin from vegetables, primarily onions, he theorizes. Cooking does not destroy the quercetin, so cooked onions are just as good in this respect as raw ones.

Bronchitis Preventive. UCLA's Dr. Ziment advises his patients with chronic bronchitis and emphysema to eat pungent foods, including garlic, onion, and hot peppers, at least three times a week to help keep airway passages open and clear. In surveys among Hispanic populations he has also found that eating lots of hot, spicy foods lowers the chances of developing these smoking-related lung diseases. Dr. Ziment attributes the therapeutic benefit to capsaicin in the hot foods, the compound that gives peppers their fire.

There's new evidence giving Dr. Ziment's advice added validity. In British tests people with mild cases of asthma were able to breathe better after inhaling capsaicin; it dilated their air passages. Similarly, Austrian researchers cured all symptoms of a particular sinus problem (vasomotor rhinitis), including sinus headaches, by applying capsaicin to the inside lining of the nasal passages.

In a strange twist Joel Schwartz, a senior scientist at the Environmental Protection Agency, has discovered another compound in peppers that also seems to fight off lung disease—plain old vitamin C. His analysis of the diets of 9,000 adults found that those who eat foods containing 300 milligrams of vitamin C daily are only 70 percent as likely to have a case of chronic bronchitis as those who eat foods providing 100 milligrams of C per day. Thus this vitamin, which is a potent antioxidant, may be one more reason peppers help protect lungs, particularly from the ravages of cigarette smoke.

Surprisingly few people know that peppers of all kinds, including ordinary mild green and red bell peppers, are super sources of vitamin C, outranking the most common source, oranges. In fact one red bell pepper contains 140 milligrams of vitamin C compared with 70 milligrams in one orange; a green bell pepper contains 95 milligrams of vitamin C. Hot chili peppers contain the same high concentrations of vitamin C. A one-and-a-half-ounce chili pepper has about 110 milligrams of vitamin C. (For foods high in antioxidant vitamin C, see page 7.)

A Burning Question. Some people shun peppers, fearing they damage the stomach. But recent tests reveal that eating hot chili peppers will not cause ulcers or otherwise harm normal stomachs. Researchers at Baylor College of Medicine in Houston, by taking photos of stomach cells flooded with hot peppers, have disproved the suspicion that spicy foods irritate or inflict damage on the lining of ordinary stomachs.

The researchers asked twelve healthy volunteers to eat four different test meals and then examined their stomachs via videoendoscopy—a procedure that takes close-up pictures of the interior stomach surface. None of the subjects ordinarily ate spicy foods. Meal number one was a bland steak-potatoes-peas dinner; two was the same dinner plus three aspirin tablets; three was a Mexican meal with an ounce of jalapeño peppers; and four was a pizza with an ounce and a quarter of pepperoni sausage.

There was no evidence of harm (cell erosion or bleeding) after any of the meals, except those containing aspirin.

Just to be sure, the investigators ground up an ounce of fresh jalapeño pepper in a food processor and dumped it directly into stomachs through a tube. Still no damage.

The conclusion: eating highly spiced meals does not cause visible stomach or duodenal damage to the lining in normal individuals.

If peppers bother you, you shouldn't eat them. However, even if you have an ulcer, such peppers need not be banned from your diet. Research in India a few years ago found that eating chilies did not hinder the healing of duodenal ulcers. One group of ulcer patients was given a normal hospital diet without peppers. Another group additionally got three grams of red chili powder daily—the average amount consumed in the Indian diet. At the end of four weeks the healing rate in the two groups was identical. And the pepper eaters showed no damage to the stomach lining.

Do your health a favor: remember to eat garlic, onions, and peppers regularly—raw or cooked; chop them, mince them, put them in casseroles or on hamburgers; use them as a flavoring, as a side dish, as a vegetable, or as a condiment.

PART TWO

New Food Pharmacy Facts, Cook's Advice, Doctor's Advice, Recommendations, and Recipes

Food Pharmacy Bottom-Line Recommendations

Here are the most important food pharmacy recommendations for better health and a longer life.

• Eat more fruits and vegetables. The evidence is overwhelming that people who eat more fruits and vegetables enjoy better health—have lower rates of cancer, heart attacks, and strokes as well as certain other chronic diseases. Strive for at least five servings every day.

• Use fresh fruits and vegetables when possible; they contain more active pharmacological agents. Freezing does not seem to significantly destroy the beneficial agents, but canning may.

• Eat vegetables raw as well as cooked to be sure you are getting maximum benefit. Some pharmacological agents are diminished or destroyed by heat. The best way to preserve pharmacological agents in cooked food is to use a microwave oven.

• Eat some garlic and onion every day. The bulbs may help prevent numerous problems, including cardiovascular disease and cancer. Use fresh garlic and onions. Garlic and onion powder or salt lack the active ingredients needed for a therapeutic effect.

• Eat more beans. Probably no other food is as underrated as the lowly legume; that includes all kinds of white beans, black beans, pinto beans, fava beans, lima beans, chick-peas, soybeans, split peas, and lentils. All pack a powerful therapeutic and disease-preventive punch. Eat some soybean products, including tofu (soybean curd).

• Be sure to eat yogurt that contains live cultures, preferably yogurt that includes acidophilus cultures. Be aware that if you heat yogurt you destroy the cultures along with much of the therapeutic benefit.

• Eat seafood at least twice a week or more, especially the fattier fishes like salmon, tuna, mackerel, sardines, and herring. It's okay to include some shellfish. Mussels, clams, and oysters are particularly high in beneficial omega-3 fatty acids. Scallops are rock-bottom low in fat. Although shellfish has a reputation for being high in cholesterol, most types, except squid, have only moderate amounts. Tests show that eating shellfish generally benefits blood cholesterol. Shrimp appears neutral—neither lowering nor raising cholesterol.

• Broil, grill, bake, steam, or poach fish, using little or no fat. Frying seafood, especially deep-frying, increases seafood's fat content about twelve times, according to research. Such fat can flood the cells with undesirable types of polyunsaturated fatty acids, undoing some of the benefits of eating seafood in the first place.

• Eat less meat, but if you do eat meat, be doubly sure to eat lots of fruits and vegetables, for studies indicate that these are apt to help soften some hazards of eating meat, notably cancer. Try to think of meat as Asians do, not as an entrée but as just one more ingredient in a main dish that incorporates vegetables, legumes, and grains.

• Eat less fat. Probably no other item in your diet has more pharmacological impact on the functioning of your cells than fat. The health of your cells depends on the amount and type of fat and the proper ratio of each. Generally considered worst are saturated dairy and animal fats. Best: omega-3 fish fat and monounsaturated fat found in olives, avocados, and almonds. Also excellent: canola oil and flaxseed oil. When possible, use *extra-virgin* olive oil.

• Trim meat of all visible fat. Remove skin from poultry. Substitute low-fat or nonfat yogurt for sour cream. Use low-fat or skim milk instead of whole milk. Go easy on butter and high-fat cheese and also on margarine, as well as corn, soybean, and safflower oils, all containing high amounts of omega-6 fatty acids that are increasingly suspect as disease contributors. Trimming the fat off meat and poultry to be grilled also makes it safer, because it is less likely to drip fat and create smoke that rises and deposits cancer-causing agents on the surface of the food.

• Eat only moderate amounts of cholesterol. Old evidence: eating cholesterol, as in egg yolks, actually raises blood cholesterol levels in 30 to 50 percent of individuals. So some thought they didn't have to worry. However, new evidence suggests that those who eat the most cholesterol trim several years off their life spans, regardless of any effect on blood cholesterol.

• Whether or not you have high cholesterol, restrict your intake of egg yolks, even though each yolk has about 213 milligrams of cholesterol, 22 percent less than previously thought. Eat all the egg whites you want. The American Heart Association advises not more than four yolks a week.

• If you are a smoker, or have been a smoker in the last ten years, be sure to eat foods rich in antioxidants. They may help block the development of smoking-related diseases such as lung and throat cancer and chronic bronchitis. Such foods include carrots (beta-carotene), green leafy vegetables (folacin, various carotenoids, quercetin, indoles, glutathione, vitamin C), and oranges (vitamin C). Broccoli is an all-around antioxidant superstar. However, no diet can fight off the damage from continued smoking.

• If you have polyps (small growths) of the colon, increasing your risk of colon cancer, eat more high-fiber wheat cereals, such as a serving of All-Bran once or twice a day, and vegetables, notably cruciferous vegetables (cabbage, broccoli, Brussels sprouts, kale, cauliflower).

• If you have a history of strokes in your family, be sure to eat lots of high-potassium foods, which have been shown to dramatically lower stroke risk. (For such foods, see page 21.)

• If you are worried about lung or breathing problems, eat more pungent, hot foods, such as onions, garlic, and fiery chili peppers. Hot peppers are highly recommended for smokers or ex-smokers and people with emphysema, chronic bronchitis, sinus problems, bronchial asthma, or congestion due to a cold.

• If you drink alcohol, limit it to two drinks a day and make it wine or beer. Both wine and beer in low doses have medicinal properties that may help ward off cardiovascular disease and promote longevity. More than two drinks a day can shorten life.

• Drink small amounts of caffeine if it makes you feel better. Studies show that moderate amounts of caffeine and coffee drinking do not seem to encourage heart disease or other chronic diseases. Low doses (a cup or two a day) can elevate mood and increase mental concentration and performance, but caffeine is highly individual in its effects. If it makes you jittery or produces other adverse effects, avoid it. Caffeine is addictive.

• Use restraint in eating sodium. The old theory was that sodium's only danger is raising blood pressure, and thus only certain people prone to high blood pressure and in whom salt acts as a booster need worry. New theory, according to animal studies: sodium may harm arteries, leading to death, in ways independent of raising blood pressure. Also, research shows that high-salt diets cause the body to lose more calcium, which could be quite detrimental to the bones of older women.

• Use common sense. Don't eat large amounts of only a few fruits, vegetables, grains, legumes, or seafood while avoiding others. Various plant foods have varying pharmacological benefit, and science is not advanced enough now to know where a new natural drug of critical importance may turn up. Also, overdosing on anything can be hazardous, and all plants contain toxins and carcinogens as well as antitoxins and anticarcinogens.

At present it's smartest to choose from a wide range of such foods, although admittedly it also makes sense to eat those for which there is substantial evidence of specific benefit. As Dr. James Duke, expert on medicinal plants at the U.S. Department of Agriculture, says, "Variety in your diet may not only be the spice of life; it may be the guardian of life."

• Do not substitute food remedies for current medications without consulting with your physician. Often food and medicine can work together for increased benefit, resulting in lower doses of a medication. But such an experiment needs monitoring by a physician for benefits as well as adverse effects.

A Word About the Recipes

Obviously the recipes are chosen for their specific therapeutic and disease-preventive potential. Additionally, all have been analyzed nutritionally by Hill Nutrition Associates to determine their calorie, fat, cholesterol, sodium, vitamin, and mineral contents.

Low in Fat. Because fat is detrimental to good health in many ways, the recipes are consistently low in fat. When the fat content is relatively high, it comes from monounsaturated fat, as in olive oil, nuts, and seeds, or omega-3-type fat in seafood. You will find very little saturated fat, from meat and dairy products, in the recipes.

How to Make Low-Fat Recipes Even Lower in Fat. Even so, if you wish, you can further reduce fat in the recipes. Many recipes in the book follow the tradition of sautéing or stir-frying onions, garlic, and other vegetables in small amounts of oil, usually a tablespoonful. Often you can get by with a teaspoon or two of oil, or sometimes none in a nonstick pan. Also, you can reduce the fat needed for sautéing to virtually zero if you skip the oil and simply sauté the onion, garlic, and other vegetables in a quarter to half a cup of water, defatted chicken or vegetable broth, wine, tomato juice, or other nonfat liquids. Microwaving is an excellent way to sauté vegetables without any added fat. Simply put the vegetables in a dish with a small amount of nonfat liquid, cover, and microwave. After the vegetables are softened, continue with the recipe.

Low in Cholesterol. The recipes are also low in cholesterol. When some is present, it is almost always from sources that are highly beneficial in other ways, such as seafood. In recipes that call for eggs—of which there are very few in this book—you can use egg substitutes. Be aware that egg substitutes sometimes have three times the amount of sodium as a whole egg. You can also cut back on the egg yolk. If a recipe calls for two eggs, use one whole egg and two egg whites.

Low in Sodium. The ingredients used in the recipes are almost always very low in sodium. Noted exceptions are canned anchovies, sardines, and mackerel, which, however, are full of beneficial omega-3 oil. What generally raises the sodium content of recipes is added salt. Because of the great variations in salt preference and tolerance, and to give you the widest options, in this book no specific amount of salt is called for except in rare cases. The recipes nearly always call for "salt to taste." This means that added salt has not been calculated in the nutritional analysis of the recipes; only the amount of natural sodium in ingredients has been counted. Thus adding salt raises the sodium count; one teaspoon of salt contains about 2,000 milligrams of sodium.

When chicken broth is an ingredient, you can make your own, adding as little or as much salt as you like. Otherwise the recipes call for "low-sodium" chicken broth, with the sodium count based on Campbell's canned "low-sodium" chicken broth, which contains 53 milligrams of sodium per cup. Those who find this unpalatable can substitute broth with more sodium; a cup of Campbell's "reduced sodium" chicken broth, for example, contains 640 milligrams of sodium.

Since regular canned tomato juice can be fairly high in sodium, the tomato juice used in the recipes is "low sodium," containing about 24 milligrams of sodium per cup. Be aware that if you substitute regular canned tomato juice (with added salt) the sodium count per cup is about 880 milligrams. Of course, if you want an in-between salty taste you can use low-sodium tomato juice and add a little extra salt.

When butter or margarine is an ingredient, the analysis figures assume that it is lightly salted. If you use unsalted butter or margarine, the sodium count will go down slightly.

Pepper. Unless otherwise designated, pepper called for in the recipes is black. Here, too, the amount is generally left up to your taste buds. Freshly ground black pepper straight from a pepper mill is preferable because it is coarsely ground and has more flavor and punch. Thus freshly ground pepper is called for in the recipes. Of course you can substitute ready-to-use finely ground black pepper if you wish. Or you can also buy ready-to-use pepper that is coarsely ground. But if you don't already have one, a pepper mill is a good, inexpensive investment.

A Tomato Tip. When a recipe calls for fresh tomatoes that are to be cooked, and the only ones around are the hard, tough, tasteless variety, you are better off substituting canned whole tomatoes. Especially good are the canned whole pear-shaped Italian tomatoes, also known as plum tomatoes. Simply chop the canned tomato and substitute it for the amount of fresh tomato in the recipe. I've done that when making many of the recipes in this book, and the results are terrific. Of course canned tomatoes cannot substitute in recipes requiring fresh tomatoes to be used raw.

How to Read the Nutrient Analysis. When an ingredient is listed as optional, it is not included in the analysis. In all cases the first ingredient or measure is the one included in the analysis when a choice of ingredients and amounts is given. If a recipe states that it serves "4 to 6," the nutrient analysis is for four, not six; the more conservative first serving size is used. If you divide a recipe into more servings, the calorie, fat, cholesterol, and sodium counts will be lower.

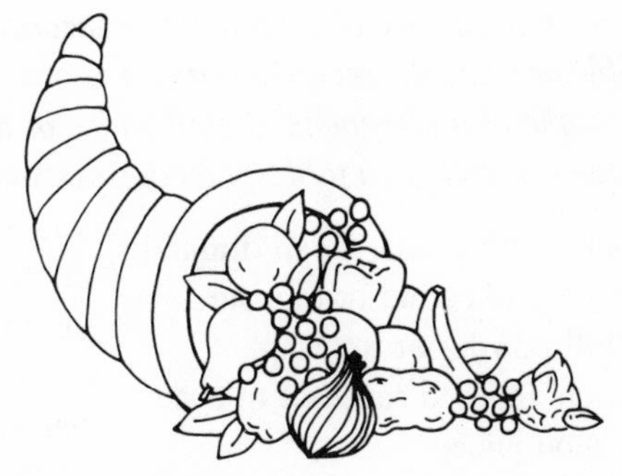

Appetizers, Starters, and Snacks

Quick Mexican Bean Dip

About 2½ cups

This is a quick and simple cholesterol-reducing dip with no added fat. It's great for a party. You whip it up in a blender in thirty seconds. And, of course, you can easily double or triple the recipe to serve a crowd. If you want more seasoning, add a couple of tablespoons of chili sauce or Mexican salsa, a finely minced jalapeño pepper, or a tablespoon of freshly chopped cilantro.

2 15-ounce cans pinto beans, 1 can drained
1½ teaspoons ground cumin or to taste
¼ teaspoon chili powder or to taste
¼ to ¾ teaspoon Tabasco sauce or to taste
2 teaspoons lemon juice
Salt to taste

Place the drained can of beans in a food processor or blender. Add the other can of beans with their liquid. Add the cumin, chili powder, hot sauce, lemon juice, and salt. Blend at high speed until it becomes smooth and creamy.

Serve with fresh vegetables, tortillas, or crackers.

Note: For a thicker dip, drain both cans of beans before processing.

Per tablespoon:

Calories	16
Total fat	.03 g
Saturated fat	0
Cholesterol	0
Sodium	80 mg

FOOD PHARMACY FACT

No Beans About It

Eating dried beans—legumes—can depress blood cholesterol whether you are on a low-fat or high-fat diet. Dr. James Anderson at the University of Kentucky College of Medicine found that eating a cup of cooked beans, such as navy or pinto beans or even canned baked beans, every day decreased blood cholesterol an average of 19 percent. And the beans worked on people eating a moderately high fat diet—36 percent of calories from fat. Dr. David Jenkins at the University of Toronto found that a daily regimen of beans (kidney beans, pinto beans, chick-peas, or red or green lentils) depressed cholesterol an average of 7 percent in men with high cholesterol who were already on a low-fat diet.

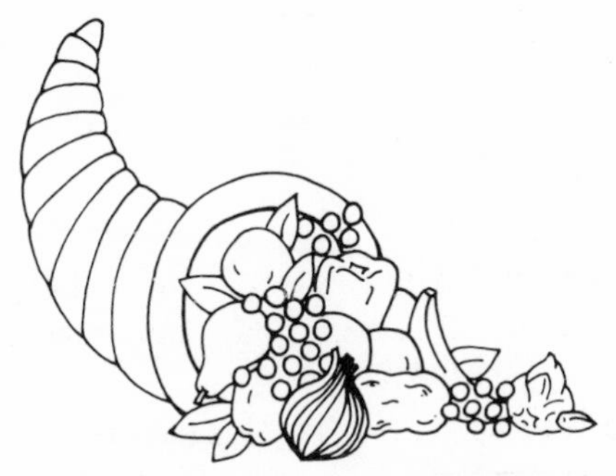

Guacamole

Serves 2

The secret to good guacamole is an extra-ripe avocado. After that I prefer this very simple version. Avocado, contrary to what you have heard, will not kill you with all its fat. In fact the fat is mostly the same good type as found in olive oil. However, the avocado is high-fat and fairly high calorie—so it should be regarded as a treat, not an everyday staple.

1 small to medium avocado, peeled, pitted, and cut into chunks
1 teaspoon lemon juice (more if needed to preserve the avocado's color)
1 garlic clove, crushed
1 tablespoon finely minced onion
1 heaped tablespoon coarsely chopped tomato
5 drops Tabasco sauce or to taste
Salt and freshly ground pepper to taste

In a bowl, mash the avocado coarsely. Add the remaining ingredients and mix but do not puree.

Serve with vegetables and/or tortilla chips (recipe follows) or as a garnish.

Per serving:

Calories	147
Total fat	13 g
Saturated fat	2 g
Cholesterol	0
Sodium	16 mg

LOW-FAT TORTILLA CHIPS

Spray both sides of a corn tortilla with olive oil. Cut into quarters. Put on a cookie sheet in a 375-degree oven for about 12 to 15 minutes until crisp.

IN DEFENSE OF THE AVOCADO

The avocado is often maligned because it is high in fat. But the fact is most of avocado's fat is good fat. Fully 70 percent of the fat in a California avocado and 60 percent in a Florida avocado is monounsaturated; that's the same type that predominates in olive oil and is credited with olive oil's artery-protecting, heart-disease-fighting properties.

Moreover, the monounsaturated fat in avocado is 95 percent oleic acid, and that's good news, because oleic acid, researchers recently discovered, is an antioxidant; that means it can help destroy vicious disease-causing oxygen free radicals. Oleic acid is the stuff that also makes up virtually all of olive oil's monounsaturated fat, which is so widely heralded by scientists for its anti-artery-clogging, cholesterol-lowering abilities. If oleic acid makes olive oil the lifesaver it is, then the avocado qualifies too. Additionally, avocado contains lots of stroke-fighting potassium.

THE WONDROUS MEDITERRANEAN DIET

For a quarter of a century scientists have been marveling over something they call "the Mediterranean diet." They think it is a prime reason that people of southern Italy and Greece, countries bordering the Mediterranean Sea and the Mediterranean island of Crete, have some of the lowest rates of heart disease in the world. If only Americans, they say, would eat more like Mediterranean peoples, heart disease rates would drop. And what does that mean? According to Gene Spiller, director of the Health Research and Studies Center, Los Altos, California, and author of a book *The Mediterranean Diets in Health and Disease,* it means more fruit, vegetables, seafood, and monounsaturated fats, such as olive oil. It means less fatty meat and cheese.

Surprisingly, people practicing this diet do not necessarily eat a Spartan, fatless diet; in fact, in Crete the population eats more than 40 percent of its calories in fat. But the fat calories come almost entirely from olive oil and nuts—the monounsaturated-type fat—and seafood with its omega-3s. Thus all fat is not always bad—indeed it may even be protective—if it's the Mediterranean type. And if the rest of the diet too is "Mediterranean"—rich in fruits and vegetables.

Tzatziki

About 4 cups

If you've ever been to Greece or even to a Greek restaurant, you know how tempting this cucumber yogurt mixture is when scooped onto bread, eaten alone, or used as a sauce. And don't forget that the cultures in yogurt fight off bacteria like E. coli, *the most common cause of "traveler's diarrhea." I generally eat yogurt, but I make it a special point to do so when I travel in foreign countries where upset stomach and gastrointestinal bugs are apt to be problems. This tzatziki is a delicious way to get protection—at home or away. Thanks to Mary and Lee Koromvokis, who have made this authentic tzatziki more times than they can remember.*

3 cucumbers, peeled, seeded, and finely chopped
1 small onion, finely minced
2 garlic cloves, minced (more if desired)
3 cups plain nonfat yogurt

Mix all ingredients together and refrigerate for at least 2 hours so flavors blend.

Note: To make a thicker tzatziki, use 4 to 5 cups of yogurt and let it strain for two or three hours, as in making yogurt cheese (page 73).

Per 1/4-cup serving:

Calories	31
Total fat	.1 g
Saturated fat	.06 g
Cholesterol	1 mg
Sodium	35 mg

Chick-Pea Dip (Hummus)

Serves 6

Of all the hummus recipes I have seen, I think this is the best. You can make it in a jiffy and feel virtuous eating it because chick-peas are one of the richest sources of anticancer compounds called protease inhibitors; *chick-peas also help lower blood cholesterol. Use this as a dip for vegetables or spread for all kinds of bread; the traditional one is pita. It's great as an appetizer, sprinkled with parsley, or a snack or sandwich. It also freezes well. Nearly all the fat, of which 87 percent is unsaturated, comes from the tahini, which is high in antioxidant vitamin E.*

1 16-ounce can chick-peas, drained
½ cup tahini (sesame seed paste)
Juice of 2 lemons
1 teaspoon chopped garlic
Salt to taste
¼ teaspoon ground cumin
Snipped parsley for garnish

Place all ingredients except the parsley in the bowl of a food processor. Process, using the steel blade, until the mixture is smooth. You can also do it in a blender, but the processor is quicker and easier. Serve chilled or at room temperature, sprinkled with snipped parsley.

Per serving:

Calories	212
Total fat	11 g
Saturated fat	1.6 g
Cholesterol	0
Sodium	249 mg

FOOD PHARMACY FACT

Olive Oil: The Winner!

Olive oil is better than a low-fat diet in lowering cholesterol, report researchers at the Catholic University of Nijmegen, the Netherlands. In the study of forty-eight healthy people, half ate a low-fat diet (22 percent of calories from fat), and the other half ate a high-fat diet (41 percent of calories from fat) but the fat was almost entirely monounsaturated, as in olive oil. After thirty-six days the average blood cholesterol of the low-fat group fell seventeen points, with the good-type HDLs down three points. The cholesterol of the olive-oil eaters, although they had eaten nearly twice as much fat per day, dropped even more—by twenty points, with no reduction in protective HDLs.

The point is not to overdose on olive oil, which can add lots of unwanted calories, but to substitute olive oil for other saturated animal fats and polyunsaturated oils (like corn and safflower). In other words, when you must eat fat, make it olive oil.

Rena's Syrian Baba Ghanouj (Eggplant Dip)

Serves 4

What makes this Baba Ghanouj so authentic is both its first-generation Syrian origin and the plentiful amount of lemon juice, which, Rena Dweck says, is what makes it taste so good. She has been making it for fifty years, just as her grandmother did. But it's not only taste that makes it special. Eggplant, several studies show, has properties that help protect the arteries and lower blood cholesterol, even helping fight some ill effects of high saturated fat in meat and dairy products.

1 large eggplant, pierced with a fork in several places
1/2 cup tahini (sesame seed paste) or more to taste
3 medium garlic cloves, minced
Salt to taste
1/2 cup plus 2 tablespoons lemon juice (more if needed)
1/2 teaspoon ground cumin
Chopped parsley for garnish

Preheat the broiler and broil the eggplant, turning it at least once, until it is soft to the touch. The skin will be charred.

When cool, split the eggplant and remove the eggplant pulp, discarding the skin.

In a bowl, combine the eggplant pulp, tahini, garlic, salt, and lemon juice and stir to blend. Add cumin and stir.

Sprinkle parsley on top. Serve with toasted or heated pita bread.

Per serving:

Calories	173
Total fat	11 g
Saturated fat	1.5 g
Cholesterol	0
Sodium	38 mg

Radicchio with Garlic

Serves 4

For a taste adventure, try lightly grilling or broiling radicchio as Italians do. This red leaf chicory is full of carotenoids, as revealed by the reddish color; the bits of garlic and olive oil are good for your cardiovascular system.

2 orange-size heads radicchio
1 tablespoon olive oil
4 garlic cloves, minced
4 teaspoons balsamic vinegar or to taste
Salt and freshly ground pepper to taste

Cut the heads of radicchio in half. Sprinkle the cut side of each piece of radicchio with 3/4 teaspoon of olive oil and 1 minced garlic clove.

Preheat the broiler and place the radicchio halves under the heat source on the lowest rack for 2 or 3 minutes, until the top is slightly browned. Or put cut side down on a grill for a minute or two. The radicchio should be slightly heated but still crisp.

Drizzle a teaspoon of balsamic vinegar or more on each half; add salt and pepper to taste. Serve as an appetizer, salad, or vegetable.

Per serving:

Calories	55
Total fat	3.7 g
Saturated fat	.5 g
Cholesterol	0
Sodium	11 mg

Bruschetta

Serves 6

"Once you've lived in Italy, one thing you can never do without is bruschetta," says my friend Kathleen Drew. It's the original grilled garlic bread, and she prepares it in summer on the grill, in winter under the broiler. In both cases you can pass the ingredients and let the guests make their own. Be sure to use good-quality olive oil. This simple appetizer is undoubtedly one more reason for Italians' healthy hearts.

6 slices crusty Italian bread
3 garlic cloves, peeled and cut in half
2 tablespoons extra-virgin olive oil
1 to 2 tablespoons chopped fresh basil
Salt and freshly ground pepper to taste
6 plum tomatoes, chopped

Toast or grill the bread. While the bread is still hot, rub cut garlic over one side of each slice. Drizzle on a teaspoon of olive oil. In the meantime, add the basil, salt, and pepper to the tomatoes.

Top the bread with a portion of the seasoned tomatoes.

Per serving:

Calories	126
Total fat	5 g
Saturated fat	.7 g
Cholesterol	.3 mg
Sodium	169 mg

FOOD PHARMACY FACT

Garlic vs. Cancer

In tests by Sidney Belman at New York University Medical Center, animals that had garlic and onion oils rubbed onto their skin were not as likely to develop skin cancer. Similarly, Michael Wargovich at the University of Texas System Cancer Center in Houston exposed animals to cancer-causing agents, then fed half of them a dose of diallyl sulfide, a compound in garlic. The garlic chemical prevented colon cancer in 75 percent of the animals.

I Matti's Beans and Onions

Serves 4

What makes these beans distinctive is the large amount of onion, says Roberto Donna, a distinguished chef and owner of I Matti and Galileo, two of Washington, D.C.'s highly rated Italian restaurants. I have had the dish often at I Matti and made it many times. You can serve the beans as a side dish or as an appetizer heaped onto a slice of thick, sturdy Italian bread, as they do at the restaurant. Then it's called bruschetta al fagioli e cipolla, and unquestionably it's good for your health.

1 large onion, chopped
2 tablespoons olive oil (less if desired)
1 19-ounce can cannellini beans (white kidney beans) with liquid
1½ tablespoons chopped fresh sage *or* 1 teaspoon dried, crushed
1 teaspoon dried thyme
1 teaspoon balsamic vinegar (optional)

In a large skillet, sauté the onion in the olive oil over medium heat until the onions are translucent and soft. Add the beans, sage, and thyme and cook over low heat for about 20 to 30 minutes. Add the vinegar if desired. Serve at room temperature or lightly chilled with Italian bread.

Per serving:

Calories	184
Total fat	7 g
Saturated fat	1 g
Cholesterol	0
Sodium	468 mg

Dr. David's Caponata (Eggplant Appetizer)

Serves 12 (9 to 10 cups)

Caponata is a kind of ratatouille, except it has vinegar and sugar, and I can definitively say this version is the best I have ever had. It is made often by Dr. David Rall, former director of the National Institute of Environmental and Health Sciences, the government group that does all those studies to ferret out which compounds may cause cancer. You can be sure this recipe has all the right stuff.

2 medium eggplants (2 pounds)
Salt
2 to 3 tablespoons olive oil
3 medium onions, thinly sliced
4 celery stalks, sliced
¼ to ½ pound Kalamata or other Greek-type black olives, pitted and halved
1 28-ounce can crushed Italian tomatoes
5 tablespoons drained capers
3 tablespoons raisins
3 tablespoons pine nuts
¼ cup red wine vinegar
1 tablespoon sugar
Salt and freshly ground pepper to taste

Peel the skin from half of the eggplants. (This is for variety, so some pieces still have skin.) Cut all into 1-inch cubes. Put the eggplant in a colander and sprinkle generously with salt. Let it sit for about 20 minutes to draw out moisture and bitterness. Rinse with cold water to remove some of the salt.

Put the olive oil in a large saucepan and sauté the onions and celery until translucent and soft. Blot the eggplant with paper towels, then add it to the skillet and sauté for about 20 to 25 minutes, until the eggplant is cooked but not mushy.

Add the remaining ingredients and simmer for about 10 minutes.

Per serving:

Calories	93
Total fat	4.6 g
Saturated fat	.6 g
Cholesterol	0
Sodium	388 mg

Gazpacho Vegetable Pâté

Serves 6

What a powerhouse of vitamin C is this brightly colored and taste-filled appetizer or salad. And it's so refreshing—very pretty, too, when served as part of a buffet dinner, perhaps during holidays. Need I say that it has very high protective value for your cardiovascular system and a great deal of anticancer potential?

3 cups undrained canned plum tomatoes
1 medium green bell pepper, cut into eighths
1 cucumber, peeled, seeded, and cut into large pieces
1 medium onion, quartered
2 tablespoons olive oil
3 tablespoons tomato paste
3 tablespoons red wine vinegar
Salt to taste
2 teaspoons ground cumin
1/2 teaspoon celery seed
1/4 teaspoon cayenne pepper
3 tablespoons (3 packages) unflavored gelatin
1/2 cup dry white wine
1 ripe but not soft avocado, peeled, pitted, and cubed
1 medium green or yellow bell pepper, minced
Watercress or shredded lettuce for garnish
Reduced-calorie mayonnaise for serving (optional)

Puree in a food processor (or in two batches in a blender) the plum tomatoes, green pepper, cucumber, onion, olive oil, tomato paste, vinegar, salt, cumin, celery seed, and cayenne. Transfer to a large bowl.

In a small bowl, combine the gelatin with the wine and place the bowl in a larger bowl filled with hot water. Stir until dissolved.

Combine the vegetable puree with the softened gelatin. Mix in the cubed avocado and minced green pepper.

Oil a 9- by 5-inch loaf pan and pour in the mixture. Chill up to several days before serving or until the mixture is firm and set.

To unmold, run a small knife around the edges of the pan and dip the pan into a larger pan of hot water for a couple of seconds. Invert onto a platter. Slice the pâté about an inch thick and place on individual salad plates garnished with watercress or shredded lettuce. Add a dollop of reduced-calorie mayonnaise if you wish.

Per serving:

Calories	157
Total fat	10 g
Saturated fat	1.5 g
Cholesterol	0
Sodium	272 mg

FOOD PHARMACY FACT

Veggies vs. Cataracts

In a group of people between ages forty and seventy, those who had the highest levels of carotenoids in their blood were only 18 percent as likely to have cataracts as those with the lowest carotenoid levels, reported researchers at U.S. Agriculture Department's Human Research Center on Aging at Tufts University in Boston. Nearly half of all Americans over age seventy-five have cataracts, which causes the lens to become opaque, reducing eyesight. Carotenoids in the blood come from eating fruits and vegetables—especially tomatos, carrots, and dark green leafy vegetables.

Yogurt Cheese

You can easily convert yogurt into a soft, creamy "cheese" without the calories and fat of ordinary cheese and with lots of medicinal value. If you have never done this, try it, for it will give you a whole new world of possibilities for using this ancient medicinal food with its newly documented benefits.

All you do is take plain, preferably nonfat or low-fat, yogurt made without gelatin and drain it until it loses most of its liquid and becomes like a soft cheese. Low-fat yogurt forms a slightly firmer, thicker cheese than nonfat yogurt, but nonfat yogurt works very well if you wish to avoid all fat.

Put the yogurt in a colander or strainer lined with a porous material—for example, several layers of cheesecloth, a cotton kitchen towel, or, my favorite, a cloth napkin. Put the colander or strainer in a bowl to collect the excess moisture. Refrigerate overnight or for at least five hours. The longer you strain the yogurt, the thicker it tends to become. Four cups of yogurt will make from 1½ to 2 cups of yogurt cheese.

Use this cheese as a base to make spreads, dips, low-fat desserts, cheese balls or logs, and sauces. It can almost double for fat-rich cream cheese. It is also an excellent substitute for sour cream or crème fraîche. Use a dollop of yogurt cheese to top soups and omelets instead of sour cream.

Yogurt Cheese and Lox

Serves 8

This can really satisfy people who love cream cheese and lox but don't like all the saturated fat in cream cheese. It has the rich taste of cheese without the fat; most people think it is a high-fat cheese. And the fat you get from the lox is good fat that helps your heart and the rest of your body. You can use it as a dip or as a spread on crackers—or, of course, on bagels, where it belongs.

1 cup nonfat yogurt cheese (page 73)
2 ounces lox or smoked salmon, chopped
1/4 cup finely chopped scallions, including green parts
Salt and freshly ground pepper to taste

Combine all ingredients and chill for at least an hour to let flavors mingle.

Per serving:

Calories	35
Total fat	.4 g
Saturated fat	.1 g
Cholesterol	3 mg
Sodium	173 mg

Herbed Yogurt Cheese

Serves 8

If you love boursin or herb-flavored goat cheese but don't love the saturated fat and calories, this is an excellent substitute. Serve it with crusty French bread, crackers, or vegetables. It is also excellent alongside or atop sliced fresh tomatoes.

1 cup nonfat yogurt cheese (page 73)
1 tablespoon minced scallions
1 tablespoon minced parsley
1 tablespoon minced fresh basil
1 teaspoon finely minced garlic
Salt and freshly ground pepper to taste

Put the yogurt cheese in a small bowl. Stir in the scallions, parsley, basil, garlic, salt, and pepper.

Per serving:

Calories	27
Total fat	.1 g
Saturated fat	.1 g
Cholesterol	1 mg
Sodium	31 mg

Yogurt-Roquefort-Walnut Dip

About 7/8 cup

Try this dip using slices of fruit as a scoop. It's marvelous with pears. You can also slice fresh pears and put a dollop of the dip on top. Or halve pears, scoop out the cores, and fill with dip. It's also good with crackers, but it makes a superb appetizer surrounded by slices of apples and pears. The Roquefort adds some saturated fat, but not much, because little Roquefort is needed to produce a strong flavor.

1/2 cup nonfat yogurt cheese (page 73)
2 tablespoons Roquefort cheese, crumbled
1/4 cup chopped walnuts

Blend together the yogurt and Roquefort cheese. Mix in the walnuts and refrigerate.

Per tablespoon:

Calories	26
Total fat	1.7 g
Saturated fat	.4 g
Cholesterol	1.4 mg
Sodium	31 mg

PHARMACEUTICAL NUTS

Some people shun nuts because they are high in fat. True, they are. But nuts are a terrific pharmacological package. Nuts are definitely not just a high-fat, empty-calorie food. If you do not eat nuts, you may cheat yourself of vitamin E, an antioxidant linked to lower rates of cancer. Walnuts also are extremely high in the marvelous omega-3 fatty acids, as well as antioxidants, such as ellagic acid. Almonds, hazelnuts, and pistachios are rich sources of monounsaturated fat, in particular oleic acid, which has recently been revealed as an antioxidant. Eating almonds has lowered blood cholesterol in human tests. One major study decidedly linked low rates of heart disease with consumption of nuts. People who eat nuts seem to have a lower risk of Parkinson's disease.

As Dr. David Jenkins, University of Toronto, points out, the almond is full of the right stuff; most of its fat is monounsaturated; it is exceptionally low in saturated fat (even lower than olive oil); it is full of vegetable protein and fiber. It also helps keep blood sugar and insulin levels steady and thus may help fight high blood pressure, diabetes, obesity, and general atherosclerotic damage to arteries. Nuts also have anticancer compounds.

This does not mean, of course, you should risk gaining weight by eating nuts. But it does suggest that nuts, as Dr. Jenkins says, are a potent pharmaceutical food and should be included in a healthful diet.

FOOD PHARMACY FACT

Shellfish Anointed

It's official. It's okay—in fact, advisable—to eat oysters, clams, mussels, and crabs. That's what Dr. Marian Childs, a lipid expert at the University of Washington, says after feeding the shellfish to men with normal cholesterol. When a group of eighteen men substituted these shellfish for the protein they usually got from meat, cheese, and eggs, their total cholesterol dropped significantly. Clams depressed cholesterol an average of 13 percent; crabs, 10 percent; oysters, 9 percent; and mussels, 5 percent. More dramatic was the drop in triglycerides, falling 59 percent from eating clams, 52 percent from oysters, 51 percent from mussels, and 25 percent from crabs. Further, oysters and mussels improved the good-type HDL ratios, thought to help protect against heart disease. All-around best for cholesterol, said Dr. Childs, were oysters, clams, and mussels.

In the study, shrimp neither raised nor lowered cholesterol; squid was detrimental.

Steamed Clams Portuguese

Serves 4

Contrary to popular opinion, clams are not laden with cholesterol and forbidden to people who are concerned about their cardiovascular systems. In fact studies done at the University of Washington found that eating clams twice a day depressed triglycerides—a blood fat linked to heart disease—by an astonishing 61 percent.

3 pounds or 3 dozen steamer clams
2 ounces prosciutto
2 tablespoons olive oil
1 medium onion, diced
2 garlic cloves, minced
2 teaspoons imported paprika
2 tomatoes, peeled, seeded, and coarsely chopped
3 tablespoons chopped parsley
1 cup dry white wine or more if needed
1 tablespoon wine vinegar

Scrub the steamers. Cut the prosciutto into tiny slivers. Heat the oil in a large saucepan and sauté the ham, onion, and garlic for 3 to 4 minutes, or until the onions are translucent and soft but not browned. Pour off any fat.

Add the remaining ingredients, cover the pan, and cook over high heat for 4 to 6 minutes, or until the steamer shells just open. (Discard any clams that have not opened.) Serve at once, with crusty bread for dipping in the broth and a bowl for the empty shells.

Per serving:

Calories	188
Total fat	8.8 g
Saturated fat	1.9 g
Cholesterol	34 mg
Sodium	432 mg

Cucumber Rounds with Anchovy Topping (Tapénade)

About 20 pieces

Here's a way to work anchovies, rich in omega-3 oils, into your diet along with tuna, also high in the health-promoting oils. Plus, cucumbers have been known to help lower blood cholesterol. These appetizers do get a high proportion of their calories from fat—but all of it is from either beneficial fish oil or olive oil, which helps lower blood pressure and cholesterol. Go easy on these if you're on a sodium-restricted diet.

8 anchovy fillets
2 ounces canned white water-packed tuna, drained
3 tablespoons drained capers
Freshly ground black pepper
1 teaspoon lemon juice or to taste
Approximately 1/4 cup olive oil
2 cucumbers, sliced into 1/2-inch-thick rounds
20 black olives, pitted (optional)

In a blender or a food processor fitted with the steel blade, puree the anchovies, tuna, capers, pepper, lemon juice, and enough olive oil to make a thick paste.

Using a piping bag fitted with a wide star tip, pipe the anchovy mixture onto the cucumber rounds. Or heap the mixture on with a teaspoon. Decorate each with a pitted olive if desired.

Per piece:

Calories	34
Total fat	2.9 g
Saturated fat	.4 g
Cholesterol	2 mg
Sodium	103 mg

FOOD PHARMACY FACT

Fish Is an Anti-Arthritis Drug

The oil in fish helps relieve the symptoms of rheumatoid arthritis, according to six well-conducted clinical investigations, says Dr. Joel Kremer, associate professor of medicine, Albany (New York) Medical College, and a leading researcher in the field. There's no doubt that fish oil is an anti-inflammatory agent, says Dr. Kremer. Furthermore, in an exciting new discovery he found that fish oil also acts directly on the immune system to suppress the release of trouble-causing compounds called *cytokines* that help destroy joints. When patients with rheumatoid arthritis took moderate doses of fish oil in addition to their regular medication for six months, Dr. Kremer found their production of a certain cytokine (interleukin 1) dropped by 40 to 55 percent.

He also found in his study of forty-nine patients that fish oil suppressed various symptoms of arthritis. Fish-oil eaters had fewer tender and swollen joints and less pain and fatigue as well as other improvements based on twenty-four different measurements.

The dose: five or six grams of fish oil daily. That's comparable to a couple of cans of sardines a day or a seven-ounce serving of salmon or mackerel, says Dr. Kremer. "There's no reason to think the oil from eating fish will not work the same way," he says.

Mackerel Salad Spread

Serves 8 as an appetizer, 4 as sandwiches

If you think mackerel is not addictive, try this sandwich or cracker spread. I couldn't stop eating it. Canned mackerel is one of the best, least expensive oily fishes that can help fight blood clots, lower your blood pressure, and help protect you from psoriasis, rheumatoid arthritis, migraine headaches, and other health problems. This also is not low-sodium diet fare, although studies have shown that canned mackerel lowered blood pressure despite its higher sodium content.

2 teaspoons lemon juice
1 15-ounce can mackerel, drained and flaked, any skin removed
½ cup diced celery
½ cup diced onion
1 tablespoon sweet or dill pickle relish
½ cup reduced-calorie mayonnaise
Salt and freshly ground pepper to taste
1 teaspoon Dijon mustard

Add the lemon juice to the mackerel. Combine the remaining ingredients, add them to the mackerel, and mix thoroughly. Chill.

Spread on bread or eat with crackers. For a sharper taste, add 1 to 1½ teaspoons Dijon mustard.

Per serving:

Calories	115
Total fat	6.8 g
Saturated fat	1.7 g
Cholesterol	39 mg
Sodium	281 mg

Molly's Chopped Herring

Serves 4

If you're not accustomed to making chopped herring—or even if you are—I heartily recommend this simple and delicious version given to me by Molly Schuchat, who often makes it for her husband, Michael, and her children. It's an old family recipe from Mike's mother. I have served it to chopped herring aficionados, who proclaimed it superb. And it's a snap to make in a food processor. There is no better way to get lots of omega-3s than from herring, which is one of the leading sources of the healthful oils.

2 medium *or* 1 large tart apple, peeled, cored, and cut into chunks
1 12-ounce jar pickled herring, drained and skin removed
2 to 3 hard-cooked eggs, shelled and thickly sliced
White or red wine vinegar to taste

In a food processor fitted with the steel blade, chop the apples; add the herring and pulse quickly to chop, then add the eggs and pulse again. Do not overprocess, or the mixture will become too smooth. It should be chunky.

Stir in the vinegar a teaspoon at a time, tasting until the flavor meets your approval.

Serve with a dark bread, bagels, or pita bread.

Note: The Schuchats usually discard any onion that comes with the herring, but you can chop the onion along with the herring if you wish. Also, if you accidentally add too much vinegar, you can counteract it by adding a 1/2 teaspoon sugar, says Molly. The herring also keeps well in a closed jar in the refrigerator.

Per serving:

Calories	207
Total fat	14 g
Saturated fat	2.5 g
Cholesterol	141 mg
Sodium	564 mg

Salmon Pâté

6 servings

Salmon pâté is a classic, so good for company and for you. Here is a favorite of mine. It's thickened with gelatin, which makes it exceptionally low in saturated fat. Serve with raw vegetables or crackers. Thanks to nutritionist Ann Louise Gittleman; this recipe is adapted from her book, Beyond Pritikin.

- 1 15½-ounce can salmon, bones and skin removed, rinsed, liquid reserved
- 2 tablespoons lemon juice
- 1 teaspoon dried dill *or* 1 tablespoon chopped fresh dill
- 1 tablespoon agar-agar (seaweed gelatin, available in health food stores) or plain gelatin
- ½ cup chopped onion
- ¼ cup chopped parsley
- 1 tablespoon rinsed and drained capers

Place the salmon, lemon juice, and dill in a food processor fitted with the steel blade or in a blender. Blend for 10 seconds.

Dissolve the agar-agar or plain gelatin in 2 tablespoons of the salmon liquid in a saucepan and bring to a boil. Add the dissolved agar-agar or gelatin to the salmon mixture. Stir in the onion, parsley, and capers. Refrigerate for about 4 hours before serving.

Per serving:

Calories	113
Total fat	4.5 g
Saturated fat	1 g
Cholesterol	0
Sodium	445 mg

FOOD PHARMACY FACT

Fish Oil Keeps Arteries Unclogged

Heart surgeons are excited to discover that fish oil may help keep arteries open longer after angioplasty, a common surgical procedure to unclog arteries. Dr. Mark R. Milner, Washington (D.C.) Hospital Center, found that giving patients fish oil capsules for six months after surgery cut in half the rate at which arteries tended to become clogged again. In a study of eighty-four angioplasty patients those who took fish-oil capsules and ate a low-fat diet had a 19 percent arterial reclosure rate compared with twice that of another group eating a low-fat diet but not taking fish oil.

The effective therapeutic dose equaled 4.5 grams of fish oil—or about three small cans of sardines or seven ounces of Atlantic mackerel.

Dr. Milner says fish oil retards the inflammation and scarring of arterial walls that lead to the buildup of plaque and reblockage. He says he gives fish oil capsules as an "emergency measure," but that if patients ate fish regularly this would be unnecessary. "After three to six months I tell patients, 'Stop taking the capsules and eat fish once a day or every other day,' " he says.

Oriental Tuna-Stuffed Mushrooms

About 20

Since fresh and frozen tuna steaks are now readily available throughout most of the country, here's an imaginative way to use the tuna to make appetizers, buffet fare, or party nibbles. You can use large button mushroom caps or preferably shiitake or other Oriental mushroom caps, which have specific cardiovascular protecting properties. Remember that tuna is one of the most concentrated sources of the marvelous omega-3 fatty acids.

½ pound fresh or thawed frozen tuna, coarsely chopped
2 scallions, minced
2 tablespoons reduced-sodium soy sauce
¾ teaspoon ground ginger
20 large mushroom caps, preferably shiitake

Preheat the broiler. Mix the tuna, scallions, soy sauce, and ginger.

Clean the mushroom caps and stuff them with the tuna mixture.

Place the stuffed mushrooms on a baking sheet and broil for about 7 to 8 minutes. Serve with extra soy sauce.

Per piece:

Calories	23
Total fat	.6 g
Saturated fat	.1 g
Cholesterol	4 mg
Sodium	65 mg

Sardine-Avocado Sandwich

2 sandwiches

I grew up on sardines, thanks to my grandmother. So when Lynn Fischer, coauthor of the cookbook Low Cholesterol Gourmet, *told me about this new sardine sandwich she had devised, I was eager to try it. It gets raves from me. The flavors blend perfectly. You can also use plain sardines if you cannot find or do not care for the spicy ones. It also works as an open-face sandwich, and I have packed it into a pita bread pocket.*

1 to 2 teaspoons Bengal-style hot chutney
4 slices whole wheat bread
1/4 ripe avocado, peeled and cut into thin slices
1 4 3/8-ounce tin sardines in spicy sauce or plain sardines, drained
4 wafer-thin onion slices
2 large leaves cold crisp leaf or romaine lettuce *or* several watercress sprigs

Spread chutney over two slices of bread. Add the avocado and half the sardines. Top with onion slices and lettuce and the other slices of bread. Cut in half and serve.

Note: Bengal-style hot chutney has a jam consistency. You can substitute regular chutney, well mashed or blended in a food processor fitted with the steel blade.

Per sandwich:

Calories	278
Total fat	11 g
Saturated fat	1.7 g
Cholesterol	77 mg
Sodium	524 mg

Soups

Easy Pumpkin Applesauce Soup

Serves 6

Everybody needs a fantastic recipe for pumpkin soup—what better way to get all that fabulous health-promoting benefit of pumpkin's cancer-fighting beta-carotene! Pumpkin is one of the highest of all foods in beta-carotene. In this case you also get a bonus: the heart-protective benefits of apples. Plus, this soup is so easy to make with canned goods right off the pantry shelf, yet it has an elegant flavor fit for a dinner party. I like it hot, but you can also serve it cold. My thanks for this adaptation to Maxine Rapoport and Nina Graybill, coauthors of Cold Soups *and other cookbooks.*

1 teaspoon butter or margarine
½ cup chopped onion
1 cup finely sliced celery
1 16-ounce can pureed pumpkin
1 cup unsweetened applesauce
1 quart low-sodium chicken broth
1 teaspoon dried marjoram, crushed
Salt to taste
½ cup plain, nonfat yogurt mixed with grated lemon peel to taste for garnish (optional)

Place the butter, onion, and celery in a small bowl. Microwave on HIGH until the vegetables are softened and translucent—about 5 minutes.

Transfer the onion-celery mixture to a large pot. Stir in the pumpkin, applesauce, chicken broth, and seasonings. Cook, covered, over low heat for about 20 to 30 minutes, stirring occasionally. Taste for seasoning.

Ladle the soup into bowls and garnish with yogurt if desired. Or refrigerate for several hours or overnight and serve cold.

Note: The zest is the colored part of the rind of citrus fruits. Be sure not to use any of the white pith, which is bitter.

Per serving:

Calories	77
Total fat	2 g
Saturated fat	.8 g
Cholesterol	2 mg
Sodium	431 mg

FOOD PHARMACY FACT

Orange Vegetables: New Heart Savers

That stuff that makes carrots and pumpkins orange—beta carotene—seems to have unexpected abilities to protect the heart. In a major 10-year study of 22,000 male physicians, Harvard investigators have been giving high doses of beta carotene, mainly to test its powers to prevent cancer.

Then researchers decided to look at a small group of men who had entered the study with signs of heart disease, such as angina (chest pain). To their great surprise, the researchers found that beta carotene appears to slow down the process of atherosclerosis—stiffening and clogging of arteries—and to cut the risk of heart attacks dramatically.

In fact, such men taking 50 milligrams (about 80,000 international units or IUs) of beta carotene every other day for six years suffered only half as many heart attacks and strokes as similar men who took a placebo—a harmless "sugar pill."

The daily dose used in the study is comparable to the beta carotene in about two cups of carrots per day.

Spiced Carrot Soup

Serves 6

Believe it or not, carrots give you an even better jolt of life-preserving beta-carotene when they are cooked. That's because more of the beta-carotene is released from the carrot's cell walls, and this soup is off the charts for high levels of beta-carotene. This wonderful spicy soup is a favorite of mine and of diners at Leigh Stone-Herbert's family owned Gravetye Manor Restaurant north of London, recognized for its healthful food. Thanks to the restaurant for the recipe from which this was adapted. (This soup is also easy to make in a microwave.)

6 large carrots, thinly sliced
6 cups homemade chicken broth or low-sodium chicken broth
1 tablespoon butter or margarine (optional)
1/8 teaspoon ground cumin or to taste
1/8 teaspoon ground coriander or to taste
1/8 teaspoon ground cinnamon or to taste
1/8 teaspoon cayenne pepper or to taste
Salt and freshly ground pepper to taste

Simmer the carrots in a heavy saucepan with 1/2 cup of the chicken broth and butter or margarine if desired, until the carrots are tender. (You can also do this in a microwave.)

Put the carrots in small batches in a blender and puree. Then return the puree to the pan or microwave bowl.

Add the spices and stir. Add the remaining chicken broth and salt and pepper and simmer for 20 minutes on the stove or cook on HIGH for about 10 minutes in the microwave.

Per serving:

Calories	74
Total fat	1.7 g
Saturated fat	.4 g
Cholesterol	0
Sodium	88 mg

Curried Broccoli Soup

Serves 4

Green is the color researchers are raving about in evaluating foods as potential inhibitors of cancer. The green vegetables are exceptionally high in certain compounds believed to combat cancer-causing agents, according to U.S. Department of Agriculture studies. Broccoli, they say, is one of the best. In this recipe you get chunks of broccoli awash in a broccoli base. It's delicious. You can also substitute other green vegetables—peas, green beans, or asparagus—for the broccoli.

4 cups chopped fresh or frozen broccoli
2½ cups low-sodium chicken broth
1 large onion, chopped
2 large garlic cloves, chopped
1 teaspoon curry powder (more if desired)
Salt to taste
1 cup low-fat buttermilk mixed with 1 teaspoon flour

Set aside 2 cups of the chopped broccoli. Place the remaining broccoli, chicken broth, onion, garlic, curry powder, and salt in a heavy saucepan. Cover and bring to a boil. Lower the heat and simmer for 20 minutes. Cool for 10 to 15 minutes.

In batches, puree the mixture in a food processor fitted with the steel blade or in a blender. Return the puree to the saucepan and bring to a simmer, uncovered. Add reserved 2 cups broccoli and buttermilk. Bring to a simmer (do not boil), adjust seasonings, and serve immediately.

Note: The soup can also be served lightly chilled.

Per serving:

Calories	89
Total fat	2 g
Saturated fat	.6 g
Cholesterol	2.5 mg
Sodium	122 mg

BROCCOLI—AN AMAZING FOOD PILL

Broccoli is one of the most amazing pharmaceutical packages in nature's food pharmacy.

If it had a pharmacological label, it would read like this: Contains high concentrations of beta-carotene (suspected lung cancer antagonist); carotenoids (general anticancer agents); quercetin (antioxidant and anticancer agent); glutathione (antioxidant and anticancer agent); indoles (anticancer and detoxification compounds); vitamin C (powerful antioxidant); folate (anticancer agent); chromium (antidiabetic and anti-heart-disease medication); readily absorbable calcium (needed to help prevent osteoporosis—also a suspected anticancer and high blood pressure medication); calcium pectate fiber (lowers blood cholesterol). It is also a member of the famous cruciferous family of vegetables, closely tied to lower rates of cancer, notably colon cancer. In numerous studies broccoli shows up as a vegetable most preferred by those with lower rates of all kinds of cancer.

Potato and Kale Soup

Serves 6

Full of dense green kale, this soup has been described as "vigorous and deeply satisfying." It's the national soup of Portugal. I'm attracted to it mainly because kale is so underused yet is one of the super sources of carotenoids, believed to help fight off numerous diseases—from cancer to cataracts. Kale, for example, contains twice as many carotenoids as spinach, another super source. And combined with potatoes and onions, it makes a rich and flavorful soup.

1 tablespoon olive oil
1 medium yellow onion, finely chopped
1 leek, trimmed, washed, and chopped
3 garlic cloves, minced
3 large potatoes, peeled and diced
6 cups water
Salt and freshly ground pepper to taste
1/4 pound chorizo or chourico (Portuguese) sausage (optional)
1 pound kale, trimmed and shredded

In a large, heavy saucepan, heat the olive oil. Add the onion, leek, and garlic and cook over medium heat for 3 to 4 minutes or until the onions are translucent and soft.

Add the potatoes, water, salt, and pepper. Bring to a boil, reduce the heat, and simmer gently, covered, for 20 minutes or until the potatoes are very soft. With a potato masher, mash the potatoes right in the broth or puree in a food processor fitted with the steel blade.

If you are using the sausage, prick it all over with a pin and place in cold water to cover. Gradually bring to a boil, reduce the heat, and simmer gently for 6 to 8 minutes or until cooked. Let cool and cut into 1/4-inch slices. Then add the sausage to the potato mixture and simmer for 3 minutes.

Stir in the kale and simmer for a minute or 2 or just until the kale is tender. Do not overcook. The kale should remain bright green. Correct the seasonings and serve.

Note: To shred kale, after you have stemmed and washed the leaves, roll them into a tight cigar and then slice crosswise into the slenderest slivers.

Per serving:

Calories	175
Total fat	4 g
Saturated fat	.5 g
Cholesterol	0
Sodium	38 mg

Minted Pea Soup

Serves 6

It's hard to pass up peas when you can so quickly make them into a fabulous, fragrant soup like this. One night I made this soup and ate half of it myself. Peas are one of those green vegetables included in the diets of people more likely to escape cancer. The pea is also surprisingly high in fiber, which may be one more reason for its therapeutic qualities.

2 10-ounce packages (4 cups) frozen peas
2 10½-ounce cans (about 2½ cups) low-sodium chicken broth
½ cup chopped mint leaves
1 medium potato, baked or boiled, peeled, and cut into chunks
2 teaspoons lemon juice
1 cup nonfat buttermilk
Salt and freshly ground pepper to taste
1 tablespoon plain nonfat yogurt for garnish (optional)

Put the frozen peas and 1 cup of the chicken broth in a large saucepan. Heat for about 5 minutes until the peas are thawed.

Put the pea mixture in a blender or a food processor fitted with the steel blade. Add the mint, potato, and lemon juice and puree.

Return the puree to the saucepan. Stir in the buttermilk and salt and pepper. Cook just until heated through; do not boil. If desired, serve topped with a small dollop of yogurt.

Per serving:

Calories	128
Total fat	1.4 g
Saturated fat	.5 g
Cholesterol	1.6 mg
Sodium	173 mg

Tomato Basil Soup

Serves 4

The best time to make this soup is when both ripe, juicy fresh tomatoes and fresh basil leaves are plentiful. It's delicious served either cold or hot. Tomatoes are a super source of the powerful cell defenders vitamins A and C and the compound lycopene, as well as potassium, which some experts believe counters high blood pressure and strokes.

1 tablespoon olive oil
2 pounds tomatoes, peeled, seeded, and finely chopped
3 garlic cloves, minced
½ cup chopped fresh basil leaves
3 cups low-sodium chicken broth
Salt and freshly ground pepper to taste
Seasoned croutons or plain nonfat yogurt for garnish (optional)

Place the olive oil and tomatoes in a saucepan and cook over medium heat for 5 minutes. Add the garlic and basil and cook for 10 more minutes.

Pour in the chicken broth, season, and bring to a boil. Reduce the heat and simmer for 5 minutes.

If you are serving the soup cold, chill it for several hours or overnight. Serve topped with seasoned bread cubes or a dollop of yogurt.

Note: Skin tomatoes by blanching in boiling water for 10 seconds. Run under cold water to stop cooking process. Cut in half. Squeeze out the seeds, then chop.

Per serving:

Calories	101
Total fat	4 g
Saturated fat	.8 g
Cholesterol	0
Sodium	58 mg

FOOD PHARMACY FACT

The Red Tomato Alert

Eating tomatoes may help protect you from pancreatic cancer, a particularly virulent malignancy that kills 22,000 Americans yearly. So suggests a study at Johns Hopkins University. Investigators found that the blood of a group of such cancer victims was markedly low in levels of a vegetable compound called *lycopene*—a red pigment found in red vegetables and fruits, notably tomatoes and strawberries. In fact those with the least lycopene in their bloodstreams were five times more likely to develop pancreatic cancer than those with the highest blood levels of lycopene.

My Favorite Lentil Soup

Serves 6

Lentil soup is irresistible, especially on a cold day. But you can also eat this soup cold on a hot day. Lentils are one of nature's pharmacological gems, keeping blood sugar and cholesterol down, and probably blood pressure too. Lentils also, as a member of the legume family, are full of a variety of anticancer agents. Another virtue: unlike other legumes, they do not need soaking and thus are quicker to prepare, although the soup is richer if allowed to simmer for a few hours.

2 teaspoons olive oil
1 medium onion, chopped
2 quarts water
3 low-sodium chicken or vegetable bouillon cubes *or* 3 teaspoons instant bouillon
1 cup lentils
3/4 cup coarsely chopped spinach leaves
1 carrot, chopped
1/4 cup chopped celery
1 cup chopped fresh or canned tomatoes with juice
2 garlic cloves, minced
1/2 teaspoon ground allspice
1/2 teaspoon dried thyme
Salt and freshly ground pepper to taste
Juice of 1 lemon

Place the olive oil and onions in a 4-quart saucepan and sauté until the onions are translucent and soft.

Add the remaining ingredients except the lemon juice. Cover and bring to a boil. Reduce the heat and simmer until the soup is of desired thickness, from an hour to 3 or 4 hours, stirring occasionally.

Add the lemon juice just before serving or squeeze a splash of lemon juice into each bowl.

Per serving:

Calories	149
Total fat	2 g
Saturated fat	.2 g
Cholesterol	0
Sodium	23 mg

FOOD PHARMACY FACT

Beans vs. Pancreatic Cancer

Seventh-Day Adventists who ate the most lentils, peas, and beans (including soybean products) as well as dried fruit were much less likely to develop fatal pancreatic cancer, according to a study by Paul K. Mills, Department of Preventive Medicine, Loma Linda University School of Medicine. Specifically, those who ate beans, lentils, and peas more than three times a week had only 40 percent the chance of dying of pancreatic cancer of those who ate legumes less than once a week. Heavy eaters of raisins, dates, and other dried fruits (more than three times a week) had equally low odds. The anticancer agents in dried fruits were unclear, said Dr. Mills, but he credited protease inhibitors in legumes with warding off the deadly cancer.

Mariana's Salmon Corn Soup

Serves 6

This is such a pretty soup, flecked with colorful vegetables. And it's a simple, inexpensive way to get lots of omega-3-type fish oils, especially if you use lower-priced pink canned salmon. Each serving contains about 1,200 milligrams of healthful omega-3s. This low-fat soup is adapted from a recipe given to me by my friend Mariana Gosnell, who first tasted it during a visit to wintry northern Canada.

1/4 cup chopped celery
1 garlic clove, crushed
1/2 cup chopped onion
2 cups low-sodium chicken broth
1 cup diced peeled potatoes
1 cup diced carrots
1 15 1/2-ounce can salmon, drained and flaked, liquid reserved
1/2 teaspoon dried thyme
Salt and freshly ground pepper to taste
1/2 cup chopped broccoli
1 10-ounce package frozen corn kernels
1 12-ounce can (1 1/2 cups) evaporated skim milk

In a large saucepan, sauté the celery, garlic, and onion in 1/2 cup of the chicken broth until the onions are translucent and soft.

Add the potatoes, carrots, the remaining 1 1/2 cups of chicken broth, salmon liquid, thyme, salt, and pepper. Cover and simmer for about 30 minutes, until the vegetables are tender. Add the broccoli and cook for 5 minutes.

Add the flaked salmon, corn, and evaporated skim milk. Heat through and serve.

Per serving:

Calories	239
Total fat	5.5 g
Saturated fat	1.4 g
Cholesterol	2.5 mg
Sodium	512 mg

Oyster Chowder

Serves 6 to 8

Oysters are the opposite of what many people think—they are good, not bad, for your heart and cholesterol. They are extremely rich in the trace minerals copper, zinc, chromium, and selenium—all of which have been linked to better cardiovascular functioning—and selenium is an antioxidant, thought to help prevent cancer as well. I especially like this chowder because it has spinach and potatoes, which are also well endowed with pharmacological properties.

- 1 tablespoon olive oil
- 3 shallots, minced
- 2 celery stalks, finely chopped
- 1 tablespoon flour
- 1 quart bottled clam juice or fish stock
- 1 pint shucked fresh oysters, strained and liquor reserved
- 2 large potatoes, peeled and diced
- 1 cup low-fat milk
- Salt and freshly ground black pepper to taste
- 5 ounces fresh spinach, stemmed, washed, and cut into ½-inch strips

Heat the oil in a large saucepan and cook the shallots and celery over medium heat for a few minutes or until translucent and soft but not brown. Stir in the flour. Stir in clam juice and reserved oyster liquor and bring the chowder to a boil. Add the potatoes and simmer gently for 6 to 8 minutes or until tender. Add the milk and salt and pepper to taste. (The chowder can be prepared up to 24 hours ahead to this point.)

Just before serving, add the oysters and simmer for 2 minutes or until the oysters are cooked—but just barely. Stir in the spinach. The heat from the chowder should be sufficient to cook the spinach, but if not, simmer the soup for a few seconds more. Taste and correct the seasonings.

Per serving:

Calories	158
Total fat	5 g
Saturated fat	1 g
Cholesterol	48 mg
Sodium	493 mg

FOOD PHARMACY FACT

More Oysters, Please

Oysters are one of the highest of all foods in the trace mineral chromium. That may make them good heart food. In studies at Bemidji State University in Minnesota and Mercy Hospital in San Diego, researchers gave 200 micrograms of chromium supplements to people with high cholesterol—265 milligrams or higher—for forty-two days in a double-blind study. The chromium reduced the undesirable-type LDL cholesterol by 11 percent and slightly increased desirable HDLs. About 90 percent of Americans do not get enough chromium every day, according to the National Academy of Sciences. Other high-chromium foods: whole grains, liver, nuts, prunes, asparagus, egg yolks, potatoes, mushrooms, rhubarb, beer, and wine.

Seafood Minestrone

Serves 6

This mélange of seafood with Italian seasonings and vegetables helps ensure you get your daily quota of omega-3, which all your cells will appreciate; they can function better when they are supplied with good fats instead of bad fats. Shellfish, especially scallops, are quite low in fat; both mussels and clams help lower blood cholesterol. This is a hearty soup that can also serve as an entrée. It's one of many low-fat, low-calorie recipes in Ellen Brown's The Gourmet Gazelle Cookbook.

1 dozen mussels
1 dozen small hard-shelled clams
2 tablespoons cornmeal
1 tablespoon olive oil
1 leek, cleaned and chopped
½ cup chopped onion
1 garlic clove, minced
¼ cup chopped celery
¼ cup sliced mushrooms
4 large tomatoes, peeled, seeded, and diced
1¾ cups chicken stock, preferably unsalted
1 cup clam juice
2 tablespoons chopped fresh basil *or* 2 teaspoons dried
¼ teaspoon freshly ground pepper
1 cup chopped washed kale
¼ cup macaroni
¼ pound shrimp, peeled and deveined, *or* crab meat
¼ pound fillet of sole or other white fish, cut into ½-inch pieces
¼ pound bay scallops
3 tablespoons freshly grated Parmesan cheese

Scrub the mussels and clams under cold running water with a stiff brush, discarding any that are not firmly shut. Scrape off the mussels' beards with a sharp paring knife. Place the mollusks in a bowl of cold water and sprinkle cornmeal on top. Place in the refrigerator for at least 2 hours.

Heat the olive oil in a large stockpot over medium heat. Add the leek, onion, garlic, celery, and mushrooms. Sauté over medium heat, stirring frequently, for 5 minutes or until the onions are translucent and soft. Add the tomatoes, stock, clam juice, basil, and pepper. Bring to a boil, reduce the heat to low, and simmer the soup, uncovered, for 15 minutes. Add the kale and macaroni and simmer for 5 minutes.

Drain the mussels and clams, then wash again. Raise the heat to high, add the shellfish, and cover the pot. Steam the mussels and clams with the pot tightly covered for 5 to 7 minutes, depending on the size of the seafood. Shake the pot occasionally to redistribute the clams and mussels.

Remove the clams and mussels with a slotted spoon, discarding any that did not open. Set aside.

Return the soup to a boil and add the shrimp, sole, and scallops. Cover the pot and turn off the heat. Let the pot sit undisturbed for 5 minutes.

To serve, ladle the soup into shallow flat soup bowls, arrange the clams and mussels on top, and sprinkle with Parmesan cheese.

Per serving:

Calories	193
Total fat	5 g
Saturated fat	1 g
Cholesterol	54 mg
Sodium	308 mg

Dr. Ziment's Garlic Chicken Soup for Colds and Coughs

Serves 4

Brought to you by popular demand, this soup has helped countless people fight colds and chest congestion. The recipe appeared in The Food Pharmacy, *and so many people attested to its therapeutic benefits that it is reprinted here. It comes from Dr. Irwin Ziment, professor of pulmonary medicine, University of California at Los Angeles, who says he finds it more healing than most modern drugs. He advises taking it at the beginning of a meal, one to three times a day.*

1 quart homemade chicken broth
1 garlic head, about 15 cloves, peeled
5 parsley sprigs, minced
6 cilantro sprigs, minced
1 teaspoon lemon pepper
1 teaspoon minced fresh mint leaves
1 teaspoon dried basil, crushed, *or* 1 tablespoon chopped fresh
1 teaspoon curry powder
Hot red pepper flakes to taste, sliced carrots, bay leaves (optional)

Place all ingredients in a pan without a lid. Bring to a boil, then simmer for about 30 minutes.

Strain the soup—or, better yet, remove the solid garlic cloves and herbs and put them in a blender or food processor, then return the puree to the broth. Serve hot. And be sure to inhale the fumes during its preparation, urges Dr. Ziment.

Per serving:

Calories	52
Total fat	1.6 g
Saturated fat	.4 g
Cholesterol	0
Sodium	258 mg

FOOD PHARMACY FACT

Chicken Soup Fights Cold Symptoms

Let's not forget that several years ago a study in the prestigious medical journal *Chest,* to the surprise of researchers, revealed that chicken soup really is "good for you, especially if you have an upper respiratory infection." As researcher Dr. Marvin Sackner, pulmonary specialist at Mount Sinai Medical Center in Miami Beach, concluded: "There's an aromatic substance in chicken soup, not yet identified, that helps clear your airways."

He meticulously measured the effects of cold water, hot water, and hot chicken soup on the rate of flow of mucus and airflow through nasal passages. Hot water cleared congestion in airways better than cold water, but best of all was hot chicken soup. Even cold chicken soup worked to a lesser extent.

Dr. Weil's Miso Soup

Serves 4

A few years ago Japanese scientists found that those who ate miso soup regularly were about one-third less likely to have stomach cancer. There's apparently something in miso itself, which is fermented soybean, rice, or barley paste, that is protective. No book with pharmacological recipes would be complete without one for miso soup. Luckily, I discovered this recipe in a superb book, Natural Health, Natural Medicine, *by Dr. Andrew Weil, well-known medical author and faculty member at the University of Arizona College of Medicine. He says the soup was developed for one of his food and nutrition workshops.*

2 teaspoons canola oil
3 thin slices fresh gingerroot
1 large onion, thinly sliced
2 carrots, peeled and thinly sliced
2 celery stalks, thinly sliced
4 cups coarsely chopped cabbage
5 cups water
4 tablespoons light or dark miso
Scallions, including green parts, chopped, for garnish

Heat the canola oil in large pot. Add the gingerroot and onion and sauté over medium heat for 5 minutes. Add the carrots, celery, and cabbage. Stir well. Add the water. Bring rapidly to a boil, then lower heat and simmer, covered, until the carrots are just tender, about 10 minutes.

Remove the soup from the heat. Place the miso in a bowl, add a little of the broth, and stir well to a smooth paste. Add more broth to thin the mixture, then add it to the pot of soup. Let rest for a few minutes.

Serve the soup in bowls with chopped raw scallions. You may wish to remove the sliced ginger and/or add a few drops of roasted (dark) sesame oil to each bowl.

Per serving:

Calories	105
Total fat	4 g
Saturated fat	.3 g
Cholesterol	0
Sodium	670 mg

Eat Less, Live Longer

Could there be any connection between the fact that the typical Japanese eats the fewest calories and yet has the longest life expectancy among inhabitants of industrialized nations?

The average Japanese man lives 75.2 years, the average woman 80.9 years, for a combined life expectancy of 78. The U.S. ranks twelfth with a life expectancy of 74.8 years, below Sweden (77), Switzerland (77), Canada (76.5), Netherlands (76.4), Norway (76.2), Australia (76), Spain (76), France (75.6), West Germany (75.2), and Greece (74.9), according to figures from the United Nations Secretariat. The Japanese have remarkably low rates of heart disease and all cancers except stomach cancer.

And what do they eat in Japan? Less fat and meat and fewer calories. And more fish and complex carbohydrates like rice, vegetables, and soybean products. Strikingly, the average Japanese eats a mere 2,600 calories daily compared with about 3,500 daily calories for Americans. In Japan about 25 percent of the calories come from fat. In the U.S. it's about 37 percent.

A main dish in Japan is often carbohydrates like rice and noodles with meat and vegetables as condiments. In the U.S., of course, meat is the centerpiece of most meals, complemented by carbohydrates and vegetables.

That restricting calories leads to a longer life has substantial support in animal studies. Trim, lean—but not undernourished—mice that eat about 65 percent as many calories as normal mice live about 50 percent longer. Why? Nobody is sure; the subject is under intense scrutiny. One theory: the processing of calories boosts glucose or blood sugar as well as insulin levels. High amounts of glucose and/or insulin circulating in the system seem to promote cell destruction and disease, particularly heart disease, according to some experts.

Chicken or Turkey Broth

About 2 quarts

Making your own chicken or turkey broth allows you to control its amount of sodium and fat, reducing them to virtually zero if you wish. You can use this recipe for the chicken broth in the recipes in this book. And you can vary the seasonings and richness as you desire.

3 pounds chicken necks, wings, and backs, or turkey wings
3 quarts water
1 large yellow onion, chopped
3 large celery stalks, including leaves, chopped
2 carrots, peeled and chopped
2 bay leaves
5 parsley sprigs (more if desired)
1 tablespoon whole black peppercorns
1 tablespoon dried thyme (optional)
2 garlic cloves, chopped (optional)
Salt to taste

Place all ingredients in a large kettle or stockpot and bring to a boil. Simmer over very low heat for about 3½ hours. Skim the surface from time to time to remove any scum that forms.

When the flavor is of the desired richness, remove the soup from the heat. Let the broth cool slightly, then strain it into a large bowl, using a colander lined with cheesecloth or other porous material. Refrigerate for at least 3 hours, preferably overnight.

Skim off all congealed fat that has risen to the top. Keep the broth refrigerated or put into small containers and freeze. The frozen broth should keep for about 6 months.

Per 1-cup serving:

Calories	44
Total fat	1.8 g
Saturated fat	0
Cholesterol	0
Sodium	8 mg

Vegetable Broth

About 1½ quarts

You can substitute vegetable broth for chicken broth called for in recipes. Practically any vegetable will work. Here's a suggested version.

1 medium yellow onion, chopped
2 carrots, peeled and chopped
2 celery stalks, including leaves, chopped
2 parsnips, peeled and chopped
1 small turnip, peeled and chopped
Salt and freshly ground pepper to taste
2 quarts water

In a large saucepan, combine all ingredients, bring to a boil, lower the heat, and simmer for 1 hour, skimming occasionally.

When the vegetables are very soft, remove from the heat and strain through a cheesecloth-lined colander. Using a potato masher, mash the vegetables to extract all liquid.

Discard the vegetables and store the broth in the refrigerator or freezer.

Per 1-cup serving:

Calories	10
Total fat	0
Saturated fat	0
Cholesterol	0
Sodium	8 mg

Lottie's Grapefruit-Vegetable Gazpacho

Serves 6

This grapefruit-based cold soup is one of the most unusual and refreshing I have ever come across. And you get loads of fiber from the membranes and juice sacs of the grapefruit, a unique fiber shown to help lower blood cholesterol and perhaps even help reverse damage that has already occurred to arteries. And the soup is low in calories and has virtually zero fat.

4 grapefruits, peeled, seeded, and quartered
3 tomatoes, halved crosswise and seeds squeezed out
2 cucumbers, peeled, seeded, and cut into chunks
3 celery stalks, including leaves
2 red or green bell peppers, cut into chunks
1/4 cup chopped parsley
Salt to taste
1/4 teaspoon Tabasco sauce or to taste
Grapefruit juice as needed

Puree the grapefruit quarters in a food processor fitted with the steel blade or in a blender and pour into a large bowl or pitcher.

Puree the tomatoes and cucumbers and add them to the grapefruit.

Puree the celery, bell peppers, and parsley and add to the bowl or pitcher.

Stir the pureed pulp together. Stir in the salt and hot pepper sauce and add grapefruit juice as needed.

Per serving:

Calories	83
Total fat	.5 g
Saturated fat	.03 g
Cholesterol	0
Sodium	34 mg

FOOD PHARMACY FACT

Citrus Against Cancer

Nomilin—a compound that brings the sour and bitter taste to citrus fruits—may help block cancer, according to Dr. Luke K. T. Lam at the University of Minnesota. Mice given nomilin and then a potent cancer-causing agent in cigarette smoke were much less likely to develop stomach cancer. One hundred percent of the mice not given nomilin developed malignancies, compared with only 28 percent of the nomilin-treated mice.

Some experts have long speculated that the falling rate of stomach cancer in the U.S. is tied to the year-round consumption of citrus fruits. They generally credit vitamin C; nomilin may be another reason. Dr. Lam explains that nomilin probably works by tripling the activity of an enzyme that helps detoxify poisons in the body, including carcinogens.

Grape Gazpacho (Ajo Branco)

Serves 4

Even if red grapes were not super sources of quercetin and other anticancer and cell-protecting compounds, this soup would still be an all-time favorite because of its unusual texture and pleasing taste and color. It's even a favorite of my friend Daryl, who cannot abide grapes in any other form. You can use white seedless grapes, but I prefer red because they are so concentrated in the antioxidant quercetin and other known antibacterial, antiviral substances. Almonds, too, are good for you; although high in fat, most of it is heart-protective and cholesterol-lowering monounsaturated fat. This recipe, which I have modified to use red instead of white grapes, is the inspiration of Steven Raichlen, a national food writer based in Miami, who specializes in ethnic foods.

1 pound seedless grapes, preferably red
2 to 3 slices country-style white bread, crusts removed and cubed (enough to make 2 cups)
1½ cups cold water (more if needed)
3 ounces (about ⅔ cup) blanched almonds
2 to 3 garlic cloves, peeled, or to taste
2 tablespoons olive oil
2 to 3 tablespoons white wine vinegar
1 to 2 drops almond extract
Salt and freshly ground black pepper to taste

Remove the stems from the grapes. Place the bread cubes in a bowl with the water. Soak the bread until soft.

Place the grapes in a food processor fitted with the steel blade with the remaining ingredients and puree until smooth. Add the bread and water and puree. Chill the soup for at least 1 hour before serving.

Just before serving, correct the seasoning, adding salt, pepper, or vinegar to taste. The sweetness of the grapes should be balanced by the pungency of the vinegar and garlic.

Per serving:

Calories	309
Total fat	19 g
Saturated fat	2 g
Cholesterol	.5 mg
Sodium	80 mg

DON'T UNDERESTIMATE GRAPES

Nutritionally speaking, the grape does look puny. It has only a smidgen of vitamin C and not much potassium to speak of—and those are its strong points. That has caused some conventionally minded nutrition experts to write off or denigrate the grape. But to scientists who see beyond nutrients to other molecular aspects of food power, the grape is far from a wimp.

Red grapes are one of the richest of all foods in a powerful antioxidant called *quercetin* that can protect animals against cancer. It is also high in caffeic acid, another anticancer agent in animal and lab studies. Blue grapes, commercial grape juice, and pure tannins extracted from grapes have been found extremely potent in inactivating viruses in test tubes. Wine, notably red wine, is an antibiotic; it contains compounds shown to work in similar fashion to penicillin. Grapes are also rich in boron, a newly discovered trace mineral linked to keeping bones strong and the brain alert. Dietary surveys link grapes to a lower incidence of gum disease (considered an infection), and raisins—dried grapes—to lower rates of both cancer of the pancreas and deaths from all cancers.

So don't neglect grapes just because they are "nutritionally" lightweight; in other ways they are capable of delivering knockout punches regularly to save your cells from damage, researchers insist.

FOOD PHARMACY FACT

Almonds—Good for the Heart

Almonds, though high in fat, still may help fight heart disease, according to Dr. Gene A. Spiller, a noted researcher and director of the Health Research and Studies Center in California.

In an experiment Dr. Spiller asked a group of men and women with moderately high cholesterol (average around 240) to eat three-and-a-half ounces of almonds a day for three to nine weeks. Other groups in the study ate the same amount of fat from cheese or olive oil. Everybody ate equal amounts of grains, vegetables, and fruits.

Surprise! The almond-eaters' cholesterol dropped from 10 to 15 percent compared with the cheese eaters' cholesterol. Olive oil also reduced cholesterol, but almonds were slightly better.

Dr. Spiller explains it this way: most of the fat in almonds is the same type as that in olive oil—monounsaturated, which is linked to healthier blood and less heart disease. However, this does not give you license to eat tons of almonds to lower blood cholesterol—because almonds, like olive oil, are high in fat (one ounce of almonds has about 175 calories). The point is that almonds, like olive oil, can substitute for other fats in a health-promoting diet.

Other nuts exceptionally high in monounsaturated fat are filberts (hazelnuts) and pistachios.

Avocado Ceviche

Serves 4

I flipped over this when I found it on the menu of the Four Seasons Hotel in Beverly Hills. I had it as an appetizer for dinner and again the following day at lunch and immediately asked the chef for the recipe. It is like a gazpacho with a marvelous hot spicy flavor offset by the mellow avocado. It's full of vitamin C from the tomatoes and limes, the best cell-protecting vitamin known, with horseradish and jalapeños to clear your sinuses and avocado to help keep your blood pressure down. Many thanks to Pascal Vignau, executive chef.

6 plum tomatoes, seeded and diced
1 small cucumber, seeded and diced
1 avocado, peeled, pitted, and diced
½ red onion, finely diced
2 jalapeño peppers, seeded and diced
1 large bunch cilantro, chopped (at least 1 cup)
Juice of 2 limes
1 quart tomato juice
1 teaspoon horseradish
Salt and freshly ground pepper to taste
Additional avocado slices for garnish (optional)
Tortilla chips for serving (optional)

Combine all ingredients. Adjust the seasoning and chill. Garnish with a fan of avocado slices and serve with crisp tortilla chips.

Note: Low-sodium tomato juice was used in the analysis.

Per serving:

Calories	151
Total fat	8 g
Saturated fat	1.3 g
Cholesterol	0
Sodium	38 mg

Peachy Ginger Soup

Serves 6

A lovely-to-look-at, mellow blend of peaches and ginger, this is a most pleasant way to get some beta-carotene, plus the other largely unidentified health-promoting compounds in peaches. The ginger, in case you have forgotten, is a rather potent blood "thinner," according to tests, and a stomach soother. This chilled soup is glorious on a hot summer day. It is definitely not too sweet as a prelude to dinner, although the degree of sweetness depends on the natural sugar in the peaches. You can sweeten it to use as a dessert soup.

4 cups sliced peaches (about 5 or 6 large) *or* 2 16-ounce packages frozen peaches; reserve 1 whole peach or 2/3 cup frozen peaches
1/4 cup minced candied ginger
1/4 cup plain nonfat or low-fat yogurt
1 1/4 cups skim or 1 percent milk
Salt to taste
1/4 teaspoon ground nutmeg (preferably freshly grated)
1/4 teaspoon ground cinnamon

In a food processor fitted with the steel blade or in a blender, puree the peaches (except for the reserved peach) and ginger until smooth. Transfer the peach mixture to a large bowl. Add the yogurt, milk, salt, nutmeg, and cinnamon. Blend well.

Peel and cut the remaining fresh peach or frozen peaches into small dice. Stir in the diced peach. Chill until serving time.

If desired, garnish with a small dollop of yogurt sprinkled with additional slivers of candied ginger.

Per serving:

Calories	109
Total fat	.3 g
Saturated fat	.1 g
Cholesterol	1 mg
Sodium	40 mg

Chilled Cantaloupe Soup

Serves 6

Lovely to look at, this soup is also lovely for your heart and cells in general because it is packed with vitamin A (beta-carotene), vitamin C, and potassium and is virtually nonfat.

3 very ripe cantaloupes, peeled and seeded
1 6-ounce can frozen orange juice concentrate
½ cup honey
½ teaspoon ground cardamom
½ teaspoon ground cinnamon
¼ cup peach brandy (optional)
Fresh mint leaves, if available, for garnish

Place the cantaloupe chunks in a food processor fitted with the steel blade or in a blender and puree. Add the remaining ingredients and blend until smooth.

Pour into a pitcher or container and serve in small bowls, mugs, or goblets, garnished with mint. Serve well chilled.

Per serving:

Calories	237
Total fat	1 g
Saturated fat	0
Cholesterol	0
Sodium	26 mg

Cranberry Soup

Serves 6

A cranberry soup recipe is a must for anyone interested in the pharmacological properties of food. And this delicately flavored blend of fruit, vegetables, and Indian spices makes a wonderful hot or cold soup for any season. Cranberries have been used to prevent and treat bladder and urinary tract infections for at least a century. Even cranberry juice watered down to 1 percent has some pharmacological activity, lab tests show, but the whole berry is more potent.

1 12-ounce bag fresh cranberries
2 cups chopped carrots
1/2 cup chopped onions
1 cup water
3 cups homemade chicken stock or canned low-sodium chicken broth
1/2 cup drained canned tomatoes, strained to remove seeds
1/4 cup frozen unsweetened orange juice concentrate
1/2 teaspoon ground cinnamon
3/4 teaspoon ground cardamom
3 tablespoons sugar
Salt to taste

In a heavy saucepan, simmer the cranberries, carrots, and onions in the water for about 25 to 30 minutes or until all liquid is absorbed and carrots are soft.

Stir in the remaining ingredients. Add to a blender or a food processor fitted with the steel blade in small batches and puree. Taste for seasoning. Serve hot or refrigerate to chill until very cold.

Per serving:

Calories	128
Total fat	1 g
Saturated fat	.2 g
Cholesterol	0
Sodium	74 mg

Salads, Relishes, and Chutneys

Cabbage-Pepper Coleslaw

Serves 8

Coleslaw is one of the best ways to eat cabbage. Some studies suggest that raw *cabbage and peppers have more of certain cancer-fighting compounds than the cooked vegetables. Also, you won't get any possible cancer-promoting fat in this recipe. Absolutely no fat is added, making it as low-fat as a coleslaw can get. Yet I find it exceptionally good. One of the keys to its excellent flavor is the balsamic vinegar.*

1½ pounds green cabbage, cut into chunks
1 medium onion, quartered
1 green bell pepper, cut into chunks
1 yellow bell pepper, cut into chunks
1 red bell pepper, cut into chunks
Salt and freshly ground pepper to taste
3 tablespoons balsamic vinegar
2 teaspoons sugar

This can be made entirely in a food processor. Using the slicing blade, process the cabbage. Then add onions and peppers and process.

Transfer the vegetables to a bowl and add the salt, vinegar, and sugar. Marinate in the refrigerator for at least an hour.

Per serving:

Calories	36
Total fat	.3 g
Saturated fat	.01 g
Cholesterol	0
Sodium	16 mg

Apple Coleslaw with Peanuts

Serves 6

Adding apples, carrots, and nuts to cabbage gives more variations of crunch and disease-fighting properties. Peanuts are high in boron, a trace mineral thought to help keep bones strong and the brain alert. The lemony yogurt gives this salad an appealing taste without the fat found in typical coleslaw. This easy-to-make dressing is also terrific on other fruit and vegetable salads.

3 cups shredded cabbage
1 cup shredded carrots
1 large tart apple, cored and diced
1/3 cup raisins
1/4 cup chopped dry-roasted peanuts

DRESSING

1/2 cup lemon low-fat or nonfat yogurt
1 tablespoon low-calorie mayonnaise
1 tablespoon lemon juice

Combine the coleslaw ingredients in a bowl and toss with the dressing.

Per serving:

Calories	118
Total fat	4 g
Saturated fat	.7 g
Cholesterol	1.6 mg
Sodium	39 mg

FOOD PHARMACY FACT

Strong-Bone Foods

Nuts, particularly peanuts and almonds, as well as dried fruits, surprisingly may help prevent the crippling bone disease osteoporosis. These foods are high in the trace mineral boron, now thought critical in producing hormones that help regulate calcium metabolism. Tests by Dr. Forrest H. Nielsen, at the U.S. Department of Agriculture's Human Nutrition Research Center in Grand Forks, North Dakota, found that women on low-boron diets were more apt to lose calcium and magnesium, essential for keeping bones strong. But when given three milligrams of boron a day for three months, their calcium losses dropped by 40 percent. People who eat lots of fruits and nuts get an average three milligrams daily, says Nielsen. One of the richest sources: peanuts. Three-and-a-half ounces contain two milligrams of boron.

Dr. Duke's Anticancer Slaw

Serves 8

Dr. James Duke, chief of the medicinal plants section at the U.S. Department of Agriculture, eats cabbage slaw every other day. He's convinced it may help ward off colon cancer, prevalent in his family. Here's one of his favorite recipes, and he notes that every single ingredient has shown anticancer potential. For example, radishes, like cauliflower, are a member of the cabbage family well endowed with anticancer compounds. "Hot peppers contain capsaicin, another potent chemopreventive. Ginger absorbs and neutralizes gastrointestinal toxins and acids and is an immune stimulant," he says. And, of course "onions and garlic were added because they contain sulfurous compounds with cancer preventive properties."

1 small firm green cabbage, shredded
1 large carrot, shredded
2 cups cauliflower florets, steamed until tender-crisp
½ green bell pepper, chopped
4 radishes, thinly sliced
4 scallions, thinly sliced

DRESSING

2 teaspoons grated fresh gingerroot *or* ½ teaspoon ground ginger
2 garlic cloves
¼ to ½ teaspoon hot red pepper flakes
½ cup white wine vinegar
2 tablespoons tamari or reduced-sodium soy sauce
2 tablespoons olive oil or dark sesame oil
2 tablespoons toasted sesame seeds or slivered almonds (optional)

Place all the salad ingredients in a large bowl.

Place all dressing ingredients except the optional sesame seeds or almonds in a blender and process until smooth. Stir in the sesame seeds or almonds if desired.

Add the dressing to the vegetables to taste and toss. Refrigerate any remaining dressing.

Per serving:

Calories	71
Total fat	3.6 g
Saturated fat	.5 g
Cholesterol	0
Sodium	276 mg

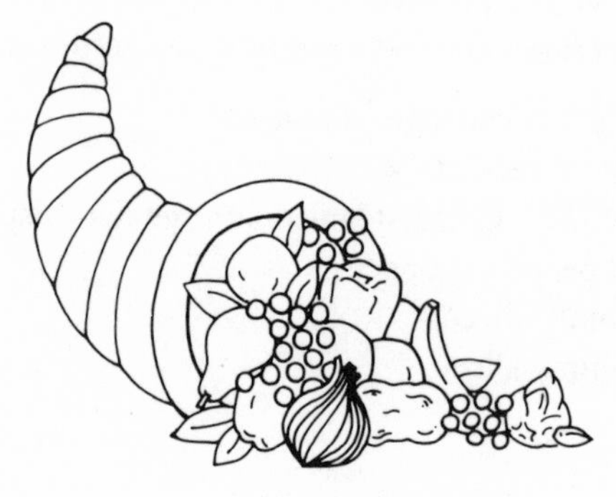

Turnip Slaw with Banana Dressing

Serves 4

"Turn on to turnips" might be a slogan of some researchers. Turnips are one of the cruciferous vegetables known to have several compounds believed to help cells resist damage leading to cancer. Frankly, I love raw turnips, and the addition of apples and the banana dressing in this recipe makes it outstanding—a real turn-on. Many thanks to my friend Pat Krause for this imaginative combination.

4 cups peeled and grated white turnip
1/2 cup grated onion
2 unpeeled apples, preferably tart, chopped
2 tablespoons frozen unsweetened orange juice concentrate
2 tablespoons lemon juice
1 teaspoon celery seeds
1 teaspoon caraway seeds
Salt and freshly ground black pepper to taste
1 cup Banana Dressing (recipe follows)

Combine all ingredients and refrigerate for at least 3 hours, preferably overnight.

Per serving:

Calories	138
Total fat	.7 g
Saturated fat	.1 g
Cholesterol	0
Sodium	93 mg

BANANA DRESSING

2 1/2 cups

2 medium bananas
2 small onions, chopped
1/4 cup frozen unsweetened apple juice concentrate
12 drops Tabasco sauce
Freshly ground black pepper to taste

Puree all the ingredients in a blender and refrigerate.

Per 1-tablespoon serving:

Calories	9
Total fat	.02 g
Saturated fat	.01 g
Cholesterol	0
Sodium	.73 mg

FOOD PHARMACY FACT

Pineapple for Strong Bones

To preserve strong bones and guard against the crippling bone disease osteoporosis, you need not just calcium but also other minerals, including manganese. And pineapple is full of manganese, says Dr. Jeanne Freeland-Graves, professor of nutrition at the University of Texas at Austin. "When we want to up the levels of manganese in the diet, we tell women to eat pineapple or drink pineapple juice," she says.

Her studies find that women with osteoporosis have about one third less manganese in their blood than healthy women. Further, when given manganese the diseased women absorbed twice as much, proving their bodies needed it. There's no question animals deficient in manganese develop severe osteoporosis, says Dr. Freeland-Graves.

Other good sources of manganese: oatmeal, nuts, cereals, beans, whole wheat, spinach, and tea. However, you're not as likely to absorb the mineral as well from these foods as from pineapple, she says.

Cold Grated Carrot Salads

"A fluffy pile of orange shreds, light, cold, moist as snow" is the way Phyllis Richman, restaurant critic of The Washington Post, *describes freshly grated carrots, saying she has loved them since childhood. But now she combines them with a variety of fruits, vegetables, nuts, and flavors. Grating or shredding raw carrots, say experts, is one of the best ways to obtain their therapeutic benefits, because grating breaks down cell walls, enabling you to absorb more beta-carotene, the carrot compound that is thought to help protect against cancer and some of the effects of aging.*

With some imagination there's virtually no end to combinations you can think up with grated carrots. Here are some of Richman's suggestions: diced orange sections, crushed pineapple, diced red or green bell peppers, diced bananas, shredded red cabbage, raisins, grapes, cantaloupe, green or black olives, coconut, onion, avocado, shredded cucumbers, nuts, parsley, scallions, garlic, diced candied ginger, shredded mint, dill, caraway seeds, cumin seeds, celery seeds, nutmeg, mustard, hot pepper, oregano, paprika, anise, oil and vinegar, citrus juice, yogurt, low-fat mayonnaise.

Here are some of my favorite combinations.

CARROTS WITH PINEAPPLE, RAISINS, AND WALNUTS

Serves 4

3 cups grated carrots (4 large carrots)
1 cup canned, crushed pineapple in unsweetened juice
1 teaspoon lemon juice or to taste
1/4 cup chopped walnuts

In a bowl, mix all ingredients together. This salad needs no dressing; the pineapple juice takes care of that.

Per serving:

Calories	121
Total fat	4.8 g
Saturated fat	.4 g
Cholesterol	0
Sodium	30 mg

FOOD PHARMACY FACT

Surprising Anti-Parkinson's Foods

It's a small study, but it offers a hint about what foods may hold off Parkinson's disease, a nervous-system disorder characterized by shaky hands and a shuffling gait. Researchers at the University of Medicine and Dentistry of New Jersey asked eighty-one Parkinson's patients (average age sixty-five) and their same-sex siblings of similar age who were free of the disease which foods they were most likely to have eaten in earlier years. Those free of Parkinson's were more apt to have eaten nuts and seeds, particularly walnuts and sunflower seeds, and salad oil or dressing.

The researchers speculate such foods share a common protective factor: vitamin E, which is concentrated in nuts, seeds, and oils. A study of actual Parkinson's patients at Columbia University did find fewer symptoms in those taking megadoses of vitamin E. Thus some researchers conclude that vitamin E may help prevent Parkinson's and reduce its severity.

CARROTS WITH A TOUCH OF CUMIN

Serves 4

4 large carrots, peeled and grated
2 to 3 tablespoons frozen orange juice concentrate diluted with half as much water
½ teaspoon ground cumin or to taste
2 to 3 tablespoons pine nuts (optional)

Put the grated carrots in a bowl and pour the diluted concentrate over them. Add the cumin (and pine nuts if desired) and mix well.

Per serving:

Calories	58
Total fat	.2 g
Saturated fat	0
Cholesterol	0
Sodium	36 mg

DOCTOR'S ADVICE

If you're a smoker or ever have been one, eat lots of deep orange foods high in beta-carotene; they may cut your chances of lung cancer, says Phyllis Bowen, associate professor of nutrition and medical dietetics at the University of Illinois at Chicago and an expert in beta-carotene. Studies show, she says, that smokers and former smokers who consume the most beta-carotene foods are only half as likely to develop lung cancer as those who skimp on such foods. Highest in beta-carotene: deep orange vegetables like carrots and deep green leafy vegetables like spinach.

MINTED CARROTS WITH LIME JUICE

Serves 4

Thanks for this suggestion to Molly O'Neill, food writer, The New York Times.

- 4 large carrots, shredded or grated
- ½ cup shredded fresh mint leaves
- 2 to 3 teaspoons lime juice
- 2 teaspoons olive oil
- Black pepper to taste, preferably freshly ground

Combine all ingredients and let marinate in the refrigerator for 30 to 60 minutes.

Per serving:

Calories	65
Total fat	2.5 g
Saturated fat	.3 g
Cholesterol	0
Sodium	35 mg

Tomatoes and Onions with Fresh Basil

Serves 4

My family loves this summer treat, claiming to have a craving for it. It's an excellent way to get the cholesterol-fighting benefits of raw onions and the varied protection from raw garlic. The fresh basil makes it all very pleasant to swallow.

2 large vine-ripened tomatoes, cut into 1-inch cubes
1 large mild onion, such as Vidalia or red, chopped
6 to 8 large fresh basil leaves, shredded
2 tablespoons raspberry vinegar
3 tablespoons olive oil
2 garlic cloves, crushed
Salt and freshly ground pepper to taste

Combine the tomatoes and onions and add the basil.

Combine the vinegar, olive oil, salt and pepper and garlic. Add the dressing to the tomato-onion mixture and let chill for an hour.

Per serving:

Calories	136
Total fat	10 g
Saturated fat	1.4 g
Cholesterol	0
Sodium	8 mg

DOCTOR'S ADVICE

Be sure to eat at least some of your garlic and onions raw. So advises Dr. William Blot, Ph.D., epidemiologist and biostatistician at the National Cancer Institute. It's unclear, he says, whether garlic and onions work equally well raw and cooked. "Nobody knows for sure," he says, "but we suspect that the active cancer-fighting compounds in garlic and onion are most potent in the raw form. In animal studies researchers usually use garlic or onion oils or garlic and onion extracts from raw bulbs to test anticancer potency, not the cooked version. Garlic and onion may also be anticancer when cooked, but we just don't know at this time."

Footnote: quercetin, an anticancer agent in yellow and red onions, is not destroyed by heat. Allicin, in garlic, is.

Red and Yellow Onion Rings

About 1½ cups, 4 servings

If you are in constant quest of the raw onion, as you should be, here's a treat that can be eaten as a relish with meat or poultry or added to green salads—it comes complete with its own low-calorie vinegar dressing. If it needs repeating, raw onions may boost your good-type HDL cholesterol, and both yellow and red onions are incredibly rich sources of quercetin, an antioxidant and anticancer agent.

1 tablespoon balsamic vinegar or cider vinegar
1 tablespoon rice vinegar or white wine vinegar
1 tablespoon plus 1 teaspoon honey
2 teaspoons Dijon or any spicy mustard
Freshly ground pepper to taste
1 small red onion, thinly sliced
2 small yellow onions, thinly sliced

In a small bowl, thoroughly mix the vinegars, honey, mustard, and pepper.

Separate the onions into rings and add the dressing. Cover and let stand at room temperature for 30 minutes or refrigerate until serving time.

Note: You can also coarsely chop the onions to make a relish.

Per serving:

Calories	36
Total fat	.2 g
Saturated fat	0
Cholesterol	0
Sodium	76 mg

Raw Onion Salsas or Relishes

In California they call them salsas, and they are like what most people know as relishes—chopped-up fruits and vegetables, spiked with herbs and a little vinegar and/or oil. Regardless, they are wonderful accompaniments to almost any main course. And I love them because they can be a vehicle for getting a daily quota of raw onions, shown in tests by Dr. Victor Gurewich, professor of medicine at Tufts, to boost good-type HDL cholesterol by an average whopping 30 percent. Consequently people are always asking me: "How can I get more raw onions into my diet?" The following five salsas are one of the most pleasant ways I know. Try them; you'll love them too, not just for their health qualities but also for their unique flavor and great colors.

They can turn a plain grilled fish, for example, into a spectacular event. Heap the salsa on top of or beside the fish. You can also use salsas as a colorful accompaniment to many vegetable or meat main dishes or sandwiches.

PEACH, ONION, AND BELL PEPPER SALSA

Serves 4

3 unpeeled peaches, cut into 1/2-inch dice
1/3 cup sliced scallions, including some of the green
1/4 cup diced red bell pepper
1/4 cup diced green bell pepper
2 to 3 tablespoons lime juice
1/4 cup chopped parsley or cilantro
3 tablespoons chopped flat-leaf parsley
1 tablespoon olive oil
1/2 teaspoon ground cumin
Salt and freshly ground pepper to taste
Minced jalapeño pepper or hot red pepper flakes to taste (optional)

Combine all ingredients and allow to rest for about 30 minutes.

Per serving:

Calories	51
Total fat	.2 g
Saturated fat	0 g
Cholesterol	0
Sodium	4 mg

FOOD PHARMACY FACT

Onion Juice for Bronchial Asthma

German studies at the University of Munich by Dr. Walter Dorsch have shown that onion juice may be antiallergenic, helping ward off bronchial asthma attacks. In one test those who drank onion juice prior to being exposed to irritants had about half the number of bronchial asthma attacks. Also, when onion juice solution was rubbed on arms that had been exposed to allergens, there was delayed swelling and less inflammation in nine out of twelve cases. Onion compounds are known to inhibit the formation of prostaglandins in the blood; prostaglandins are cellular messengers that can encourage the allergic process.

CANTALOUPE AND PEAR SALSA

Serves 4

1½ cups diced cantaloupe
⅓ cup finely chopped celery
⅓ cup chopped red onion
2 scallions, including some green, minced
¼ cup lime juice
1 tablespoon olive oil
1 tablespoon minced fresh mint
¼ cup chopped parsley or cilantro
1 teaspoon hot chili oil
1 tablespoon grated fresh gingerroot
⅓ cup chopped peeled pear in ½-inch dice
⅓ cup chopped unpeeled pear in ½-inch dice
Salt and freshly ground pepper to taste
Pinch of sugar to taste

Mix all the ingredients except the pears, salt, pepper, and sugar. Add these last ingredients just before serving.

Per serving:

Calories	80
Total fat	3.7 g
Saturated fat	.5 g
Cholesterol	0
Sodium	18 mg

FOOD PHARMACY FACT

The Vidalia Phenomenon

The county in Georgia famous for producing Vidalia onions has an unusually low death rate from stomach cancer. Residents of the county are only one third as likely to die of stomach cancer as other Americans and one half as likely to die of the disease as other Georgians. Experts can only speculate it's because the residents who grow so many onions also eat more of them, helping protect them from the cancer.

TOMATO-ONION SALSA

Serves 4

- 3 large tomatoes, peeled, seeded, and minced
- ½ large red onion, minced
- 1 red bell pepper, minced
- 1 cucumber, minced
- 2 tablespoons lime juice
- 3 or 4 tablespoons chopped flat-leaf parsley, cilantro, or fresh basil *or* 2 tablespoons chopped fresh oregano
- 2 tablespoons dark brown sugar
- 1 tablespoon olive oil
- Salt and pepper to taste
- Tabasco sauce to taste

Mix all ingredients in a bowl and marinate for 30 minutes.

Per serving:

Calories	99
Total fat	3.8 g
Saturated fat	.5 g
Cholesterol	0
Sodium	16 mg

CONFETTI JICAMA SALSA

Serves 4

1 small jicama or apple, peeled and diced
2 carrots, peeled and diced
1 red bell pepper, diced
1 medium onion, chopped
1 jalapeño pepper, seeds and veins removed, minced
2 to 3 garlic cloves, minced
½ cup rice vinegar
Salt and freshly ground pepper to taste
½ teaspoon hot red pepper flakes
1 teaspoon dried oregano
3 tablespoons chopped parsley or cilantro *or* 1 tablespoon each chopped fresh parsley, basil, and mint
1 teaspoon dark brown sugar (optional)

Put the diced vegetables in a bowl.

Using a fork, beat together the garlic, vinegar, salt and pepper, pepper flakes, oregano, parsley or cilantro, and optional sugar. Pour the dressing over the diced vegetables and marinate for at least 2 hours before serving.

Per serving:

Calories	60
Total fat	.4 g
Saturated fat	0
Cholesterol	0
Sodium	23 mg

FOOD PHARMACY FACT

Proof of Onion's Anticancer Powers

Experimenters at Harvard have found that putting ground-up yellow onions in the drinking water of hamsters saves them from oral cancer. Every day for four weeks the researchers put fresh onion in the animals' drinking water. Other hamsters were given no onions. Then the scientists painted a cancer-producing agent inside the mouths of both sets of animals. The onion-eating hamsters had only one third as many oral cancers and much smaller tumors than carcinogen-painted hamsters given no onions. The onion reduced the "total tumor burden" by about tenfold.

The researchers suspect that several compounds in the onions, including allicin, the chemical that brings tears to the eyes, are active cancer-preventive agents.

ONION-RHUBARB SALSA

Serves 4

2 pounds rhubarb stalks, diced
2/3 cup chopped onion, preferably Vidalia
1/2 cup chopped green bell pepper
1/2 cup chopped yellow bell pepper
1 jalapeño pepper, minced
1 tablespoon grated fresh gingerroot
2 tablespoons lime juice
2 tablespoons dark brown sugar or to taste
Salt and freshly ground pepper to taste
2 tablespoons balsamic vinegar
Chopped parsley, cilantro, fresh oregano, or fresh mint to taste

Blanch the rhubarb in boiling water for about 10 to 20 seconds. Drain and submerge in cold water for a few minutes.

Thoroughly drain the rhubarb and combine it with the onion, peppers, ginger, lime juice, sugar, salt, and pepper. Add just a little balsamic vinegar.

Add the chopped herbs last, using just one or a combination of them.

Note: Since this salsa tends to soften, it is best to use it fairly soon after making it.

Per serving:

Calories	93
Total fat	.6 g
Saturated fat	.01 g
Cholesterol	0
Sodium	14 mg

Chopped Broccoli-Pepper Salad

Serves 4

Here's a broccoli salad with a simple, no-fat tomato juice dressing. Broccoli is one of the best-tested and best-analyzed vegetables, full of disease-fighting vitamins and minerals as well as at least half a dozen antioxidants and anticancer agents.

1 pound broccoli, trimmed and broken into small florets, upper stems peeled and cut into ½-inch pieces
1 cup inch-long red bell pepper strips
½ cup finely chopped red onion

TOMATO DRESSING

¾ cup tomato juice
10 to 12 large fresh basil leaves, torn in half
2 teaspoons fresh thyme or oregano
2 teaspoons prepared mustard
¼ teaspoon pepper, preferably freshly ground (more to taste)

Place broccoli in a microwave-safe dish. Cover with plastic wrap and cook for 1 minute on HIGH. Remove and blanch broccoli in cold water, drain, and pat dry.

Toss the broccoli, red pepper strips, and chopped red onion together in a bowl.

In a blender or food processor, mix together the tomato juice, herbs, mustard, and pepper. Blend just until the leaves are finely chopped. Pour the dressing over the vegetables and toss to coat. Chill before serving.

Per serving:

Calories	58
Total fat	.7 g
Saturated fat	.1 g
Cholesterol	0
Sodium	230 mg

HOW CARROTS, CABBAGE, AND BROCCOLI CAN LOWER CHOLESTEROL

Peter D. Hoagland, Ph.D., and Philip E. Pfeffer, Ph.D., at the U.S. Department of Agriculture's regional research center in Philadelphia, have discovered a major cholesterol-lowering constituent in carrots, cabbage, and broccoli. It is a peculiar type of pectin fiber called *calcium pectate.* It works just like some cholesterol-lowering drugs, such as cholestyramine.

In laboratory experiments Drs. Hoagland and Pfeffer have demonstrated that both carrot pectin and particularly calcium pectate bind to bile acids. This is critical, for bile acids are digestive substances in the intestine that are made from cholesterol. Bile acids normally are reabsorbed after use, but small amounts are lost and the body must make more by drawing cholesterol out of the system. Thus, if vegetable fiber grabs onto bile acids and whisks it out of the body, the body is forced to take cholesterol out of the blood to make more bile acids. Consequently cholesterol levels in the blood drop. Carrot fiber is very potent in binding to bile acids; both broccoli and cabbage have high amounts of calcium pectate.

Broccoli-Cauliflower Garlic Salad

Serves 4

What makes this salad so special is that the cruciferous vegetables are totally raw, meaning that all the antioxidant glutathione and indoles so plentiful in broccoli and cauliflower are totally intact and at full power. Add to that the antioxidant quercetin in red onions and all the therapeutic benefits of raw garlic, and this salad is a real health winner. It is not for the timid; the garlic gives it real zing, but if the garlic is too overwhelming for your taste, you can reduce the amount. It is always better to get some garlic than none.

3 cups broccoli florets
2 cups cauliflower florets
½ cup chopped red onion
½ cup Garlic Dressing (recipe follows)

Combine all ingredients and toss.

Per serving:

Calories	69
Total fat	.5 g
Saturated fat	0
Cholesterol	.6 mg
Sodium	53 mg

GARLIC DRESSING

1 cup plain nonfat yogurt
4 large garlic cloves, roughly chopped
⅓ cup tightly packed fresh basil leaves
2 teaspoons frozen orange juice concentrate (optional)
Salt and freshly ground pepper to taste

Put ½ cup of the yogurt in a blender or a food processor fitted with the steel blade with the garlic and basil and process until blended. Stir in the remaining yogurt, orange juice concentrate if desired, and salt and pepper. Use half on the salad and save the rest for another salad.

Lynn's Caesar Salad

Serves 4

Who doesn't love Caesar salad? Scientifically it's a favorite because romaine lettuce is one of the darkest green varieties and therefore overstuffed with carotenoids, chlorophyll, and other disease-fighting agents. Here's a fantastic-tasting version by Lynn Fischer, coauthor of The Low Cholesterol Gourmet, *that lacks all that traditional fat and cholesterol except for the good fat of anchovies and olive oil. Everyone I know who has tasted it has asked for the recipe.*

1 head chilled romaine lettuce
Olive oil cooking spray
1/2 teaspoon Worcestershire sauce
1/2 teaspoon anchovy paste *or* 4 anchovy fillets, patted dry
2 large garlic cloves, minced
2 tablespoons lemon juice or to taste
1/4 cup freshly grated Parmesan cheese
Coarsely ground black pepper to taste
Garlic croutons (optional; recipe follows)

Wash and shake dry the romaine. Spray the leaves all over with olive oil.

In a separate dish, mix the Worcestershire sauce, anchovy paste, minced garlic, and lemon juice. Toss the salad and sprinkle with cheese, black pepper, and croutons if desired.

Per serving:

Calories	66
Total fat	2.8 g
Saturated fat	1.3 g
Cholesterol	7 mg
Sodium	280 mg

GARLIC CROUTONS

2 slices toast
1 large garlic clove, cut in half
Olive oil cooking spray

Preheat the broiler. Rub the toast with the garlic. Spray lightly with olive oil. Put under the broiler until browned a little more. Remove, cut into cubes, and add to the salad.

Per serving:

Calories	36
Total fat	.6 g
Saturated fat	.08 g
Cholesterol	.4 g
Sodium	62 mg

Spinach with Strawberries and Honey Dressing

Serves 4–5

It's hard to say enough for spinach pharmacologically, since it more than any other green leafy vegetable except broccoli and kale is full of identified compounds that protect cells in numerous ways. For example, it is extremely high in beta-carotene, being tested for its anticancer properties. Strawberries also contain disease-fighting antioxidants and frequently turn up in the diets of people who have less heart disease and cancer. I'm also crazy about this no-fat dressing, and I use it on many other green salads.

6 ounces fresh spinach (about 6 to 7 cups), torn into bite-size pieces
1 cup thickly sliced strawberries
1 tablespoon toasted sesame seeds *or* 1/4 cup chopped pecans (optional)
1 small red onion, thinly sliced (optional)

HONEY MUSTARD DRESSING

2 tablespoons balsamic vinegar
2 tablespoons rice vinegar
1 tablespoon plus 1 teaspoon honey
2 teaspoons Dijon mustard
Salt and freshly ground black pepper to taste

Wash and thoroughly dry the spinach.

In a separate container, whip together the vinegars, honey, mustard, salt, and pepper. Add to the spinach and toss lightly.

Add the strawberries and optional ingredients and toss again lightly.

Note: You can also spray the spinach leaves with olive oil, then add the mixture of vinegar, garlic, and salt before tossing.

Per serving:

Calories	47
Total fat	.4 g
Saturated fat	0
Cholesterol	0
Sodium	111 mg

DOCTOR'S ADVICE

Eat the greenest vegetables you can find. Cancer-fighting vegetables have shown their true colors—and one is definitely dark green. The deeper the green color, the more cancer-inhibiting carotenoid compounds a vegetable has, says Dr. Frederick Khachik of the U.S. Department of Agriculture's Research Service. His analysis found that kale, known for its deep green color, has the highest concentrations of three important carotenoids, twice as much as spinach. Fortunately, in tests, he says, cooking—by boiling, steaming, or microwaving—did not lessen the protective carotenoids in broccoli, green beans, or spinach. "Even after boiling green beans for one hour, we ended up with the same amounts," he says. It's unlikely heat destroys the carotenoids in other green vegetables either, he says.

Bitter Greens with Tangy Avocado Dressing

Serves 6

All kinds of dark green leafy vegetables appear tops on the diets of people who escape numerous diseases. That's probably because the greens are so high in carotenoids as well as folic acid and often vitamin C—all three disease-fighting antioxidants. Here's a particularly good way to use a variety of flavorful greens with a salad dressing that gives you only the beneficial monounsaturated fats in the avocado; it's the same type as is in olive oil. You can also add reddish radicchio for contrast; its red color reveals that it too has carotenoids.

½ head escarole
½ bunch chicory or curly endive
1 head radicchio
1 bunch watercress
2 seedless oranges, peeled and cut into 1-inch chunks (optional)
¾ cup Tangy Avocado Salad Dressing (recipe follows)

Wash and dry the greens thoroughly and tear them into bite-size pieces. You should have about 8 cups.

In a large bowl, just before serving, toss the greens (and oranges if desired) with about ¾ cup of avocado dressing or until the leaves are well coated.

Per serving:

Calories	81
Total fat	3 g
Saturated fat	.5 g
Cholesterol	.4 mg
Sodium	125 mg

TANGY AVOCADO SALAD DRESSING

About 1½ cups

1 ripe avocado, peeled, pitted, and cut into chunks
2 tablespoons white wine vinegar
3 tablespoons lemon juice
2 teaspoons Dijon mustard
10 drops Tabasco sauce or to taste
¼ teaspoon salt or to taste
1 cup skim milk

Put all the ingredients in a blender or food processor fitted with the steel blade and process until smooth and creamy.

Note: Use half of the dressing for the greens; save the rest by putting it in a tightly closed container and refrigerating.

Per tablespoon:

Calories	18
Total fat	1.3 g
Saturated fat	.2 g
Cholesterol	.2 mg
Sodium	43 mg

A Guide to Greens

The greening of the diet may be as important to survival as the greening of the planet, say some authorities. The green stuff is packed with a variety of compounds—carotenoids, chlorophyll, glutathione, folic acid, vitamin C—all thought to protect cells from myriad types of damage.

Here are some of the greens you should be including in your diet:

Arugula (Rocket): Dark green leaves with a pungent, peppery bite. Use arugula as a salad green alone or to add spice to other salad greens. Tear leaves into pieces and toss into soups and stir-frys.

Bibb Lettuce (Butterhead, Limestone): A small, roundish head lettuce with delicate, buttery-flavored pale green to dark green leaves. Use in salads with a light dressing.

Boston Lettuce (Butterhead, Cabbagehead): Larger than Bibb lettuce, with a similar taste but slightly less crunchy texture and usually deeper green leaves. Use in salads with a light dressing.

Collard Greens: Similar to kale, but with straighter, smoother leaves, this is the so-called "cabbage" beloved among ancient Romans, according to Waverley Root's book *Food*. Collards have a distinctive, robust flavor and like kale are usually cooked, notably in the South, with other greens.

Curly Endive (Chicory): A stalk with frizzled, curly green leaves, cultivated in ancient Egypt and probably referred to in the Bible as "bitter herbs." Because of its distinctive taste, it is often mixed with other greens in salads.

Escarole (Chicory, Endive): Large, broad leaves with a slightly bitter, tangy taste, but not as bitter as curly endive. Add to other salad greens or sauté as a vegetable or tear into pieces and add to soups and stews.

Kale: A member of the cruciferous or cabbage family, kale leaves are slightly curled and crimped (kale in French is "curly cabbage") and strongly flavored. Kale is often sautéed, steamed, or boiled alone or with other greens, such as collards and turnip greens. Shred it and add to soups, stews, and stir-frys. To eat it raw in salads, remove the stems and center veins and tear into small pieces.

Lamb's-Lettuce (Mâche, Field Salad): Small, delicately flavored round leaves with a light, creamy texture. Popular in Europe, rarer and more expensive in the U.S. Serve with very lightly flavored dressings and herbs.

Looseleaf Lettuce (Leaf or Bunching Lettuce): Sweet, delicate, and crisp, with green and/or reddish leaves. Excellent for salads.

Mustard Greens: The leaves are a vivid green and not surprisingly have a somewhat sharp, mustardy taste, which is diminished with cooking. Can be eaten raw in salads or lightly cooked.

Parsley: One of the world's oldest and most universal greens, widely used in ancient Roman cuisine. Common supermarket parsley with its frilly, curly leaves has a pleasant light, peppery taste; Italian parsley, with broader flat leaves, tastes stronger and sharper. Chinese parsley is actually cilantro, or coriander. Use parsley in salads, sauces, and dressings, to stuff fish, to sprinkle on vegetables, and as a vegetable on its own.

Radicchio (Red Chicory or Treviso): Actually this green usually is bright red and crunchy with a mild to bitter taste. Commonly used in Italy, radicchio is fairly new to the U.S. Heads are small and tightly wrapped, ranging from golf-ball to grapefruit size. Add to other green salads for color and distinctive taste.

Romaine (Cos): Large dark green crunchy leaves with a strong, nonbitter taste. Ideal for salads and very versatile. Used in the classic Caesar salad, romaine derives its name from "Roman" and was cultivated by the ancient Greeks on the island of Cos.

Spinach: Extremely popular in the U.S. Leaves vary from large to small and flat to crinkly and are of a sharp taste and strong texture. Spinach is of fairly recent cultivation, not known in ancient cultures. Wash and dry it thoroughly and use it in salads, steam it, stir-fry it, or toss it into soups, casseroles, stews, sauces, and meat loaves of all types.

Swiss chard (Leaf Beet): Actually the leaf of the beet plant, chard is similar to spinach and is most popular in France. Sometimes available in the U.S., it is usually steamed, sautéed, or cooked like spinach.

Watercress: Almost always available, watercress was cultivated in ancient China and is still used extensively in stir-fried dishes. Its peppery taste adds spice and pungency to salads as well as soups, stews, stir-frys, and casseroles.

Greens with Apples and Blue Cheese Dressing

Serves 6

Mixing fruit with greens is always a good idea, and apples are a natural. Among lettuces, dark green romaine and Boston are among the best, far better choices than pale iceberg, because darker green lettuces have more disease-fighting compounds. In this salad the greens and fruit are complemented with a pungent blue cheese low-fat dressing that produced raves among tasters. You can also use the dressing on other greens or fruit salads.

1 large bunch dark green leaf lettuce, cleaned and torn into bite-size pieces
1 large head romaine or Boston lettuce, cleaned and torn into bite-size pieces
1 cup diced celery
3 apples, cored and diced
Blue Cheese Dressing (recipe follows)

Put the greens on a large salad plate or in a bowl. Sprinkle the celery and apple over the greens. Pour the dressing over the salad.

Alternate: Combine greens, celery, and apples in a large bowl. Pass salad and salad dressing separately.

Per serving:

Calories	128
Total fat	2.4 g
Saturated fat	1.2 g
Cholesterol	5 mg
Sodium	148 mg

BLUE CHEESE DRESSING

- 1/4 cup crumbled blue cheese
- 1 teaspoon vinegar
- 1/4 teaspoon Worcestershire sauce
- 1/2 teaspoon prepared mustard
- 1/2 teaspoon sugar
- 2 tablespoons frozen orange or apple juice concentrate
- 1 cup plain nonfat yogurt

Put the blue cheese in a small bowl and mash with a fork. Add the remaining ingredients and combine. Cover and chill for several hours so flavors blend.

FOOD PHARMACY FACT

Vitamin C vs. Breast Cancer

Surprisingly few foods or nutrients have been linked to the prevention of breast cancer. But a recent analysis of sixteen breast-cancer studies by researchers at Canada's National Cancer Institute found that eating lots of vitamin-C-rich foods, like green leafy vegetables and fruits, may provide striking protection.

The institute's Dr. Geoffrey R. Howe estimated that if all women over age twenty were to eat enough fruits and vegetables to take in 380 milligrams of vitamin C a day, the breast-cancer rate might drop by 16 percent. Eating more vitamin C seemed to have a greater impact on breast cancer than cutting back on saturated animal and dairy fats, longtime suspected promoters of breast cancer.

Dr. Howe predicted that if women past menopause cut consumption of saturated fats to 9 percent of calories, their breast-cancer rate would probably go down 10 percent. If they cut back on fat and ate foods containing 380 milligrams of vitamin C daily, their breast cancer rate might fall a whopping 24 percent.

Hashed Brussels Sprouts with Dates

Serves 6

It's not often you find recipes for raw Brussels sprouts, but new tests find that some of the anticancer agents are more plentiful in uncooked sprouts. When I mentioned this to cookbook author Maxine Rapoport, she came up with this imaginative recipe for raw Brussels sprouts, which makes me wonder why we don't treat Brussels sprouts more like cabbage, which is commonly made into slaw. After all, Brussels sprouts are of the cabbage family and contain many of the same wonderful pharmacological agents, notably related to preventing cancer.

½ pound Brussels sprouts, shredded or chopped (about 2 cups)
2 medium carrots, peeled and coarsely grated
15 pitted dates, coarsely chopped
1 tablespoon olive oil
2 tablespoons balsamic vinegar
2 tablespoons frozen apple juice or citrus blend concentrate
⅛ teaspoon freshly ground pepper

Mix all ingredients together and chill at least 1 hour before serving.

Per serving:

Calories	114
Total fat	2.5 g
Saturated fat	.3 g
Cholesterol	0
Sodium	20 mg

FOOD PHARMACY FACT

Brussels Sprouts Zap Cancer

In tests at Cornell University, researchers fed one group of animals Brussels sprouts while a second group was fed ordinary rat chow. Both groups were injected with a powerful carcinogen. After fifteen weeks only 13 percent of the Brussels sprouts eaters had developed breast tumors compared with 77 percent of the chow-eaters. A possible reason: Brussels sprouts have high amounts of a compound called *glucobardssicin* that aids the liver in neutralizing and eliminating potential carcinogens.

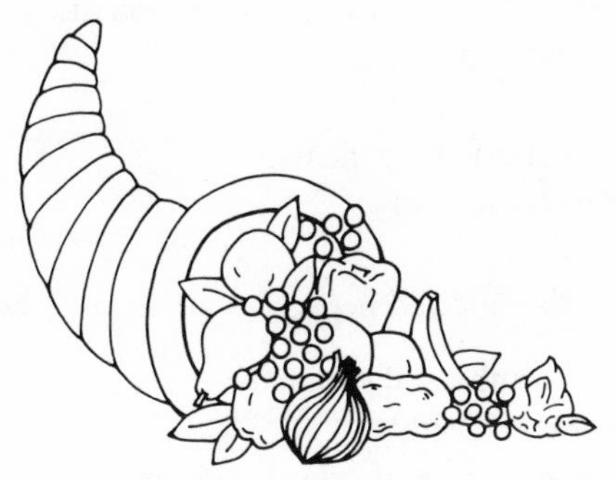

Dilled Potato Salad

Serves 10

There must be enough different potato salad recipes to stretch to another galaxy, but this one really is different and is always described as not just good but sensational. I like it because it combines so many healthful vegetables in an interesting way, and of course the dill pickles give it that extra punch. The pickles also are high in sodium, which should be noted by those on a low-sodium diet.

4 large red potatoes, cooked and diced
1/4 pound green beans, cut into 1-inch pieces and cooked until tender-crisp
2 cups sliced carrots, cooked
1 10-ounce package frozen peas, thawed, boiling water poured over them, then well drained
3 large dill pickles, diced
1 tablespoon minced fresh dill *or* 1 teaspoon dried
1 teaspoon caraway seeds
1/4 cup plain low-fat yogurt
1/4 cup reduced-calorie mayonnaise
2 teaspoons Dijon mustard
Salt to taste
1/4 teaspoon freshly ground pepper

In a large bowl, combine the potatoes, green beans, carrots, peas, pickles, dill, and caraway seeds.

Mix the yogurt, mayonnaise, mustard, salt, and pepper together and add to the salad mixture. Mix thoroughly, cover with plastic wrap, and refrigerate for several hours before serving.

Per serving:

Calories	135
Total fat	2 g
Saturated fat	.4 g
Cholesterol	2.3 mg
Sodium	535 mg

Black Bean Salad with Feta Cheese and Mint

Serves 4

The beans, cheese, and mint are a stunning combination, and the mint is a well-documented carminative that helps counteract the gaseous qualities of the beans. I think you will be surprised how fantastic this salad is—I was. It's the fresh mint that makes the difference, so use every bit called for. Since the mint tends to lose flavor if stored for many hours or overnight, the salad needs to be eaten within a few hours after being made—but that has never been a problem in my house.

1 cup dried black beans, soaked overnight, cooked, and drained, or 2 to 2½ cups canned, drained and rinsed
¼ pound feta cheese, drained and crumbled
2 to 3 teaspoons minced red onion
⅓ cup tightly packed fresh mint leaves, finely chopped
3 tablespoons olive oil
Juice of 1 lemon or to taste
Salt and freshly ground black pepper to taste

Place the beans in a large mixing bowl. Add the crumbled feta cheese and onions. Stir the mint leaves in with the oil, lemon, salt, and pepper and add to the beans. Let the beans marinate for 30 to 60 minutes. Correct the seasonings before serving.

Per serving:

Calories	333
Total fat	16 g
Saturated fat	5.7 g
Cholesterol	25 mg
Sodium	320 mg

Three-Bean Salad with Poppy Seed Dressing

Serves 6 to 8

One of the joys of beans is that you can so easily combine various types. In this salad I use one that is too often neglected in this country—soybeans. Soaked and cooked, they are as delicious in taste and texture as other commonly used legumes and yet have some added attributes. According to tests, soybeans are the most thoroughly documented among legumes for their singular anticancer capabilities. All legumes help fight blood cholesterol. Even if you substitute other beans for soybeans, you still get some soybeans from the tofu in the low-calorie, low-fat salad dressing.

- 1½ cups cooked black-eyed peas *or* 1 15-ounce can, drained and rinsed
- 1½ cups cooked black beans *or* 1 15-ounce can, drained and rinsed
- 1½ cups cooked soybeans, or chick-peas, any type of bean, or even whole-kernel corn
- 1 large green bell pepper, chopped
- 1 large red onion, chopped (1 cup)
- Salt and freshly ground pepper to taste
- 1 to 2 tablespoons cilantro, parsley, thyme, or other fresh herb (optional)
- Poppy Seed Dressing (recipe follows)

Combine all ingredients in a large bowl. Add dressing and toss until all ingredients are well coated.

Per serving:

Calories	236
Total fat	5.9 g
Saturated fat	.9 g
Cholesterol	0
Sodium	8 mg

POPPY SEED DRESSING

½ cup firm tofu
¼ cup frozen orange juice concentrate
¼ cup rice vinegar
1 garlic clove, minced
2 teaspoons lemon juice
2 teaspoons poppy seeds

Put all the ingredients except the poppy seeds into a blender or a food processor fitted with the steel blade and blend until smooth. Remove to a jar or bowl and stir in the poppy seeds.

FOOD PHARMACY FACT

The Soybean-Poppy Seed Cirrhosis Defense

Worried about liver damage from drinking alcohol? Lecithin, rich in soybeans and poppyseeds, may be an antidote. That's the remarkable finding of a group of top alcohol researchers.

In a ten-year study, Dr. Charles S. Lieber and colleagues at Mount Sinai School of Medicine in New York City, fed baboons the human equivalent of eight cans of beer per day. They also gave some animals about three tablespoons a day of soy lecithin. The lecithin-fed baboons showed only slight liver scarring and no cirrhosis. However, seven of nine baboons not given lecithin developed severe liver damage and two progressed to full-blown cirrhosis.

Although tests on humans need to be done, Dr. Lieber, a noted expert on alcohol, believes the new study indicates that lecithin delays and possibly prevents cirrhosis of the liver. It may also reverse the early stages of liver scarring.

Soybeans have 15,000 to 25,000 parts per million of lecithin; mungbeans have about 16,000 ppm, peanuts have 5,000 to 7,000 ppm, and poppy seeds have 28,000 ppm; dandelion flowers beat all with 29,700 ppm, according to U.S. Department of Agriculture expert, Dr. Jim Duke.

FOOD PHARMACY FACT

Tofu vs. Cholesterol

Eat tofu instead of cheese, and your blood cholesterol will most likely drop. That's what a study by nutritionists Carolyn Dunn and Michael Liebman, University of North Carolina at Greensboro, found. They asked twelve lacto-ovo-vegetarian men to eat tofu instead of cheese. At the end of three weeks the men's cholesterol had dropped sixteen milligrams. The probable reason: Tofu contains mostly unsaturated fat, whereas cheese is packed with saturated fat—the type that boosts blood cholesterol.

FOOD PHARMACY FACT

Cancer Drug in Soybeans

Why do Asian women have less breast cancer? Maybe it's their high diet of soybeans. Soybeans contain plant hormones (phytoestrogens) very similar chemically to a common drug tamoxifen, used quite successfully to block the spread of breast cancer in certain women. So discovered Dr. Stephen Barnes, associate professor of pharmacology and biochemistry at the University of Alabama in Birmingham.

He fed soybeans to one group of rats, regular chow to another group. Then he dosed them all with cancer-causing agents. Sure enough, the soybean-eating rats had 40 to 65 percent fewer breast cancers than the non-soybean-eating rats. Dr. Barnes suspected the anticancer agent to be plant hormones (phytoestrogens). But soybeans also contain anticancer compounds called *protease inhibitors.* So he removed the protease inhibitors from the soybeans—and the beans still curbed breast cancer in rats. "That told us it was probably the phytoestrogens blocking the cancer," says Dr. Barnes.

Soybean products highest in anticancer phytoestrogens are whole soybeans, tofu (bean curd), miso (fermented soybean paste), and soy milk. Processed soy flour may have some phytoestrogens, but soy sauce has none, says Dr. Barnes.

Waldorf Salad with Sardines

Serves 3

This unlikely combination turns an old-time favorite into a modern source of fish high in the beneficial omega-3-type oils. Add walnuts—one of the best plant sources—and you have even more omega-3s. You can use plain sardines, but smoked sardines are even more scrumptious, the smoky taste blending well with the apples and nuts. Don't worry about the fat; nearly all of it is the good omega-3-type from the fish. The rest is from the walnuts, also high in omega-3, vitamin E, and beneficial antioxidants.

1 cup diced apples
2 teaspoons lemon juice
2 3¾-ounce tins sardines, drained
½ cup diced celery
¼ cup chopped walnuts
¼ cup plain nonfat yogurt or reduced-calorie mayonnaise or a mixture

Toss the apples with the lemon juice to help the apples retain their color. Cut sardines into bite-size pieces. Lightly mix the apples, celery, sardines, walnuts, and yogurt.

Per serving:

Calories	228
Total fat	13 g
Saturated fat	1.5 g
Cholesterol	87 mg
Sodium	343 mg

Herring Salad with Potatoes and Beets

"A land with lots of herring can get along with few doctors," goes an old Dutch proverb. That's because people who load up on fish like herring, full of omega-3 fatty acids, are less likely to get heart disease, high blood pressure, cancer, diabetes, psoriasis, arthritis, and migraine headaches. It's time to make herring more popular in the U.S. For a start, try this appetizer salad with onions and apples that also give your heart a boost. Thanks to Joan Nathan, author of Jewish Holiday Kitchen.

1 cup pickled herring, drained and cut into ½-inch cubes
2 beets, peeled, cooked, and cut into ½-inch cubes
4 medium potatoes, peeled, boiled, and cut into ½-inch cubes
1 large unpeeled Granny Smith apple, cored and cut into ½-inch cubes
3 slices medium red onion, diced

VINAIGRETTE DRESSING

2 tablespoons balsamic vinegar
2 tablespoons olive oil
1 clove garlic, minced or crushed
Salt and freshly ground pepper to taste
Pinch of sugar
Herbs of your choice
2 tablespoons chopped walnuts
Lettuce leaves (optional)

Remove and discard any onion that might come with the herring.

Let the cooked vegetables cool. Then combine the herring, beets, potatoes, apple, and onion.

For the dressing, whisk together the vinegar, olive oil, garlic, salt, pepper, sugar, and herbs.

Add the vinaigrette dressing to the herring salad and toss. Sprinkle with walnuts. Serve on lettuce leaves if you wish.

Per serving:

Calories	221
Total fat	10 g
Saturated fat	1.3 g
Cholesterol	3 mg
Sodium	218 mg

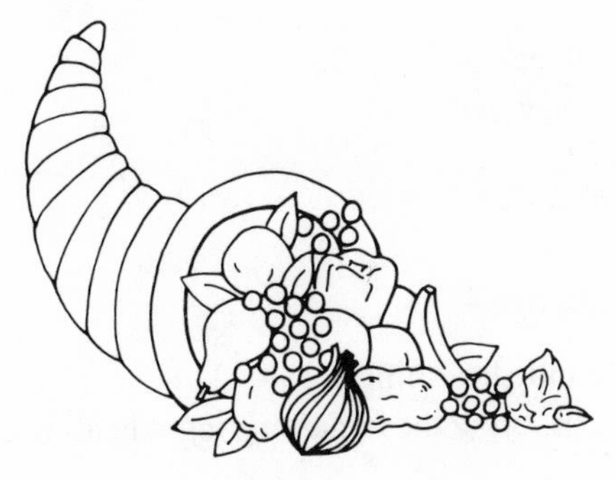

Orange-Sangria Salad

Serves 6

Oranges are so good for you, and not only because of their vitamin C, which is gaining a reputation as a health protector that not even its strongest advocate, Linus Pauling, thought possible. Vitamin C looks as if it can help zap a whole gamut of chronic diseases, including bronchitis, cancer, and heart disease. Citrus, however, has other, newly discovered cancer-fighting compounds. This excellent recipe comes from British food writer Elaine Hallgarten, as published in the London Daily Mail. *She advises serving it as a cold salad or as a warm accompaniment to poultry.*

6 oranges
1 cup dry red wine
1 cup fresh orange juice
1 tablespoon sugar
1 cinnamon stick
4 cloves
Sliver of orange zest

Peel the oranges and slice thinly.

In a small saucepan, bring the remaining ingredients to a boil and simmer for 5 minutes.

Pour the hot wine-juice mixture over the oranges. Serve warm or cold.

Per serving:

Calories	112
Total fat	.4 g
Saturated fat	.04 g
Cholesterol	0
Sodium	2.6 mg

FOOD PHARMACY FACT

Oranges for High Blood Pressure?

Too little vitamin C may make you more susceptible to high blood pressure. That's what a large-scale study by researchers in Finland noted. They found "marked high blood pressure" among those with the lowest blood levels of vitamin C and selenium. Both vitamin C and selenium are antioxidants.

It's the first evidence that antioxidants may help depress blood pressure, say the investigating scientists. For foods highest in vitamin C, see page 7.

Mango, Banana, and Blueberry Salad

Serves 6

At least six of the ingredients in this salad have been shown to be either antibacterial or antiviral, according to laboratory tests—mango, blueberry, yogurt, ginger, cayenne, and honey. They are a winning combination. The dressing is one of my favorites, a rare treat with minimal fat and few calories. Try it also on other fruit salads.

1 large *or* 3 small ripe but firm mangoes, peeled and cut into chunks (about 1 1/2 pounds with seeds and skin)
2 bananas, sliced
1 1/2 cups blueberries, rinsed and picked over
3 teaspoons lemon juice

HONEY-GINGER DRESSING

3/4 cup vanilla nonfat or low-fat yogurt
1 teaspoon honey or to taste
2 teaspoons minced candied ginger
1/8 teaspoon ground cumin (optional)
Pinch of cayenne pepper or to taste

1 bunch watercress or leaf lettuce

In a bowl, combine the fruit with the lemon juice to prevent discoloration.

Combine all the dressing ingredients in a small bowl.

Place the fruit on a bed of watercress or lettuce and top with the dressing.

Per serving:

Calories	145
Total fat	.5 g
Saturated fat	.1 g
Cholesterol	.8 mg
Sodium	38 mg

FOOD PHARMACY FACT

Mangoes Halt Herpes Virus

Scientists have found that in test tube studies two components of the mango behaved like antiviral drugs against the herpes simplex virus. In fact the mango compounds (mangiferin and isomangiferin) were found superior to commonly used antiviral compounds—acyclovir, idoxuridine, and cyclocytidine—which the scientists also tested. Apparently the mango compounds prevented the virus from replicating, causing it to die off.

Joanna's Cranberry Fantasy

Serves 8

Everyone thinks this tastes as if it took hours to make, yet it's so easy, says my friend Joanna Simon who has served it often. You can, of course, make the sauce from fresh cranberries instead. So there's no excuse for not getting your quota of cranberries, now found to contain ellagic acid, an antioxidant that protects cells from various kinds of damage. Walnuts are also high in this beneficial antioxidant. Joanna says the combination is fabulous with any roasted poultry or game. I agree.

3 cups canned whole cranberry sauce
1 cup canned crushed pineapple packed in natural juice
1 cup chopped walnuts

Mix all ingredients together and refrigerate for 2 hours before serving.

Per serving:

Calories	271
Total fat	9 g
Saturated fat	.8 g
Cholesterol	0
Sodium	32 mg

FOOD PHARMACY FACT

Doctors for Cranberries

Cranberry juice for urinary infections has passed muster with the American Medical Association, although it's still unclear, they say, exactly how the berry works. An article in the *Journal of the American Medical Association* speculated on possible mechanisms: Cranberry juice raises acidity of the urine, killing off infection-causing bacteria. But that effect appears temporary. Also, cranberry agents may help prevent bacteria from sticking to the lining of the urinary tract. Regardless, the journal noted research showing that 73 percent of patients with such infections improved after drinking about two cups of cranberry juice daily for twenty-one days. Thus the AMA suggests using liberal amounts of cranberry juice in conjunction with drug therapy as a possible preventive for such urinary tract and bladder infections.

Spicy Indian-Style Fruit Salad

Serves 6

The spicy apple butter sauce turns this ordinary salad into a spectacular one. You can mix the sauce in with the fruit or serve the sauce in a bowl surrounded with fresh-cut fruit for dipping. This recipe was inspired by a salad called chat *served at the Taste of India restaurant in Dayton, Ohio. The restaurant uses tamarind paste, a tart and tangy paste available in Indian and Middle Eastern specialty stores. But the manager suggested using spicy apple butter as a substitute to the food consultant Howard Solganik, who came up with this delightful recipe.*

4 cups sliced fruit (combination of bananas, strawberries, raspberries, blueberries, kiwifruit, peaches, mango, and papaya)
1 11-ounce jar apple butter
Juice of 1 lemon
1/8 teaspoon salt
1/2 teaspoon ground ginger
1/4 teaspoon ground nutmeg
1/4 teaspoon ground cinnamon
1/4 teaspoon cayenne pepper
1/4 teaspoon black pepper, preferably freshly ground

Place the sliced fruit in a large bowl. Whisk together the remaining ingredients, toss gently with the fruit, and serve chilled.

Per serving:

Calories	156
Total fat	.7 g
Saturated fat	.07 g
Cholesterol	0
Sodium	49 mg

FOOD PHARMACY FACT

Fruit Every Day May Keep Cancer Away

A National Cancer Institute study found that eating fruit such as apples, bananas, oranges, strawberries, orange juice, or canned fruits only once a day cut the odds of developing pancreatic cancer by 40 percent. Eating fruit twice a day cut the risk by 60 percent. The study was done among residents in southern Louisiana, where the rate of pancreatic cancer is unusually high.

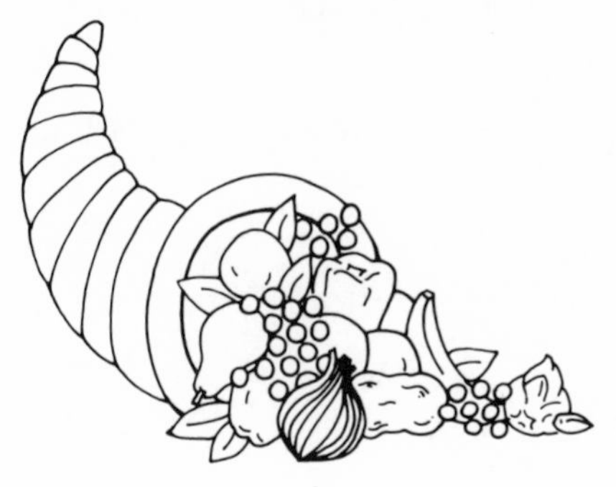

Indian Raitas

Raita is the classic yogurt-based accompaniment to hot curried dishes in India. But you can serve it with any hot spicy food, even chili. It soothes the palate and cools the fire in the mouth, taking away the burning sensation, according to experts. Not to mention that yogurt also soothes the stomach and may help keep ulcers away, according to new French research. Here are three variations on raita.

BANANA RAITA

Serves 3

1 cup plain nonfat or low-fat yogurt
1 teaspoon lemon juice
1/4 teaspoon grated fresh gingerroot
1/4 teaspoon cumin seeds, toasted
1 ripe banana, diced

Combine all ingredients and let chill for at least 1 hour.

Per serving:

Calories	78
Total fat	.3 g
Saturated fat	.2 g
Cholesterol	1 mg
Sodium	58 mg

MINT RAITA

Serves 2

1/2 cup chopped fresh mint
1/2 cup minced onion
1/2 green bell pepper, minced
3/4 cup plain nonfat or low-fat yogurt
Salt to taste

Combine all ingredients and chill before serving.

Per serving:

Calories	69
Total fat	.4 g
Saturated fat	.1 g
Cholesterol	2 mg
Sodium	66 mg

GREEN PEPPER AND WATERCRESS RAITA

Serves 4

1 cup minced green bell pepper
½ cup minced watercress leaves
1 teaspoon minced garlic
1 cup plain nonfat or low-fat yogurt
1 to 2 teaspoons ground cumin
½ teaspoon sugar
Pinch of salt
Pinch of freshly ground pepper

Combine all ingredients and refrigerate.
Note: Best made a day in advance.

Per serving:

Calories	45
Total fat	.4 g
Saturated fat	.1 g
Cholesterol	1 mg
Sodium	80 mg

FOOD PHARMACY FACT

Collards to the Rescue

Mice fed cabbage or collard greens and then injected with breast cancer cells had fewer spreading (metastasized) cancers, according to experiments at the University of Nebraska's Eppley Cancer Institute. Collards in other tests have exhibited extraordinarily active anti-mutagenic agents that help block genetic changes in cells that promote tumors.

RAW OR COOKED—WHICH IS BETTER?

Eating vegetables raw, as our Stone Age ancestors did, is undoubtedly a good idea—sometimes. Numerous studies indicate that some of the powerful antioxidants, body detoxifiers, and anticancer agents are diminished by cooking. On the other hand, recent evidence shows that cooking vegetables is not as detrimental to certain pharmacological compounds as previously thought, and in fact cooking in some cases can boost absorption of life-enhancing chemicals. Also, too much of a raw vegetable, as in the case of garlic, may cause trouble.

Here's the latest evidence on the pros and cons of eating vegetables both raw and cooked.

• Raw crucifers have more anticancer indoles. Canadian scientists at the University of Manitoba found that indole glycosinolates in cruciferous vegetables, such as cabbage, cauliflower, broccoli, and Brussels sprouts, sank by 30 to 50 percent when steamed for 10 minutes or boiled for 40 minutes. These indoles are known to prevent a broad array of cancers in laboratory animals and are thought to be active anticancer agents in humans. The Canadian researchers think any vegetable protection against stomach and colon cancer should be credited to "the consumption of raw vegetables."

• Indeed experts at the National Cancer Institute suspect that raw vegetables are highly responsible for keeping certain cancers in check. Numerous epidemiological studies single out raw vegetables and salads as protective. A study of Seventh-Day Adventists done by Harold Kahn in 1984 found that eating "green salads" was linked to lower death rates from all types of cancer.

Similarly a 1988 study by Belgian researcher Albert J. Tuyns of the International Agency for Research on Cancer declared that "all raw vegetables had a clear protective effect for both colon and rectal cancer." Eating a mere three ounces of raw vegetables a week appeared to cut the odds of colon cancer by about 40 percent. And the risk dropped with the consumption of more raw vegetables.

• One of the powerful antioxidants and anticancer agents, glutathione, heavily concentrated in green leafy vegetables, is 25 to 50 percent lower in cooked vegetables, according to tests by Dr. Dean P. Jones, associate professor of biochemistry, Emory University School of Medicine. Protective glutathione is almost entirely wiped out when vegetables are canned, he notes.

• The discovery that vitamin C is a powerful antioxidant dramatically elevates its role as a disease preventer and makes conserving it even more critical than ever. Unfortunately vitamin C in vegetables appears more fragile than previously suspected. New U.S. Department of Agriculture tests found that freezing, boiling, blanching, steaming, or cooking broccoli in any fashion cuts its vitamin C content roughly in half.

However, contrary to long-standing belief, says USDA researcher Dr. Joseph T. Vanderslice, vegetables do not lose more vitamin C when cooked in large amounts of water than when steamed in very little water. His tests showed that a stalk of broccoli retained the same amount of vitamin C when cooked in ½ cup of water or four cups of water. The best way to conserve vitamin C in cooked vegetables, he says, is to microwave them. Microwaved broccoli lost a mere 15 percent of its vitamin C.

• Dr. Victor Gurewich, professor of medicine at Tufts University School of Medicine, finds that half a raw onion a day or a comparable amount of onion juice boosts beneficial HDL cholesterol in most people by an average 30 percent. But this particular therapeutic benefit of onions lessens with cooking and disappears when onions are cooked to the limp stage. However, cooked onions retain their anticoagulant powers, he says.

• Garlic, too, loses some of its therapeutic benefits when cooked, but not nearly as much as generally believed, says Dr. Robert I. Lin, chairman of the first international scientific conference on garlic held in Washington, D.C., in August 1990.

Allicin, the major antibiotic in garlic, is destroyed by heat, but it's a myth to think allicin is the only, or even the major, medicinal compound in garlic, argues Dr. Lin. He says that most of garlic's therapeutic benefits come from the bulb's 200 or so other chemicals, most of which survive heat and do not have a strong taste or smell. Garlic does not have to give off the heavy allicin-inspired garlic odor to be good for you, he says. He explains that garlic is often pickled in China, which destroys the allicin. Yet studies show Chinese who eat the most garlic have lower rates of certain cancers.

Further, Dr. Lin notes that eating too much raw garlic could be hazardous. Chewing on raw garlic cloves could injure the mouth, stomach, and esophagus, he says. In an experiment he also found that healthy men who ate a special powdered garlic equal to seven-and-a-half raw garlic cloves a day developed diarrhea that lasted a week. "In high doses the allicin in raw garlic can be toxic," he warns.

Dr. Lin favors cooking garlic for two or three minutes, as is common in stir-frying, especially if you eat much of it. He makes it a point to average a large garlic clove daily but thinks that "two or three cloves a day are okay."

• A recent study in India by researcher-cardiologist Arun Bordia of Tagore Medical College backs up Dr. Lin. In the test Dr. Bordia had half of 432 patients with heart disease eat two or three garlic cloves a day for three years. The other half got no garlic. In the second year fatalities among garlic eaters dropped by 50 percent and sank by 66 percent in the third year.

Important: It made no difference in warding off heart attacks whether the garlic was eaten raw or cooked, concluded Dr. Bordia. Both worked equally well, indicating that garlic's heart-protective powers were not compromised by cooking. However, the raw garlic eaters grumbled more about side effects, such as flatulence.

• Nor does cooking destroy the "blood thinning" abilities of garlic and onions, according to Drs. Amar Makheja and John M. Bailey, biochemists at George Washington University School of Medicine. They found that a chemical called *adenosine* is mainly responsible for the allium vegetables' powers to reduce blood platelet stickiness (aggregation). Adenosine is not harmed by heat, they say.

There's other evidence that vegetables' disease-fighting properties can survive cooking. Studies by Dr. Terrance Leighton, University of California at Berkeley, found that quercetin, an antioxidant and anticancer agent heavily concentrated in onions, broccoli, red grapes, and yellow squash, is not damaged by cooking.

Similarly, experiments at the U.S. Department of Agriculture find that the widely acclaimed family of carotenoids, found in tomatoes, green leafy vegetables, and orange vegetables like carrots, is not ruined by cooking. Additionally, tests show that your body is better able to absorb one of the carotenoids, beta-carotene, from vegetables like carrots and broccoli that have been cooked lightly or moderately.

Researchers are still in the early stages of sorting out how these newly discovered exotic natural compounds in food are affected by cooking and modern processing. In the meantime it makes sense to eat vegetables both raw and cooked.

Vegetables and Legumes

Whole Roasted Garlic

Serves 4

If you have never had this, you are in for a treat. And don't be overwhelmed by the amount of garlic. It mellows with the cooking. For the ultimate garlic bread, squeeze the soft garlic cloves onto toasted Italian bread. Or use the garlic on vegetables or meat.

4 large heads garlic
1/4 cup olive oil

Preheat the oven to 350 degrees.

Pull off the loose papery layers around the top of the garlic and stand the heads upright in a baking dish. Drizzle the olive oil over the garlic, letting it run between the cloves.

Bake, covered, basting from time to time, for about 30 to 40 minutes or until the garlic is soft.

Place each garlic head on a plate. To eat, pull off a garlic clove and squeeze out the garlic paste onto bread, vegetables, or meat.

Per serving:

Calories	137
Total fat	3.7 g
Saturated fat	.5 g
Cholesterol	0
Sodium	12 mg

QUICK, EASY WAYS TO USE GARLIC

- Add a couple of crushed or minced garlic cloves to cheese or yogurt dips.
- Add two cloves of fresh crushed or minced garlic to all standard salad dressings.
- Rub a salad bowl with a cut clove of garlic before adding other ingredients.
- To make instant aïoli—the French garlic mayonnaise—simply put two or three crushed or finely chopped garlic cloves in one cup of reduced-calorie mayonnaise. You can use this as a dip or sauce for cooked or raw vegetables or with meats and fish.
- Add slivers of garlic to a bowl of ripe pitted olives. Mix in a couple of tablespoons of olive oil and refrigerate for two or three hours until the oil and olives have absorbed the garlic flavor. The garlic slivers will also stick to the olives and be eaten along with them as appetizers.
- Toast Italian or French bread slices in the oven. Pass the bread with fresh peeled garlic cloves and a small pitcher of olive oil. Rub a garlic clove over the toast and top with a little olive oil.
- Nibbles: Sauté peeled garlic cloves, sprinkled with oregano, in a little oil until the cloves are slightly browned. Drain and sprinkle with a little coarse salt if desired. Serve as a snack with drinks.
- When steaming or microwaving fresh or frozen vegetables, add a clove or two of crushed or minced garlic.
- Use garlic to thicken sauces. Simply toss unpeeled garlic cloves into a stew or soup. When done, remove the cloves, put them through a fine-mesh sieve, and return to the stew.
- Make a garlic and olive oil paste by putting five heads of peeled garlic cloves in a quart of good-quality olive oil. Store for a week, then put the cloves and oil through a food processor to form a paste. Use to spread on bread, to toss into stews or casseroles or pastas, or to rub on meat or poultry before roasting.
- Add a little fresh garlic to vegetable juices, such as tomato or V8 juice. Put juice and garlic in a blender until the garlic is pureed.
- Sprinkle chopped garlic over salads before tossing.

FOOD PHARMACY FACT

Oriental Cancer Fighters

Chinese who eat about three ounces a day of garlic, onions, scallions, and leeks are only 40 percent as likely to develop stomach cancer as those who eat only an ounce of the allium vegetables daily. That's what a group of National Cancer Institute and Chinese scientists found in Shandong Province, a region of China known for its high stomach cancer rates. The researchers believe that regularly eating small amounts of the garlic and onion since childhood accounts for the protection. A medium onion or one half cup of raw chopped onions weighs about three ounces.

Italian Baked Onions

Serves 4

It's impossible to imagine how wonderful these onions taste just from looking at the recipe. I was completely and pleasantly surprised when I first tasted them in the test kitchen of food consultant and TV chef Howard Solganik in Dayton, Ohio. I find them particularly good at holiday meals when you need all the help you can get in trying to counteract some of the ill effects of eating saturated fat. And onions, studies show, can help rev up your clot-dissolving capabilities, helping defeat the detrimental effects of fatty foods.

4 medium onions
2 tablespoons olive oil
2 tablespoons balsamic vinegar
1/4 cup finely chopped parsley
1/4 cup fresh bread crumbs
1/4 cup freshly grated Parmesan cheese
1/2 teaspoon Italian seasoning (more if desired)
Salt to taste
1/4 teaspoon freshly ground pepper

Preheat the oven to 375 degrees. Cut the onions in half crosswise. Peel and trim the ends so they stand flat. Use the large end of a melon baller and remove a scoop from the center of each onion half. Reserve.

Place 1 tablespoon of the olive oil in the bottom of a baking dish and rub the onions in it to coat the tops and sides. Place the onions upright in the dish and sprinkle each half with balsamic vinegar. Cover with foil and bake for 15 minutes.

Meanwhile, finely chop the remaining onion balls. Mix them with the parsley, bread crumbs, Parmesan, and seasonings. Stir in the remaining tablespoon of olive oil.

Remove the dish from the oven, remove the foil, and place about 1 tablespoon of filling in the center of each onion, mounding it slightly on top. The dish can be prepared up to this point and covered and held until baking time. (If you are not going to bake them right away, preheat the oven again to 375 degrees before baking.)

Bake, uncovered, for 15 to 20 minutes or until the onions are golden brown.

Per serving:

Calories	126
Total fat	9 g
Saturated fat	2 g
Cholesterol	4.9 mg
Sodium	133 mg

Carrot Puree

About 3 cups, serves 6

Simple yet dazzling is this puree of carrot with its rich grainy texture and touch of dill. Experts say cooking and pureeing carrots is the best way to guarantee that your body absorbs and utilizes carrots' enormous amounts of health-promoting beta-carotene.

2 pounds carrots, cut into 1/2-inch rounds
4 teaspoons butter or margarine
1 teaspoon dried dill (more if desired)
Salt to taste
1/4 teaspoon freshly ground pepper or to taste

Boil the carrots in water to cover for 25 minutes. Drain. Cool slightly, then puree in a food processor.

In a nonstick saucepan, brown the butter, add the puree, dill, salt, and pepper, and heat gently.

Note: for a more exotic taste, substitute 1/2 teaspoon ground cardamom for the dill.

Per serving:

Calories	88
Total fat	2.8 g
Saturated fat	1.6 g
Cholesterol	6.9 mg
Sodium	79 mg

COOK'S ADVICE

Smash That Carrot

To get the most beta-carotene from a carrot you need to break down its cellular structure. That releases more beta-carotene for absorption, says James Olson, a leading expert on carotenoids at Iowa State University. There are two ways to do it: by cooking carrots slightly or by chopping, grating, pureeing, and liquefying carrots. This allows your digestive juices to come in better contact with the carrot's beta-carotene. "If you actually nibble on a raw carrot Bugs Bunny style, you absorb very little of the carotene—about 5 percent," says Olson. "Cooking it makes 25 to 30 percent of the beta-carotene available, and pureeing cooked carrots allows your body to absorb about 50 percent," he says.

Honey-Lemon Carrots and Apples

Serves 4

The sweet-tart-lemony flavor of this side dish makes it unusually appealing, as do its festive colors. It's also a winning combination for health. Both carrots and apples (partly because of their fiber) and the high monounsaturated fat in the olive oil have been shown to help reduce blood cholesterol levels and possibly protect the heart in other ways. Carrots, apples, and lemon peel all contain cell-protecting antioxidants.

4 medium carrots, peeled and cut into 1/4-inch rounds
2 tablespoons honey
1 tablespoon olive oil
1 teaspoon grated lemon zest
Salt to taste
2 tablespoons water
2 unpeeled Golden Delicious apples, cored and quartered

Put the carrots, honey, olive oil, lemon peel, salt, and water into a saucepan and simmer, covered, for 20 minutes.

In the meantime, cut the apple quarters in half crosswise, then into 1/4-inch slices. Add the apple slices to the carrots and stir. Cover and simmer for about 10 minutes or until the carrots and apples are tender.

Per serving:

Calories	144
Total fat	3.8 g
Saturated fat	.5 g
Cholesterol	0
Sodium	26 mg

FOOD PHARMACY FACT

Carrot Compound Stimulates Immunity

Beta-carotene, the stuff in carrots and green leafy vegetables, can increase immune functioning. Tests show that in cell cultures beta-carotene boosted the ability of neutrophils (white blood cells) to kill bacteria and improved functioning of macrophages, immune system regulators of infection fighters such as interferon and tumor necrosis factor.

Scientists are particularly excited by animal research showing that feeding beta-carotene spurred the production of immune products that directly killed tumor cells; beta-carotene animals had tumors only one-seventh the size of those in animals not given beta-carotene. In men large doses of beta-carotene (180 milligrams daily for two weeks) increased the numbers of T helper cells that help produce antibodies.

CARROTS VS. CANCER

Why is the National Cancer Institute giving a carrot compound in a capsule to thousands of people in fourteen large-scale studies to see if it helps ward off all types of cancer, in particular lung, colon, esophageal, and skin cancer? Because animal and dietary studies throughout the world link this carrot chemical, called *beta-carotene,* first isolated from carrots 150 years ago, with substantially lower risks of cancer, notably lung cancer.

In fact about twenty epidemiological studies, say experts, now show that the most prodigious eaters of foods high in beta-carotene have lung cancer odds that are about half those of people who skimp on these foods. Of twenty-two animal studies all but one found that beta-carotene blocked the development of cancer. Additionally, low levels of beta carotene in the blood—which is tied closely to low intakes of beta-carotene foods—are grisly predictors of who is more apt to get lung cancer. And what is the critical amount of beta-carotene that separates the low-risk from the high-risk cancer candidates? Roughly the amount in one carrot, according to studies.

Squash Puree with Apricot

Serves 2

Acorn squash is one of those yellow-orange vegetables that constantly show up in the diets of those least likely to develop certain types of cancer. Here is a really simple but elegant way to prepare it without fat.

1 acorn squash (about 1½ pounds)
2 to 4 teaspoons apricot preserves
Salt to taste

With a fork, pierce the squash. Place it on a paper towel in the microwave. Microwave on HIGH for 8 to 10 minutes, turning it after 4 minutes. Let it stand for 5 to 10 minutes before cutting.

Cut the squash in half, remove the seeds, and scoop the pulp from the shell. Place the pulp in a food processor fitted with the steel blade and blend with preserves to desired sweetness. Mix in salt to taste. Serve warm.

Per serving:

Calories	130
Total fat	.3 g
Saturated fat	0
Cholesterol	0
Sodium	9 mg

Spinach with Soy and Sesame Seeds

Serves 6

You can never have too many simple recipes for spinach, because of its great taste and its potential as a fighter of various diseases, including cancer and cataracts. It's all in the green stuff's heavy concentration of carotenoids and other anticancer compounds such as folic acid. Also, hardly anything can compare with the flavor of fresh spinach, either steamed or microwaved. I prefer the microwave because it is so simple, and preserves more disease-fighting properties. You may want to do no more than add a little lemon juice. But you can also toss the spinach in an Oriental sauce given here. Soy sauce has also been found to have an anticancer effect in test tubes. This recipe even makes young children like their spinach.

1½ pounds fresh spinach, stemmed and washed thoroughly

SAUCE

1½ tablespoons reduced-sodium soy sauce
1 tablespoon rice vinegar
1 teaspoon dark sesame oil
1 teaspoon sugar
1½ tablespoons orange juice
1½ tablespoons white sesame seeds, toasted

Put the spinach with the water clinging to its leaves in a large microwave bowl. Cover with plastic wrap and microwave on HIGH for 3 minutes. Stir spinach, then microwave on HIGH for another 2 to 3 minutes. The leaves should be bright green and still hold their shape.

Drain spinach in a colander. Squeeze gently with a paper towel to remove any excess liquid. Then chop spinach coarsely.

Whisk together all the other ingredients except the sesame seeds and pour the sauce over the spinach. Toss to coat the leaves and sprinkle with toasted sesame seeds.

Per serving:

Calories	45
Total fat	2.1 g
Saturated fat	.3 g
Cholesterol	0
Sodium	215 mg

FOOD PHARMACY FACT

Attention Smokers, Another Reason to Eat Your Spinach!

Green vegetables are full of so many compounds that may help lessen damage to your lungs. A recently discovered one is folic acid, or folate, a vitamin concentrated in dark green leafy vegetables, notably spinach, collards, turnip and beet greens, broccoli, and Brussels sprouts. According to tests by Dr. Douglas Heimburger and colleagues at the University of Alabama Medical Center in Birmingham, heavy smokers had much less lung cell injury after they took fairly high doses of folic acid.

Greens with Garlic and Walnuts

Serves 6

Proclaimed by one of my guests as "the best greens I ever tasted," this wonderful mixture of green leafy vegetables gives you bountiful amounts of cell-protecting carotenoids and other disease-fighting antioxidants. This recipe is truly a rave even among people who profess not to like greens. It was inspired by Annemarie Colbin, director of the Natural Gourmet Cookery School/Institute for Food and Health in New York City, and author of several books, including The Natural Gourmet.

1 pound mixed greens, such as mustard greens, kale, and collards, washed and tough stems removed
1/2 pound spinach, washed and trimmed
1 tablespoon olive oil (more if needed)
4 large garlic cloves, minced
Salt and freshly ground pepper to taste
1/3 cup chopped walnuts

Put half the washed greens with the water clinging to their leaves in a large microwave-safe bowl. Cover with plastic wrap and microwave on HIGH for 1 minute. Stir and microwave, covered, for another 30 to 60 seconds. The greens should be just wilted and still crispy.

Repeat the procedure above, using the remaining greens and then the spinach.

Drain the greens and spinach. Chop them coarsely and press them gently between paper towels to remove more liquid.

Heat the olive oil in a skillet, add the garlic, and sauté over medium heat for 2 to 3 minutes. Add all the greens and sauté until heated through.

Season with salt and pepper, sprinkle on the walnuts, stir, and serve immediately.

Per serving:

Calories	93
Total fat	6.7 g
Saturated fat	.7 g
Cholesterol	0
Sodium	42 mg

QUICK WAYS TO PUT GREENS IN YOUR DIET

- Tear or shred leaves and toss into soups and stews during the last few minutes of cooking.
- Mix chopped or shredded greens into meat loaf, turkey loaf, or salmon loaf.
- Add chopped greens to yogurt or reduced-calorie mayonnaise and whirl in a blender to add flavor, color, and health benefits to salad dressings.
- Serve grilled or broiled seafood or poultry on a bed of raw or slightly cooked mixed greens.
- Sprinkle chopped greens over baked potatoes and other lightly cooked vegetables.
- Fold chopped greens into an omelet.

New Southern-Style Collard Greens

Serves 4

Collard greens are one of the best and most neglected vegetables in the food pharmacy. Here's a great way to get more of them in your diet without adding lots of bad fat. The darker green a leafy vegetable, the more carotenoid-type health-promoting compounds it contains. And collards are one of the deepest, brightest greens of any edible leaf. But being prepared with bacon or pork fat, as they often are, discourages many people from eating them. Here's a version that replaces that bacon with low-fat smoked turkey, adding a smoked flavor without the fatty hazards.

1 tablespoon olive oil
1 small onion, minced
1 jalapeño pepper, seeded and minced (optional)
1 ounce smoked chicken or turkey, cut into 1/4-inch slivers
1 pound fresh young collard greens, washed, stems removed, and leaves cut into 1-inch pieces
Salt and freshly ground black pepper to taste
2 teaspoons vinegar
1 splash of Tabasco sauce
1/4 cup water

Heat the olive oil in a large sauté pan. Add the onion, jalapeño, and chicken or turkey and sauté over medium heat for 2 to 3 minutes or until the onion is soft.

Add the greens, salt and pepper, vinegar, Tabasco, and water. Cook, uncovered, over medium heat for 3 to 4 minutes or until the greens are just tender. Correct the seasoning, adding salt, vinegar, or hot sauce to taste.

Per serving:

Calories	54
Total fat	3.8 g
Saturated fat	.5 g
Cholesterol	3 mg
Sodium	87 mg

Stir-Fried Kale

Serves 4

Kale, with its broad crimped leaves, is popular in many places of the world and is wonderful prepared Oriental style. In fact one study from China found that women who ate the most kale were less likely to have lung cancer. It's understandable, because kale is full of beta-carotene and is twice as high as spinach in other types of carotenoids believed to help protect cells from cigarette smoke damage.

1 tablespoon reduced-sodium soy sauce
1 tablespoon dark sesame oil
1 tablespoon rice wine or dry sherry
2 tablespoons chicken stock or water
1 teaspoon cornstarch
2 teaspoons vegetable oil
1 garlic clove, minced
1 scallion, minced
½-inch piece of fresh gingerroot, minced
1 jalapeño or serrano chili pepper, minced
1 pound kale, washed, stems and ribs removed, and leaves cut into 1-inch strips

Combine the soy sauce, sesame oil, rice wine, stock, and cornstarch in a small bowl and stir to dissolve cornstarch.

Just before serving, heat the vegetable oil to almost smoking in a wok. Add the garlic, scallion, ginger and chili pepper and cook until fragrant, 15 to 30 seconds.

Add the kale and stir-fry for 1 minute. Add the soy sauce mixture to the kale and cook for 30 seconds or until the sauce is lightly thickened and the kale is tender. Serve at once.

Per serving:

Calories	86
Total fat	4.5 g
Saturated fat	.6 g
Cholesterol	0
Sodium	182 mg

COOK'S ADVICE

Don't overcook greens. It will ruin the color as well as some of the pharmacological properties. Greens cooked too long in too much water turn from bright green to brownish green. Also, cooking greens in an aluminum pan is detrimental to the color and flavor of greens. Use stainless steel, other noncorrodible metal, or glassware pots. When blanching greens, remove them from the hot water and immediately plunge them into cold water to preserve and fix the green color.

Mustard Greens

Serves 4

If you have never had mustard greens, you are in for a treat. Not surprisingly, the greens have a sharp but pleasant bite. They are great raw in salads and also wilted as in this recipe. Mustard greens are one of those deep green leafy vegetables packed with carotenoids and folic acid and reputed to help discourage cancer, especially smoking-related cancers.

1 pound fresh mustard greens
2 tablespoons raspberry or red wine vinegar (more if desired)
1 teaspoon imitation bacon bits or to taste

Put the mustard greens in a large bowl, cover with plastic wrap, and microwave on HIGH for 2 minutes. Stir greens, then microwave, covered, on HIGH for another 2 or 3 minutes or until wilted.

Toss the mustard greens with the vinegar and bacon bits.

Per serving:

Calories	33
Total fat	.3 g
Saturated fat	0
Cholesterol	0
Sodium	39 mg

Gingered Green Beans

Serves 6

Green vegetables of all types—and that includes green snap beans—seem most likely to help ward off cancer, even breast cancer, according to recent research. Of all spices, ginger has been best scrutinized for its pharmacological properties, and it appears to be a very versatile health tonic; new discoveries of its powers turn up regularly. That's what makes this dish a winner.

1½ pounds green beans, each bean cut into thirds
2 teaspoons peanut or dark sesame oil
1 tablespoon minced fresh gingerroot
1 garlic clove, minced
1 teaspoon cornstarch
1 tablespoon reduced-sodium soy sauce
¼ cup low-sodium chicken broth
Dash of dry sherry
4 scallions, sliced
¼ cup chopped walnuts (optional)

Blanch the green beans in boiling water for about 3 minutes. Drain. Plunge into cold water, drain again, and pat dry.

Heat the oil in a large skillet or wok and add the ginger and garlic. Stir-fry over moderate heat for about a minute. Do not brown.

Add the green beans and cook for another minute.

In a small bowl, blend the cornstarch, soy sauce, chicken broth, and sherry. Add to the green beans. Bring to a boil, stirring all the while. Reduce the heat, cover, and simmer for about 4 minutes.

Add the scallions. Stir and toss briefly.

Remove the beans to a serving dish. Sprinkle with chopped walnuts if desired.

Per serving:

Calories	59
Total fat	1.7 g
Saturated fat	.3 g
Cholesterol	0
Sodium	110 mg

Sweet and Sour Cabbage

Serves 4

Cabbage with raisins was popular in biblical days, and since ancient Roman days cabbage has been touted as a cancer fighter. Indeed eating cabbage but once a week has been shown to substantially reduce the chances of colon cancer. Here's my quick and easy modern version made in the microwave.

1/2 cup raisins
1/2 cup apple juice
1/2 large head red cabbage, coarsely shredded or sliced
2 tablespoons balsamic vinegar
1 tablespoon honey
1/4 teaspoon ground cinnamon
1/2 cup chopped pecans (optional)

Soak the raisins in the apple juice for 2 hours or until plumped.

Place the cabbage in a large microwave-safe bowl. Add the vinegar and mix. Cover and microwave on HIGH for about 5 minutes.

Add the raisins, apple juice, honey, and cinnamon and mix. Microwave covered on HIGH for 3 to 5 minutes more. The cabbage should still be slightly crunchy.

Sprinkle with pecans if desired and serve.

Per serving:

Calories	140
Total fat	.6 g
Saturated fat	.1 g
Cholesterol	0
Sodium	25 mg

Cabbage and Beans with Ham

Serves 6 to 8

This old-fashioned, hearty dish combines two of nature's best medicines—cabbage and beans—in a tomato sauce that you can make as spicy as you want with the hot pepper flakes. I've served it at dinner parties as a vegetable side dish to my gourmet guests, Nancy and Kevin, and they loved it.

3 tablespoons olive oil
6 ounces lean baked ham, cut into 1-inch-long julienne strips
2 tablespoons garlic, crushed
2 medium onions, coarsely chopped
1/2 to 1 teaspoon hot red pepper flakes or to taste
3 pounds green cabbage, coarsely shredded
1/4 cup tomato paste
1 1/2 cups water
4 cups cooked Great Northern beans
1/2 cup chopped parsley
Salt and freshly ground pepper to taste

Place the oil in a Dutch oven or large kettle and sauté the ham, garlic, and onions over low heat until the onion is translucent.

Add the hot pepper and stir for 30 seconds. Add the cabbage and mix well.

In a small bowl, blend the tomato paste with the water and pour over the cabbage. Cover, reduce the heat to moderate, and cook, stirring occasionally, until the cabbage is almost tender, about 20 minutes.

Add the beans and 1/4 cup of the parsley. Cook, covered, until the cabbage is tender and the beans are heated through, about 5 minutes.

Season with salt and pepper, sprinkle on the remaining parsley, and serve.

Per serving:

Calories	320
Total fat	9 g
Saturated fat	1.6 g
Cholesterol	15 mg
Sodium	473

FOOD PHARMACY FACT

Anticancer Cruciferous Secrets

Scientists have uncovered an important clue to why a vegetarian diet may protect against breast cancer. In human tests Drs. H. Leon Bradlow and Jon J. Michnovicz of the Institute for Hormone Research in New York found that compounds (indoles) in cruciferous vegetables, such as cabbage, broccoli, Brussels sprouts, and cauliflower, bolster a process by which the body metabolizes (burns up) the female hormone estrogen. Other research shows that women with such an elevated estrogen metabolism have lower risks of hormone-dependent cancers, such as breast, uterine, and endometrial cancer.

The researchers found estrogen metabolism activity jumped about 50 percent after daily doses of 500 milligrams of indole-3-carbinol. That's the amount in about fourteen ounces of raw cabbage.

The researchers also fed the vegetable indoles to female mice; their rate of breast cancer dropped significantly.

Mapled Brussels Sprouts

Serves 6–8

Ever seeking variations of ways to prepare health-promoting Brussels sprouts, my friend Jane Stevens came up with this recipe. In case you haven't heard, the little green globes have substantial anticancer abilities.

- 2 pounds Brussels sprouts
- 3 tablespoons maple syrup
- 1 tablespoon grainy German-style mustard or Dijon mustard
- 1 tablespoon olive oil
- 3 tablespoons white vinegar
- 3 tablespoons sherry
- Salt and freshly ground pepper to taste

Wash and trim the sprouts, making an *X* in the stems.

Cook the sprouts in water or in a microwave until done but still crunchy—not mushy.

Whisk together the maple syrup, mustard, olive oil, vinegar, sherry, salt and pepper, and pour over the cooked Brussels sprouts.

Per serving:

Calories	118
Total fat	2.8 g
Saturated fat	.4 g
Cholesterol	0
Sodium	61 mg

Spicy Curried Cauliflower

Serves 4

Put more cauliflower in your life, especially if your family has a history of colon cancer. Cauliflower is a member of the cruciferous family of vegetables, which are believed to have special abilities to ward off cell changes in the colon that give rise to cancer. One study in Norway showed that people who eat the largest proportion of their calories in cruciferous veggies like cauliflower were less likely to have polyps—colon growths that can erupt into full-blown tumors. In this recipe you get a health-promoting bonus of onion, garlic, ginger, pepper, tomatoes, and lots of spices, all of which may also help inhibit various cancers. And there's very little fat.

1 tablespoon oil
1 medium onion, diced
2 garlic cloves, minced
1 jalapeño pepper, seeded and minced
1½ teaspoons minced gingerroot
Salt to taste
½ cup low-sodium tomato juice
1 medium head cauliflower, broken into equal-size florets

Curry Spices

1 teaspoon ground ginger
1 teaspoon ground cumin
½ teaspoon ground cardamom
½ teaspoon ground coriander
¼ teaspoon turmeric
⅛ teaspoon cayenne pepper or to taste
¼ teaspoon mustard seeds

Put the oil, onion, garlic, jalapeño pepper, and gingerroot in a large microwave dish. Cover and microwave on HIGH for 3 or 4 minutes, until onions are tender and translucent.

Add the curry spices, salt, and tomato juice. Microwave on HIGH for 1 minute.

Add the cauliflower and stir to coat it with the sauce. Microwave, covered, on HIGH for 5 minutes. Stir. Microwave on HIGH for another 5 minutes or just until cauliflower is tender but not mushy and sauce is bubbly.

Note: You can substitute 1 to 2 tablespoons good-quality curry powder for the curry spices.

Per serving:

Calories	74
Total fat	3.8 g
Saturated fat	.5 g
Cholesterol	0
Sodium	292 mg

FOOD PHARMACY FACT

Cauliflower, Cancer, and Men

Attention, all males! Eating more cruciferous vegetables, including cauliflower, may be your ticket to avoiding colon cancer. A study of more than 600 persons by researchers at the University of Utah School of Medicine found that men (but not women) who ate the most cruciferous vegetables were only 30 percent as likely to develop colon cancer as those who ate the least of such vegetables.

It's one of the first studies to suggest that cruciferous vegetables (cabbage, including sauerkraut, cauliflower, Brussels sprouts, broccoli) may be specifically more beneficial to men. However, both men and women who ate the most fat were about twice as likely to develop colon cancer. And both sexes who ate the most high-beta-carotene foods also had about half the risk of colon cancer.

Roasted Potatoes with Garlic and Rosemary

Serves 6

Potatoes are so entirely underrated, but they are overflowing with potassium—more per calorie even than bananas—which makes them good candidates for lowering blood pressure and preventing strokes. This easy preparation includes garlic, which also can help lower blood pressure. Rosemary contains four potent antioxidants that may also help protect arteries.

2 pounds unpeeled small red potatoes, quartered
1 tablespoon olive oil or vegetable oil spray
3 garlic cloves, slivered
2 teaspoons dried rosemary, crushed
Salt and freshly ground pepper to taste

Preheat the oven to 450 degrees. Put the potatoes on a baking sheet or in a baking pan that has been sprayed with olive or vegetable oil. Add the garlic, rosemary, salt, and lots of pepper and toss the potatoes until all are covered with oil and herbs.

Roast for about 30 minutes. Be sure to stir once during baking so the potatoes don't stick.

Per serving:

Calories	145
Total fat	2.6 g
Saturated fat	.3 g
Cholesterol	0
Sodium	12 mg

COOK'S ADVICE

You do not lose vitamin C by peeling potatoes, say Cornell University analysts. Contrary to popular opinion, they did not find in tests that most of a potato's vitamin C is just under the skin or that you destroy much of a potato's vitamin C by scraping off the skin. With or without skin, a seven-ounce baked potato, they found, has about thirty milligrams of vitamin C. That's half what conventional authorities say you need, but one fifth of what some vitamin C researchers say is adequate.

Phyllis Richman's Garlic-Stuffed Potatoes

Serves 8

Who could not love these potatoes? A version of garlic mashed potatoes, these are well worth your attention any day. They do have a little butter and cheese, giving them slightly more fat than most recipes in this book; even so, they are not ultra-caloric, and the percentage of calories from fat is but 26 percent, still relatively low and below the 30 percent government guidelines. This soul-satisfying recipe comes from Phyllis Richman, restaurant critic for The Washington Post, *who says there is no food she loves more than these potatoes.*

4 large baking potatoes
1 whole head garlic
2 tablespoons butter or margarine
½ cup low-fat milk
1 scallion, finely minced
Salt and freshly ground pepper to taste
⅓ cup freshly grated Parmesan or Swiss cheese

Preheat the oven to 375 degrees. Scrub the potatoes and dry them well. Pierce the skins with a fork.

Wrap the garlic in foil.

Place the potatoes and garlic directly on the oven rack and bake for 1 hour. Remove the garlic and continue baking the potatoes for up to 30 minutes more, until a fork pierces the center of the potato easily.

Separate the garlic cloves and squeeze each so the pulp pops out of the skin into a large bowl. Discard the skin. Mash the pulp well and beat in the butter.

Halve the potatoes lengthwise, scoop out the pulp, and add it to the bowl with the garlic butter. Reserve the skins.

Add the milk, scallion, salt, and pepper, mashing and beating until smooth. Preheat the broiler.

Refill the potato skins and sprinkle with cheese. Brown under the broiler for about 5 minutes.

Per serving:

Calories	144
Total fat	4.2 g
Saturated fat	2.5 g
Cholesterol	11 mg
Sodium	108 mg

FOOD PHARMACY FACT

Kudos for Starch

The starch in cooked potatoes, rice, and partially ripe bananas may help ward off colon cancer. So finds John Cummings, a fiber expert at Cambridge University in England. He explains that starch, broken down in the lower gut, creates butyric acid, a substance that counteracts certain cancer-causing agents.

Genevieve's Italian Potatoes and Peppers

Serves 4 to 6

A heartwarming and satisfying dish as only the Italians can make, this is always a hit and combines three pharmacological superstars—onions, garlic, and peppers. Thanks to Genevieve Trezza Hill for this recipe, which has been in her Italian family for many years.

- 2 to 3 tablespoons olive oil
- 3 medium baking potatoes, peeled, halved lengthwise, then cut into eighths or quarters
- 1 medium green bell pepper, cut into ½-inch strips
- 1 medium red bell pepper, cut into ½-inch strips
- 2 medium onions, sliced
- 2 garlic cloves, crushed, or to taste
- Salt and freshly ground pepper to taste
- 2 tablespoons chopped fresh basil *or* 2 teaspoons dried (optional)

Preheat the oven to 400 degrees. Place the olive oil in the bottom of a baking dish. Add the potatoes flat side down and bake for 15 minutes.

Add the peppers, onions, garlic, salt, pepper, and basil, and toss with the potatoes. Reduce the heat to 325 degrees and bake for 45 minutes to an hour, tossing occasionally, or until all the vegetables are cooked.

Per serving:

Calories	187
Total fat	7.1 g
Saturated fat	.1 g
Cholesterol	0
Sodium	10 mg

COOK'S ADVICE

Here's how to avoid the extra fat that comes with sautéing onions, garlic, and peppers in a pan: Sauté in a microwave without any fat. Simply chop or mince the onion, garlic, or pepper; cover; and zap them in a microwave for a few minutes. Then add them to casseroles and other dishes. You can also "sauté" garlic and onions in broth or wine, again eliminating the need for oil.

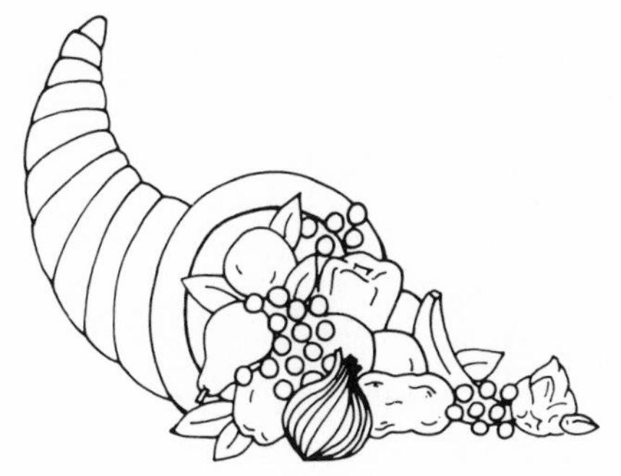

Shepherd's Pie with Curried Eggplant

Serves 8

This vegetarian version of shepherd's pie features eggplant instead of the traditional ground beef or lamb. I confess I adapted it from a meat-based recipe in The New York Times *a long time ago, and it never fails to get acclaim. Eggplant in studies has helped the blood and arteries resist damage from high-fat diets and is a vegetable high on lists of some people with lower rates of cancer.*

6 large potatoes (about 2½ pounds)
2 large eggplants (about 3½ pounds)
¾ cup finely chopped onions
1 tablespoon minced garlic
1 teaspoon olive oil
1 or 2 tablespoons good-quality curry powder
1 teaspoon ground cumin
1 teaspoon ground coriander
Salt and freshly ground pepper to taste
1 cup canned Italian crushed tomatoes
½ cup low-sodium chicken broth
¾ cup hot skim milk
1 tablespoon butter or margarine (optional)
1 cup cooked fresh or frozen green peas

Boil the potatoes, salting the water if desired, until tender.

Meanwhile, cut one unpeeled eggplant in 1-inch cubes. In a large covered bowl microwave the eggplant cubes until soft. Pour off liquid. Pierce the other eggplant with a fork several times and microwave the whole eggplant until collapsed and very soft. Split and remove the pulp, discarding the skin. Combine the eggplant pulp and cubes.

Sauté the onions and garlic in a large nonstick saucepan with the oil until translucent and soft. Add the curry powder, cumin, and coriander and cook about 3 minutes, stirring.

Add the eggplant, salt and pepper, tomatoes, and broth. Cook, stirring occasionally, for about 20 to 30 minutes.

Drain the potatoes and mash or put through a ricer or food mill. Beat in the hot milk, some salt and pepper, and butter if desired. Add the peas.

Preheat the broiler. Spoon the eggplant mixture into a shallow 8-cup baking dish. Top with the hot mashed potatoes and smooth over the top. Put the casserole under the broiler until the top is golden brown.

Per serving:

Calories	213
Total fat	1.3 g
Saturated fat	.2 g
Cholesterol	.4 mg
Sodium	82 mg

FOOD PHARMACY FACT

Let's Hear It for Eggplant, Squash, Green Beans, Spinach, and Cabbage!

All of these vegetables seem to ward off stomach cancer, according to a recent analysis in China. Scientists studied the eating habits of 482 residents of Heilongjiang Province; half had stomach cancer; half did not. Those free of cancer much preferred spinach, squash, eggplant, green beans, and especially cabbage. In fact the amount of cabbage deemed protective against stomach cancer was minuscule, according to researchers—a mere one-third cup of raw cabbage or two tablespoons of cooked cabbage per day—42 kilograms per year. Chinese cabbage is the principal vegetable eaten in the province.

Sweet Potatoes Amandine

Serves 4

These easy-to-make sweet potatoes are ever-popular at my family gatherings. The secret is the almond-flavored amaretto liqueur, which adds sweetness, richness, and an unusual flavor. It's too bad Americans eat only 3 percent as many sweet potatoes as white potatoes. The orange pigment comes from beta-carotene. One-half cup of mashed sweet potatoes has enough daily beta-carotene shown in studies to dramatically reduce the risk of smoking-related problems, especially lung cancer. Beta-carotene seems even to help "heal" the lungs for several years after a person has stopped smoking.

2½ pounds sweet potatoes, scrubbed and pierced with a fork
¼ cup amaretto liqueur
2 tablespoons almond slivers or slices, toasted (optional)

Bake the sweet potatoes in conventional or microwave oven until soft. When cool enough to handle, split the potatoes and remove the pulp.

In a bowl, mash the sweet potatoes. Add the amaretto and mash again. If the potatoes are too stiff, whip in a little heated skim milk. Top with toasted almonds if desired. Reheat in the oven or microwave if necessary.

Note: To toast almonds, use blanched, skinless almonds. Spread the nuts in a shallow pan and roast them in a preheated 350-degree oven until they are a toasty light brown.

Per serving:

Calories	255
Total fat	.6 g
Saturated fat	.1 g
Cholesterol	0
Sodium	26 mg

Slow-Baked Plantains

Serves 4

In South American folk medicine plantains are used to treat ulcers. There's truth to it, as numerous studies on both animals and humans show. Dr. A. K. Sanyal, a pioneer in the study of plantains for ulcers, recommends they be cooked slowly at a low temperature, lest their therapeutic properties be lost to high heat. Here is one way to do that Latin American style.

2 large ripe plantains
1/4 cup brown or white sugar
1/2 cup water

Preheat the oven to 350 degrees. Cut the plantains in half and run a sharp knife lengthwise down their skin, just deep enough to touch the interior. Then pull the skin off. Slice in half lengthwise.

Place the plantains in a baking dish and sprinkle with the sugar. Add the water.

Bake, covered, for about an hour, until they are golden. Turn the plantains frequently so they brown evenly.

Note: Plantains are excellent served with rice, such as Nutty Brown Rice, page 258.

Per serving:

Calories	188
Total fat	.4 g
Saturated fat	0
Cholesterol	0
Sodium	9 mg

Scalloped Corn with Peppers

Serves 4

This is a real temptation to make when fresh corn is in season, but you can substitute canned or frozen corn kernels. Corn gives you lots of cellulose, a disease-fighting fiber that has lowered cholesterol in tests and helped combat infections. Corn, like other seeds, contains anticancer protease inhibitors.

3 ears fresh corn *or* 1½ cups canned or thawed frozen corn
1 cup tortilla chips, crushed
¼ cup minced green bell pepper
1 heaped teaspoon minced hot red chili pepper
2 eggs *or* ½ cup egg substitute
1 cup skim milk
1 tablespoon butter or margarine
Salt and freshly ground pepper to taste

Preheat the oven to 350 degrees. Cook the corn, cut the kernels from the cob, and place in casserole. (If you are using canned or frozen corn, drain it.)

Add the tortilla chips, peppers, eggs, milk, butter, salt, and pepper and mix together.

Bake for about 30 minutes or until browned.

Per serving:

Calories	201
Total fat	9.1 g
Saturated fat	2.7 g
Cholesterol	115 mg
Sodium	180 mg

FOOD PHARMACY FACT

Corn Fiber Reduces Cholesterol

Jerry Earll, an endrocrinologist at Georgetown University Hospital, fed corn fiber to seven patients with high cholesterol (above 240). After six weeks the daily dose of eighteen grams of the fiber (slightly over half an ounce) reduced cholesterol by an average 20 percent. One subject's cholesterol plunged by 41 percent—down from 312 to 183. Another's dived 36 percent. However, in one case cholesterol dropped only 1 percent, and it rose 4 percent in another. Corn fiber also improved the ratio of heart-protective HDL cholesterol to total cholesterol.

Corn fiber's performance was a surprise because it is made up of 68 percent hemicellulose and 21 percent cellulose, both insoluble fibers that scientists did not think could cut cholesterol.

Turnips with Nutmeg

Serves 4

There are three basic things you should know about turnips, says my friend Joan Claybrook. Peel them before cooking. If you cook them unpeeled they have a slightly bitter taste some people find objectionable. Steam or microwave them; don't boil them in water, because they are already a watery vegetable. Season them with lots of nutmeg. Here's her recipe for scrumptious turnips that have been served for several generations in her family. Don't forget that turnips are a crucifer cousin of broccoli and cabbage and share many of the same formidable pharmacological attributes.

4 medium turnips, peeled and cut into quarters
1 teaspoon butter
Salt to taste
Ground nutmeg to taste (preferably freshly grated)

Steam the turnips until soft. Mash them with a fork and add the butter, salt, and several generous gratings of nutmeg.

Per serving:

Calories	33
Total fat	1 g
Saturated fat	.6 g
Cholesterol	3 mg
Sodium	71 mg

A SECRET CANCER FIGHTER IN BEANS, CORN, RICE, GRAINS, AND NUTS

All so-called "seed" foods, like legumes, nuts, corn, rice, and grains, possess agents called *protease inhibitors* that researchers believe help block the activity of enzymes that can instigate and promote cancer.

Legumes—chick-peas, soybeans, lentils, red and white beans—are particularly rich in one type of protease inhibitor, called the *Bowman-Birk inhibitor (BBI),* which is stirring up increasing excitement among cancer researchers. Researchers have long known that this legume compound survives cooking and digestion and thus was sure to end up in the colon, where it could conceivably help combat tumors. But what happened then was a mystery. Now researchers have discovered a specific receptor for BBI in colon cells. That means BBI has a specific docking site from which it can wage biological war against cancer-prone cells.

New clues also reveal how BBI can get into the bloodstream and thus circulate to squelch cancer. Animal studies by a leading researcher in the field, Harvard's Dr. Ann Kennedy, have confirmed that BBI can travel to far-distant sites, helping prevent both liver and lung cancer.

Experts explain that it takes only one millionth of a gram of BBI to stop the conversion of a healthy cell to a cancerous one. Soybeans have about double the BBI of other legumes.

Mexican "Refried" Beans

Serves 4

Mexican-style refried beans, in my opinion, are one of the tastiest ways to eat disease-fighting, cholesterol-lowering beans. And they need not be high in fat, notably lard, to be great-tasting, as this recipe demonstrates. There are a few canned refried beans on the market that do not contain lard, but they are often hard to find. Better to make your own.

4 cups cooked kidney or pinto beans
1½ cups finely chopped onions
½ cup low-sodium chicken broth
½ cup canned tomatoes with juice
4 garlic cloves, minced
1 teaspoon celery seeds
2 tablespoons lemon juice
10 drops Tabasco sauce (more if desired)
Salt and freshly ground pepper to taste

Combine all ingredients in a large nonstick skillet. Simmer, covered, over low heat for about 50 to 60 minutes, stirring several times, until the beans are soft and mushy and the liquid has been absorbed. Serve hot.

Per serving:

Calories	263
Total fat	1.4 g
Saturated fat	.2 g
Cholesterol	0
Sodium	65 mg

QUICK WAYS TO SOAK DRIED BEANS

Don't be discouraged from using dried beans because of the soaking time. True, dried beans—except for lentils, split peas, and black-eyed peas—must be soaked before cooking, and although many cooks think that means overnight or for twenty-four hours, most beans do not need all that time. Actually, according to *The Brilliant Bean,* a wonderful cookbook by Sally and Martin Stone, most dried beans absorb as much water as they can hold within four hours. Even so, the Stones suggest quicker methods:

1. Simply put washed and picked-over beans in a large saucepan and cover beans with two inches of fresh water. A rule of thumb is three to four times as much water as beans. Then boil for two minutes, remove from the heat, and let the beans soak, covered, for an hour. Drain and add new water for cooking.

2. Cut more time by bringing the beans to a boil and then letting them boil at medium heat for ten minutes. Then they will need to soak for only thirty minutes to be reconstituted enough for proper cooking.

Soaking the Microwave Way. You may want to soak and cook beans the microwave way, which Barbara Kafka, author of the best-selling cookbook *Microwave Gourmet,* says meant the difference to her between "almost never cooking them from scratch and feeling free to use them as an ingredient."

Here's her advice for soaking dried beans and legumes in the microwave. Place one or two cups of dried beans or legumes in a two-quart soufflé dish with two cups of water. Cover tightly with microwave plastic wrap and cook at 100 percent for fifteen minutes. Take them from the oven and let stand, covered, for five minutes. Then add two cups of very hot water, re-cover, and let stand for one hour. Drain and add new water before returning to the microwave for final cooking.

Caution: Do not add salt to dried beans either during soaking or during cooking until they are tender. Salt tends to make the skin impermeable so the liquid is not absorbed as well, leaving the beans tough despite a long cooking time. Adding highly acidic ingredients, such as tomatoes and citrus juice, before the beans are tender has the same toughening effect.

Generally one cup of dried beans makes two cups when cooked—or enough for four servings. One cup of dried soybeans or chick-peas becomes three cups.

Microwave Bean Burritos

4 burritos

For a quick cholesterol-lowering bean fix, especially for those who have frequent cravings for Mexican food, you can hardly beat this recipe. You can also use the "Refried" beans in the previous recipe.

1½ cups cooked pinto beans *or* 1 15-ounce can, drained
¼ teaspoon ground cumin
5 drops Tabasco sauce or to taste
4 flour tortillas
2 ounces reduced-fat sharp Cheddar cheese, shredded
¾ cup Salsa Cruda (page 385) or commercial tomato salsa

In a blender or a food processor fitted with the steel blade, blend the beans, cumin, and hot pepper sauce until the beans are smooth enough to spread but are still slightly chunky.

Place the tortillas flat on a plate, cover with a paper towel, and microwave on HIGH for 30 seconds to a minute, until they are soft enough to fold easily.

Place a fourth of the beans on each tortilla. Reserving 2 tablespoons, cover with one fourth of the shredded cheese. Fold two opposite sides of the tortilla toward each other, then fold over from the other direction. Sprinkle the top of each burrito with the two tablespoons reserved cheese.

Place the burritos in a shallow microwave-safe dish. Cover with plastic wrap and cook on HIGH for 2 or 3 minutes, until the cheese melts. Top with the salsa and serve immediately.

Per burrito:

Calories	263
Total fat	3 g
Saturated fat	1.6 g
Cholesterol	10 mg
Sodium	318 mg

Boston Baked Soybeans

Serves 4

The ancient Chinese called the soybean "the miracle bean," and indeed it seems to be. Highest of all beans in an anticancer compound called protease inhibitors, *soybeans have retarded cancer in animals and performed numerous other therapeutic tricks to lower blood cholesterol, blood pressure, and blood sugar. Making soybeans into the classic American baked beans is an excellent way to mainstream this much-neglected protector of health. In fact, some friends like these beans better than the traditional baked beans.*

1½ cups dried soybeans, soaked overnight
1 quart water
½ cup chili sauce
3 tablespoons dark molasses, such as Brer Rabbit
1 teaspoon dry mustard *or* 1½ teaspoons prepared mustard
½ cup water

Drain the soaked beans, transfer them to a saucepan, and add the quart of water. Bring to a boil, then simmer, covered, for about 3 hours.

Mix together the chili sauce, molasses, mustard, and ½ cup water in a 1½-quart casserole.

Drain the cooked beans and stir them into the chili mixture. Preheat the oven to 325 degrees.

Bake, uncovered, for 1½ hours, stirring occasionally.

Per serving:

Calories	360
Total fat	14 g
Saturated fat	2 g
Cholesterol	0
Sodium	473 mg

FOOD PHARMACY FACT

New Soybean Secret

Scientists know that soybeans contain several agents that can block cancer in animals and that people who eat more legumes, including soybeans, have lower rates of certain cancers. But a team of British and Egyptian researchers has discovered yet another anticancer secret in soybeans. The beans can block the formation of nitrosamines, one of the world's most dreaded cancer-causing agents. In fact soybeans worked better than vitamin C, which is added to cured meats expressly to prevent nitrosamines from forming.

In the study mice were given either soybeans, vitamin C, or a standard diet and then subjected to nitrosamine-forming chemicals. The mice fed soybeans showed no abnormalities in the liver, the prime target of nitrosamines. There was some liver damage in mice given vitamin C, and extensive damage, including tumors, in animals fed neither soybeans nor vitamin C.

Dr. Jenkins's Greek Bean Stew

Serves 4

According to Dr. David Jenkins, professor at the University of Toronto, "Food is our most intimate medicine." He and his wife and colleague, researcher Alexandra Jenkins, are particular devotees of beans, shown in Jenkins's studies as the best foods for regulating blood levels of insulin and blood sugar. This is important, says Dr. Jenkins, not only for diabetics but for everyone, and has a favorable impact on blood cholesterol. This bean main course, served with a salad, is a favorite at the Jenkins's table. Among diners at my table it is also a hit, ranking number one in recipe requests.

2 cups dried white pea beans, soaked overnight
2 medium onions, sliced
2 tablespoons olive oil
1 medium red bell pepper, sliced into strips
1 medium green bell pepper, sliced into strips
1 teaspoon minced garlic
1 28-ounce can tomatoes, chopped, juice reserved
2 tablespoons tomato paste
1 teaspoon dried marjoram
1 teaspoon Italian seasoning
Salt and freshly ground pepper to taste
1/2 cup pitted, halved black olives, such as Kalamata
2 tablespoons minced parsley

Drain the soaked beans and simmer, covered, in plenty of water for 1 to 1 1/4 hours, until almost soft. Drain and set aside.

In a large saucepan, sauté the onion in oil until brown. Add the peppers and garlic and cook gently for 10 minutes. Add the tomatoes, reserved tomato juice, tomato paste, beans, herbs, salt, and pepper. Cover and simmer for 45 minutes.

Add the olives and parsley 5 minutes before serving.

Per serving:

Calories	513
Total fat	10.6 g
Saturated fat	1.6 g
Cholesterol	0
Sodium	555 mg

David Taylor's Hoppin' John

Serves 8

My friend David says he can't stop eating this every time he makes it, and I had the same reaction when he first gave me a taste. It's spicy, and you can even add more cayenne pepper if desired. The pepper helps open up the air passages, and the black-eyed peas and onions both contain compounds for keeping the heart healthy and inhibiting cancer.

1¼ cup dried black-eyed peas, soaked overnight
½ cup imitation bacon bits
1 large *or* 2 medium onions, finely sliced
¼ teaspoon cayenne pepper
1 teaspoon Morton's Natures Seasons seasoning (optional)
2 tablespoons reduced-sodium soy sauce
2 tablespoons olive oil
½ cup rice, soaked overnight
Salt and freshly ground pepper to taste

Drain the soaked black-eyed peas, reserving 3½ cups of the liquid.

Put the peas, reserved liquid, ¼ cup of the bacon bits, onions, cayenne pepper, optional Nature's Seasons, 1 tablespoon of the soy sauce, and 1 tablespoon of the olive oil in a large pot. Cover and simmer for 1¼ hours.

Drain the rice and add it along with the remaining soy sauce, olive oil, and bacon bits, plus salt and pepper, to the black-eyed peas mixture. Simmer for 30 minutes or until the rice is cooked, then serve.

Per serving:

Calories	200
Total fat	4.8 g
Saturated fat	.5 g
Cholesterol	0
Sodium	286 mg

FOOD PHARMACY FACT

New Anticancer Agent in Legumes

It's long been known that legumes have "antinutrients" that some feared were detrimental to health. Among the suspicious agents are phytates, or phytic acid. Now researchers have discovered that phytic acid, in fact, is an antioxidant that helps guard the membranes of cells from becoming rancid and disintegrating, promoting diseases of all types, according to Dr. Ernst Graf, a food scientist with the Pillsbury Company in Minneapolis. Dr. David Jenkins suspects phytic acid may also help regulate blood sugar and insulin levels.

Lima Beans with Apple and Cinnamon

Serves 4–6

An inspired combination of spices, beans, and apple gives this North African dish a unique flavor. It's also an inspired pharmacological combination—both beans and apples lower blood cholesterol, and beans, plus apples and cinnamon, help keep blood sugar in check. Beans, apples, and turmeric also possess anticancer compounds. The cinnamony beans go especially well with rice. One of my favorite ways to serve it is with Rainbow Trout with Orange-Rice Stuffing *(page 286)*.

1 tablespoon olive oil
1 large onion, chopped
1 large tart apple, diced
1/4 teaspoon turmeric
1/2 teaspoon ground allspice
3/4 teaspoon ground cinnamon
4 cups cooked lima beans, cooking liquid reserved

Heat the oil in a large saucepan, add the onions, and sauté until the onions are golden.

Add the apple and seasonings and simmer until the apple is softened but not mushy.

Add the beans and about 1 cup of the reserved liquid. Simmer for about 10 minutes.

Microwave alternative: In a large covered bowl, microwave the onions and oil on HIGH until the onions are soft. Add the apple and seasonings and microwave on HIGH until the apples are soft but not mushy. Add the cooked beans and microwave for a few more minutes, until the beans are heated through.

Per serving:

Calories	287
Total fat	4.5 g
Saturated fat	.6 g
Cholesterol	0
Sodium	5 mg

FOOD PHARMACY FACT

A Toast to Cinnamon

Putting cinnamon in foods can boost the performance of insulin, a hormone that helps process sugar and carry it to the cells. So says biochemist Richard Anderson, U.S. Department of Agriculture's Human Nutrition Research Center in Beltsville, Maryland. In a survey of foods, to his great surprise, he found that those made with cinnamon seemed to stimulate insulin activity. In test tube experiments he discovered that most foods had little or no effect on insulin activity. But cinnamon, cloves, turmeric, and bay leaves actually tripled insulin's activity. Cinnamon was the most potent.

Such spices, he says, probably help your body metabolize sugar more efficiently with less insulin, which could be of special benefit to those with Type II (adult-onset) diabetes who produce low-activity insulin. That means that eating cinnamon might increase insulin's efficiency, reducing the amount of insulin such diabetics need. Dr. Anderson is doing tests to find out.

L & N's Bean Casserole

Serves 6 to 8

My friends Nina Graybill, a four-time cookbook author, and Lisa Berger devised this quick bean casserole while they were in a supermarket deciding what to serve at a dinner party. It was so successful, it's become part of their regular repertoire. I like it because it's an easy, fast way to use beans, one of the most therapeutic but too often neglected items in nature's food pharmacy.

1 onion, diced
1 garlic clove, minced
2 teaspoons olive oil
5 celery stalks, diced
1 green or red bell pepper, diced
4 15-ounce cans Great Northern beans, drained and rinsed (about 6 cups)
1 28-ounce can tomatoes, chopped, with juice
2 cups low-sodium chicken broth
1 teaspoon dried thyme or to taste
1 bay leaf
Salt and freshly ground pepper to taste

Preheat the oven to 350 degrees. In a casserole dish or Dutch oven, sauté the onion and garlic in the olive oil until soft and translucent. Add the celery and pepper. Cook until limp. (All these vegetables can also be cooked to this point in a microwave.)

Add the beans, tomatoes, chicken broth, herbs, salt, and pepper. Mix. Bake for 30 minutes.

Per serving:

Calories	387
Total fat	3.5 g
Saturated fat	.7 g
Cholesterol	0
Sodium	273 mg

Cuban Black Beans and Rice

Serves 4

A favorite in my family for keeping cholesterol, blood sugar, and insulin levels in check is legumes of all types. A combination of such beans and rice in various forms is popular around the world as peasant or "ordinary people food." Now researchers are discovering how really good these high-fiber, starchy foods are for you. I've adapted this recipe from that fabulous cookbook, The Brilliant Bean, *reducing the amount of oil and suggesting some hot peppers for those who also want a little pulmonary pick-me-up.*

1 to 2 tablespoons olive oil
1 medium onion, finely chopped
1 green bell pepper, finely chopped
2 teaspoons minced garlic
2 tomatoes, coarsely chopped, *or* 4 canned Italian plum tomatoes, drained and coarsely chopped
Salt and freshly ground pepper to taste
1/2 teaspoon hot red pepper flakes *or* Tabasco sauce to taste (optional)
2 cups drained cooked black beans, *or* 1 15-ounce can, drained and rinsed
2 cups water
1 cup unconverted long-grain rice

In a medium nonstick saucepan over moderately high heat, heat the oil until rippling. Add the onion, pepper, and garlic and sauté, stirring frequently, until the onion is translucent and soft. Add the tomatoes and cook, stirring, until well blended and thickened, about 3 or 4 minutes. Season with salt, pepper, and optional red pepper flakes or Tabasco. Turn the heat down to simmer.

Stir in the beans, cover, and simmer gently while the rice is prepared.

In a saucepan over high heat, bring 2 cups of salted water to a boil, add the rice, turn the heat down to simmer, and cook, covered, for 18 minutes or until the rice has absorbed all the liquid.

Mound the rice on a warm serving plate and create a well in the center. Pour the beans into the well and serve.

Per serving:

Calories	338
Total fat	4.4 g
Saturated fat	.7 g
Cholesterol	0
Sodium	9 mg

Spicy Tofu Stir-Fry with Vegetables

Serves 4

Tofu (soybean curd) has most of the good stuff of soybeans, which makes it an ideal health food. Tofu has even been found in one study to make the stomach feel better by cutting down on the production of acid. Here's a way to put more tofu into your life, as well as health-promoting peppers, squash, garlic, and ginger.

Tofu Marinade

1 jalapeño pepper, minced
2 garlic cloves, minced
1 tablespoon minced fresh gingerroot
2 teaspoons dark sesame oil
1 tablespoon rice vinegar
2 tablespoons honey
2 tablespoons reduced-sodium soy sauce or tamari
3 tablespoons lemon juice

1 pound firm or extra-firm tofu, cut into 1/2-inch pieces
1 red or yellow bell pepper
1 green bell pepper
1 medium zucchini
1 medium yellow squash
1 large carrot
2 to 3 tablespoons olive oil
1 bunch scallions, thinly sliced on the diagonal
1 tablespoon arrowroot
Soy sauce to taste (optional)
3 tablespoons sesame seeds, lightly toasted

Combine the ingredients for the marinade in a glass bowl. Add the tofu and marinate while you cut the vegetables.

Cut the peppers, zucchini, squash, and carrot into matchstick slivers. Strain the tofu, reserving the marinade.

Heat a wok over high heat. Add 1 tablespoon of the oil, and when it starts to smoke, add the peppers, carrots, and scallions. Stir-fry for 1 to 2 minutes or until crispy tender. Transfer the vegetables to a bowl using a slotted spoon.

Reheat the wok, adding more oil if necessary. Add the zucchini and summer squash and stir-fry for 1 minute or until crispy tender. Transfer to the bowl using a slotted spoon.

Reheat the wok, adding 1 tablespoon oil. Add the tofu and stir-fry for 2 minutes, constantly moving the ingredients to prevent sticking.

Meanwhile, stir the arrowroot into the reserved marinade. Add this mixture to the wok along with vegetables. Cook for 1 minute or until the sauce thickens and the vegetables are thoroughly heated. Add soy sauce to taste if desired. Sprinkle the stir-fried tofu with sesame seeds and serve at once with rice or noodles.

Per serving:

Calories	377
Total fat	23 g
Saturated fat	3.1 g
Cholesterol	0
Sodium	332 mg

Pizza, Pasta, and Grains

Pissaladière (Onion Pizza)

Serves 6

In this unique version of the classic Provençal onion pizza, you get some anchovies, one of the richest of all fishes in disease-fighting omega-3-type oil, and enough onions to make cancer researchers happy—fully one-and-a-half large onions, or more than three-and-a-half ounces cooked per serving. Studies in China found that people eating at least three ounces of onions and garlic a day were 40 percent less likely to develop stomach cancer. Reprinted from the low-fat, low-calorie cookbook Mediterranean Light, *by Martha Rose Shulman.*

1 tablespoon olive oil (more as necessary)
4 pounds (8 or 12 medium) onions, very thinly sliced
1/4 cup dry red wine
1/4 teaspoon dried thyme (more if desired)
Salt and freshly ground pepper to taste
1 recipe Three-Hour Pizza Dough (recipe follows) or prepared unbaked pizza crust (12 to 15 inches)
6 anchovy fillets, rinsed

Heat the olive oil over low heat in a large nonstick skillet. Add the onions and cook, stirring from time to time, until they are translucent and soft. Add the wine and thyme and cook gently, stirring occasionally, for 1 to 1 1/2 hours, until the onions are golden brown and beginning to caramelize. Add salt and pepper. The onions should not brown or stick to the pan. Add water if necessary. Preheat the oven to 500 degrees.

Top the pizza dough with the onions.

Cut the anchovies in half and make crisscrosses over the onions.

Bake the pissaladière for 20 to 25 minutes or until the crust is browned and crisp. Serve hot or let cool and serve at room temperature.

Per serving:	
Calories	298
Total fat	6.2 g
Saturated fat	.9 g
Cholesterol	2.2 mg
Sodium	338 mg

THREE-HOUR PIZZA DOUGH

Serves 6

For the Sponge

¼ cup lukewarm water
2 teaspoons active dry yeast
¼ cup whole wheat flour

For the Dough

½ cup plus 1 tablespoon lukewarm water
1 tablespoon olive oil
½ teaspoon salt
1 cup whole wheat pastry flour
¾ cup unbleached white flour

Mix the ingredients for the sponge and let it sit, covered, in a warm place for 30 minutes.

Add the lukewarm water and olive oil and mix well. Add the salt, then stir in the whole wheat pastry flour, then the white flour.

Scrape the dough out of the bowl and knead it on a lightly floured surface for 10 to 15 minutes. The dough will be sticky, but keep flouring your hands and add only enough flour to prevent sticking to the kneading surface.

Shape the dough into a ball and place in an oiled bowl; turn it so the greased side is up. Cover and let rise for 2 hours.

Punch the dough down and let rise again for 40 minutes.

Turn the dough out onto a lightly floured surface and roll it out until thin or press out and stretch with your hands. Line an oiled pizza pan and shape an attractive ridge around the edge with the overhanging dough.

Per serving:

Calories	166
Total fat	3 g
Saturated fat	.4 g
Cholesterol	0
Sodium	185 mg

FOOD PHARMACY FACT

Onions' Anticancer Compound

Red and yellow onions contain extraordinarily high concentrations of a compound called *quercetin.* Quercetin is an antioxidant; thus it helps protect cells from numerous attacks by rogue oxygen molecules.

Quercetin may also fight cancer in another way, says biochemistry professor Terrance Leighton, University of California at Berkeley. Cancer cells can escape normal growth controls—and thus proliferate—by activating a protein called *PKC.* Quercetin blocks the actions of PKC, thereby helping squelch the growth of cells and eventual formation of a tumor.

This is particularly critical for humans, because we all have genetically damaged cells vulnerable to turn-ons by PKC. By keeping PKC in check, quercetin may intervene when we most need it, nipping the control switch that allows such damaged cells to become truly wild and cancerous. Says Dr. Leighton, "There's enough quercetin in fifty to one hundred grams of onions (one-and-a-half to three-and-a-half ounces) to give a pretty substantial dose."

Pasta Salad with Tuna and Grapes

Serves 4

Pasta salad has become a near-universal staple for many Americans. I like this one for its low fat, its use of canned tuna—one of the easiest ways to get the fabulous fish oils—and the red grapes, which you should not pass up because of their concentrations of antioxidants and other identified virus- and bacteria-fighting compounds. This recipe was developed by the U.S. Department of Agriculture as part of its campaign to get Americans to eat within the government's health-promoting dietary guidelines.

3/4 cup macaroni
1 6 1/2-ounce can tuna packed in water, drained
1/2 cup thinly sliced celery
1 cup seedless red grapes, halved
3 tablespoons reduced-calorie mayonnaise

Cook the macaroni according to the package directions, omitting salt. Drain.

Toss the macaroni, tuna, celery, and grapes together. Mix in the mayonnaise.

Serve warm or chill until served.

Per serving:

Calories	174
Total fat	3.6 g
Saturated fat	.8 g
Cholesterol	21 mg
Sodium	222 mg

PASTA'S THERAPEUTIC PUNCH

Wheat flour made into pasta is quite different pharmacologically from the same white flour made into bread. Pasta, unlike white bread, helps keep blood sugar and insulin levels steady. This is good for your system, because too much insulin coursing through the blood may be a curse for ordinary, normal people. "Just because it's good to have enough insulin doesn't mean it's good to have too much," says Dr. David Jenkins. He explains that high insulin levels are associated with obesity, high blood pressure, lesions on artery walls (independent of high blood cholesterol), and cancer. In animals insulin can promote cancer growth. Also in animals, too much insulin, needed to process calories, is thought to help shorten life.

So not only people with diabetes but everyone has a stake in eating foods like pasta that tend to keep blood sugar and insulin levels steady, says Dr. Jenkins.

Vegetable Confetti Pasta Salad

Serves 6

A colorful display of oodles of vegetables with popular pasta makes this an all-time favorite in taste and health. Plus, the dressing is virtually nonfat. For an even heartier—pun intended—main course, you can add fish. Try a pound of salmon, sole, or halibut fillet. Simply poach the fish, let it cool, then flake it and add it to the pasta and vegetables. You can also vary the vegetables depending on what you have on hand.

½ pound medium pasta shells or rotini
2 tomatoes, diced
4 scallions, diced
1 cucumber, peeled, seeded, and diced
1 medium red onion, diced
1 medium yellow onion, diced
2 green and/or red bell peppers, diced
4 unpeeled medium red potatoes, cooked and diced
1 bunch broccoli, cooked briefly and diced
½ pound green beans, cooked briefly and diced
¼ cup minced parsley
Fresh basil to taste if available

Dressing

¼ cup balsamic vinegar
⅛ teaspoon Dijon mustard
Pinch of dried oregano
½ teaspoon freshly ground pepper or to taste
Salt to taste
1 tablespoon frozen apple juice concentrate

Cook the pasta in boiling water until al dente and drain well. Toss the pasta with the vegetables and herbs.

In a covered jar, shake the dressing ingredients until well blended, pour it over the other ingredients, and toss again. Serve at room temperature or slightly chilled.

Note: You can also use this low-calorie salad dressing for other pasta salad combinations.

Per serving:

Calories	313
Total fat	1.5 g
Saturated fat	.2 g
Cholesterol	0
Sodium	56 mg

FOOD PHARMACY FACT

Broccoli Never Quits

Think you've heard every possible reason for eating broccoli? Here's another one. You and millions of other Americans might save yourself from developing adult-onset (Type II) diabetes by eating more broccoli, which is extremely rich in the trace mineral chromium. Chromium, says Dr. Richard A. Anderson, a diabetes expert at the U.S. Department of Agriculture's Human Research Laboratories in Beltsville, Maryland, stimulates insulin to perform better in 85 percent of people with a slight glucose intolerance, which makes them vulnerable to adult-onset diabetes.

In tests Dr. Anderson put seventeen volunteers on an ultra-low chromium dose of twenty micrograms a day—which is the skimpy amount eaten by 25 percent of Americans. Then, for five weeks, Dr. Anderson put half the group on 200 micrograms of chromium daily. The chromium dramatically boosted insulin activity in those with a mild glucose intolerance. About a quarter of all Americans have this intolerance that is a precondition of diabetes.

Besides broccoli, other good sources of chromium are whole grains, especially wheat bran, oysters, organ meats, potatoes, nuts, prunes, asparagus, rhubarb, mushrooms, beer, and wine.

Spaghetti with Broccoli, Pine Nuts, and Parmesan

Serves 6

Think broccoli! It is one of the vegetables that consistently show up in dietary surveys as eaten by people less likely to develop cancer, especially lung and colon cancer. And I can hardly think of a more delicious way to eat broccoli than combined with pasta as in this marvelous recipe from that marvelous cookbook Mediterranean Light, *by Martha Rose Shulman.*

1 large bunch broccoli (about 2 pounds), broken into florets
2 tablespoons olive oil
2 large garlic cloves, minced or crushed
1 tablespoon pine nuts
Salt and freshly ground pepper to taste
1 teaspoon salt (for pasta water)
3/4 pound spaghetti, preferably whole wheat
3 tablespoons chopped parsley
1/4 cup freshly grated Parmesan cheese

Steam the broccoli for 5 to 10 minutes, until crisp-tender. Refresh under cold water and set aside.

Bring a large pot of water to a boil.

Meanwhile, heat 1 tablespoon of the olive oil in a wide, heavy-bottomed skillet over low heat and gently sauté the garlic and pine nuts until the garlic is golden. Add the broccoli and stir together over low heat until the broccoli is heated through. Set aside. Season to taste with salt and freshly ground pepper.

When the water comes to a boil, add 1 teaspoon salt, the remaining oil, and the spaghetti. Cook the pasta until al dente, drain, and toss at once with the broccoli mixture, parsley, and Parmesan. Serve at once on warm plates.

Per serving:

Calories	275
Total fat	5 g
Saturated fat	0
Cholesterol	3 mg
Sodium	102 mg

FOOD PHARMACY FACT

High-Steppin' with Pasta

Athletes are in a better mood and perform better when they eat a high-carbohydrate diet, such as pasta, rice, potatoes, and beans. So says Robert Keith, a nutrition professor at Auburn University. In tests he found that trained female triathletes could bicycle twice as far when they were on a high-carb diet instead of a low-carb diet.

Surprisingly, the women were also much calmer under stress when eating the high-carbohydrate diet. When they switched to a high-protein diet—lots of beef, pork, fish and chicken, nuts and cheese—they lost their cool and were more likely to become angry under stress. The high-carb eaters, on the other hand, scored high in vigor and low in anxiety, depression, hostility, fatigue, and confusion—just what an athlete needs to win, says Professor Keith. Thus boosting carbohydrates and eating modest amounts of fat and protein is the diet most likely to maximize both physical and mental ability in athletes.

Pasta with Asparagus and Salmon

Serves 4

This quick pasta dish with Oriental flavorings is a blending of two healthful cultures, Asian and Italian, both known for their longevity and, in particular, low rates of heart disease. You also get raw garlic and ginger, both shown to have antibiotic and blood-clot-fighting activity. There's never enough to say for omega-3-rich salmon, and asparagus is one of those green vegetables linked to lower rates of cancer. Even soy sauce has been shown to have anticancer activity. You can substitute broccoli or green beans for the asparagus. And this is a good use for leftover salmon.

1 tablespoon olive oil
3 tablespoons reduced-sodium soy sauce
4 teaspoons rice vinegar or white wine vinegar
2 garlic cloves, minced
1/4 teaspoon minced or grated fresh gingerroot
10 ounces rotini
3 cups fresh asparagus, broken into 1 1/2- to 2-inch spears, not including the tough ends
1 cup flaked cooked salmon or smoked salmon or canned salmon, skin removed
2 to 3 teaspoons sesame seeds
Freshly ground pepper to taste
Hot red pepper flakes or green nori (seaweed) flakes to taste (optional)

In a small bowl, combine the olive oil, soy sauce, vinegar, garlic, and ginger.

Cook the rotini until al dente according to the package directions. Five minutes before it is time for the rotini to be done, add the asparagus to the pot with the pasta and continue simmering for 5 minutes. Immediately drain the pasta and asparagus and put into a large serving bowl.

Add the salmon, soy sauce mixture, and sesame seeds and toss until the pasta and asparagus are coated with the sauce. Serve immediately, while still hot.

Note: Other combinations you can use with the same sauce are broccoli, poached sea scallops, and walnuts; snow peas, red pepper slivers, and crabmeat; green beans, steamed shrimp, and almonds. Adjust cooking times for each vegetable.

Per serving:

Calories	401
Total fat	8.3 g
Saturated fat	1.3 g
Cholesterol	17.3 mg
Sodium	478 mg

Pasta with Tuna-Tomato Sauce

Serves 4

Canned tuna is one of the most popular and readily available ways to get the crucial omega-3-type fish oils. Water-packed tuna is better because you lose only 3 percent of the precious omega-3s by draining away the water. When you drain oil-packed tuna, about 25 percent of the omega-3 goes down the drain. For a quick main course, high in omega-3s, this is an answer in the Italian tradition.

2 cups low-sodium canned tomatoes, drained, juice reserved
1 cup chopped onions
1/2 cup diced green bell pepper
1/2 cup minced celery
3 garlic cloves, minced
1 1/2 teaspoons dried basil *or* 2 to 3 tablespoons chopped fresh
1 7-ounce can tuna packed in water (preferably albacore), drained
1/2 pound spaghetti or small shells, cooked until al dente

Place the tomatoes in a heavy skillet or Dutch oven. Add the onions, peppers, celery, garlic, and basil and simmer for 20 to 25 minutes.

Add the tuna and 1/2 cup of the reserved tomato juice. Stir to break up the tuna. Simmer only until the mixture is heated through. Serve over cooked pasta.

Per serving:

Calories	320
Total fat	2.5 g
Saturated fat	.5 g
Cholesterol	19 mg
Sodium	215 mg

COOK'S ADVICE

When using canned fish, it's better to choose those not packed in olive oil or soybean oil. When possible, choose sardines canned in their own oil (sild), mustard, or tomato sauce or tuna packed in water. When you drain oil from canned tuna, you lose from 15 to 25 percent of the omega-3s that have leached from the fish into the oil. Draining water-packed tuna washes away only 3 percent of the omega-3s. Of course, you can also save the omega-3s by using the oil in which the fish were packed.

Linguine with Clams and Black Pepper

Serves 6

An exquisite dish, wonderful to look at and great for your health, this combines the big three: garlic, onions (shallots), and peppers. Plus, clams not only keep you away from other bad fat but help protect your heart by lowering cholesterol and especially triglycerides, according to research. My thanks to the talented chef Kenneth Juran, Park Hyatt Hotel in Washington, D.C.

1 pound fresh black peppercorn linguine or plain linguine with 2 teaspoons cracked black pepper
1/4 cup olive oil
30 littleneck clams
3 shallots, finely diced
4 garlic cloves, minced
2 bok choy stalks, cut into 1/4-inch slices on the diagonal
2 cups dry white wine
3/4 cup fish stock or clam juice
2 tablespoons chopped fresh basil
Salt and freshly ground pepper to taste
1/2 red bell pepper, diced
1/2 yellow bell pepper, diced
2 plum tomatoes, peeled and diced

Cook the pasta in boiling salted water with 2 tablespoons of the olive oil. Drain the pasta.

Heat a large, wide saucepan. Add the clams, shallots, garlic, and bok choy. Stir briefly, then add the white wine and fish stock. Cover immediately and cook for 2 to 3 minutes over high heat, occasionally shaking the pot.

Remove the clams as they open, allowing the natural juices to remain in the pot.

Reduce the liquid by boiling for 1 minute, then add the basil, remaining 2 tablespoons olive oil, salt, and pepper.

Arrange the pasta in the center of individual bowls; place 5 clams in each bowl. Ladle the sauce over the pasta. Garnish with red and yellow peppers and diced tomato.

Per serving:

Calories	484
Total fat	9 g
Saturated fat	1 g
Cholesterol	25.5 mg
Sodium	138 mg

Rotelle with Judy's Fresh Tomato Sauce

Serves 6 to 8 (about 1 quart sauce)

There is no better way to get your lycopene than by eating tomatoes. Lycopene? Yes, that's a red vegetable pigment that researchers suspect helps ward off cancer. In a Johns Hopkins study those with the highest levels of lycopene in their blood had the lowest risk of pancreatic cancer. And there's no better way to combine fresh, juicy tomatoes with fresh sweet basil than in this superlative pasta sauce passed down to my sister-in-law Judy by her Italian grandmother.

2 to 3 tablespoons olive oil
2 medium garlic cloves, minced
1 medium onion, chopped
2 pounds vine-ripened tomatoes, peeled and coarsely chopped
½ cup chopped parsley
3 tablespoons chopped fresh basil
1 teaspoon red wine vinegar
Salt to taste
1 teaspoon sugar (optional)
⅛ teaspoon freshly ground pepper or to taste
1 pound rotelle, spirals, or small shells, cooked until al dente
¼ cup freshly grated Parmesan cheese (optional)

Place the oil in a large saucepan and sauté the garlic and onion until translucent and soft. Add the remaining ingredients except the pasta and cheese and simmer, covered, slowly for 15 minutes.

Remove from the heat and let sit in the tightly covered pan for 4 to 5 hours.

When ready to serve, return the sauce to the stove and bring to a simmer. Serve immediately over cooked rotelle, spirals, or small shells. Pass the optional Parmesan cheese.

Per serving:

Calories	366
Total fat	7.1 g
Saturated fat	1 g
Cholesterol	0
Sodium	19 mg

COOK'S ADVICE

Figuring Pasta Portions

You can usually figure that four ounces of dried pasta makes about two cups of cooked pasta, or two servings:

- Four ounces or one cup of macaroni, shells, rotini or spirals, twists, cavatelli, wagon wheels, penne, or ziti makes about two-and-a-half cups when cooked.
- Four ounces or a one-inch-diameter bunch of spaghetti, angel hair, capellini, vermicelli, or linguine makes about two cups when cooked.

Jean's Marco Polo Pasta

Serves 6

Parsley is one of the prime players in this salad, and although most people think of parsley as just a pretty garnish, it actually is a top source of a compound called glutathione, *which is a highly regarded anticancer agent. Long before I knew this, I often made this pasta, which was inspired by a famous Julia Child recipe. It's amazingly quick to assemble and always gets raves. It's also terrific with ripe, juicy tomatoes in place of the red peppers.*

- ½ pound spaghetti, fettuccine, or angel hair pasta
- 1 7-ounce jar roasted red peppers (or pimientos), drained and coarsely chopped
- 2 cups chopped parsley
- ½ cup chopped walnuts
- 2 to 3 tablespoons olive oil
- 1 garlic clove, crushed
- Salt and freshly ground pepper to taste

Cook the pasta in boiling water until al dente.

While the pasta is cooking, lightly mix together the red peppers, parsley, and walnuts.

When the pasta is done, toss with olive oil and crushed garlic. Add the pepper-parsley mixture, salt, and pepper and toss again. Serve immediately or at room temperature or chilled.

Per serving:

Calories	258
Total fat	11 g
Saturated fat	1 g
Cholesterol	0
Sodium	12 mg

FOOD PHARMACY FACT

Parsley, Important at Last!

In a recent analysis parsley, along with broccoli and spinach, topped the list of 100 common foods analyzed for their content of a disease-fighting compound called *glutathione.* According to Dr. Dean Jones, associate professor of biochemistry at Emory University School of Medicine, glutathione is a potent protector of bodily cells. At least thirty cancer-causing agents are deactivated when they encounter glutathione, he notes. Further, glutathione is an antioxidant (see page 7), which means it may help turn off numerous disease processes. For example, glutathione in Dr. Jones's lab tests has neutralized peroxidized fats that help clog arteries. "It's very exciting," he says.

Other foods rich in glutathione: generally fruits and vegetables, especially broccoli and oranges. Fish has moderate amounts.

To get the most glutathione, eat foods raw. From 30 to 60 percent is lost in cooking. Processed vegetables—as in canned green beans—have virtually no glutathione, says Dr. Jones.

Tabbouleh

Serves 4 to 6

Another excellent way to get your quota of parsley is to eat tabbouleh, a cracked wheat and parsley salad that is a staple in Mideastern countries, where they put in even more parsley than this recipe calls for.

2/3 cup bulgur (makes about 2 cups)
1 cup water
2 1/4 cups finely chopped parsley
8 scallions, thinly sliced
1 1/2 teaspoons chopped fresh mint (more if desired)
1 1/2 teaspoons minced garlic
3 tablespoons lemon juice or to taste
1 small tomato, chopped
Salt and freshly ground pepper to taste
3 tablespoons chopped pecans (optional)
2 teaspoons olive oil

Cover the bulgur wheat with the water. Let soak for 30 minutes to an hour, until tender. If necessary, add more water.

Put the bulgur in a strainer and squeeze out excess moisture.

Put the bulgur in a bowl and add the parsley, scallions, mint, garlic, lemon juice, tomato, salt and pepper, and the optional pecans. Toss, add the olive oil, and toss again.

Per serving:

Calories	128
Total fat	2.8 g
Saturated fat	.4 g
Cholesterol	0
Sodium	23 mg

Bulgur with Chick-Peas

Serves 6

This is always a hit at cookouts and buffets. While the wheat fiber works wonders on your intestinal tract, the chick-peas, pecans, garlic, and scallions provide your cells with small hits of anticancer compounds of various sorts. It tastes great, too.

1 cup bulgur, soaked in cold water and drained (see preceding recipe)
2 bunches scallions, including some green, sliced
1 19-ounce can chick-peas (about 2½ cups), drained
½ cup chopped pecans
2 to 3 tablespoons olive oil
2 tablespoons balsamic vinegar
1 teaspoon lemon juice
1 large garlic clove, crushed
Salt and freshly ground pepper to taste

Place the drained bulgur in a large bowl. Add the scallions, chick-peas, and nuts.

In a small bowl, mix the olive oil, vinegar, lemon juice, garlic, salt, and pepper. Add to bulgur mixture and toss.

Serve at room temperature or chilled.

Per serving:

Calories	298
Total fat	12 g
Saturated fat	1.2 g
Cholesterol	0
Sodium	274 mg

DOCTOR'S ADVICE

Eat foods that are vitamin E powerhouses, advises Dr. James Duke, authority on medicinal plants at the U.S. Department of Agriculture. Vitamin E is a powerful, protective antioxidant. Unfortunately, information about the vitamin E content of food is scanty, because analysis is tricky. But calculations by Dr. Duke from existing foreign data found that vitamin E is present in dark green vegetables, such as green bell peppers, parsley, spinach, broccoli, and kale. It's even higher in almonds, peanuts, tomatoes, black currants, blueberries, and vegetable oils such as sunflower seed oil and notably wheat germ oil, which has the highest concentration of all foods.

Nutty Brown Rice

Serves 6

Rice has the distinction of being a prominent staple in the diet of the nation with the longest life span in the world—Japan. Although no one is sure what rice's secret longevity agent might be, rice, like other seed foods, does have protease inhibitors, which help combat cancer. Brown rice also has lots of fiber, which can lower blood cholesterol. The nuts in this recipe do add fat, but it's not saturated cholesterol-raising and artery-destroying fat. And nuts have many therapeutic properties on their own. Besides, they provide a wonderful I-can't-stop-eating-this crunch that makes me devour this dish.

1 cup brown rice
2⅔ cups water
2 teaspoons vegetable oil or butter
2 teaspoons seeded and minced jalapeño pepper *or* ⅛ teaspoon hot red pepper flakes
2 scallions, thinly sliced
¼ cup chopped walnuts
¼ cup chopped pecans
¼ cup chopped peanuts
3 tablespoons sesame seeds
Salt and freshly ground pepper to taste

Place the rice and water in a saucepan and cook according to the package directions.

Put the oil or butter in a small skillet and sauté the pepper and scallions just until soft.

When the rice is cooked, combine all the ingredients.

Per serving:

Calories	225
Total fat	11 g
Saturated fat	1.2 g
Cholesterol	0
Sodium	23 mg

Curried Apricot Rice

Serves 6

Apricots and onions both add cancer-inhibiting compounds to rice, which has its own anticancer agents called protease inhibitors. *Here you get another infusion of cancer-fighting compounds in the curry spices. This is an exceptionally quick and easy dish to make—yet adds some exotic and healthful flavors to plain rice.*

2 teaspoons butter or margarine
1/2 cup chopped onion
2 1/2 cups low-sodium chicken broth
1/4 cup chopped dried apricots
1 teaspoon curry powder
1 cup brown rice
2 tablespoons chopped parsley

Melt the butter in a medium saucepan. Add the onion and sauté until soft and translucent. Add the broth, apricots, and curry powder and bring to a boil.

Add the rice. Cover, reduce the heat, and simmer for 30 minutes or until the liquid is absorbed. Stir in the chopped parsley.

Per serving:

Calories	157
Total fat	2.9 g
Saturated fat	1.1 g
Cholesterol	3.5 mg
Sodium	39 mg

Greek Rice with Artichokes

Serves 4

Brown rice is high in bran, now known to help lower blood cholesterol. Artichokes have in some studies been found to do the same. In addition, onions are good for helping discourage blood clots. Altogether this is a satisfying, earthy dish, just what you'd expect from a country where grains are highly valued and heart disease is uncommon. It's adapted from a recipe given to me by Mary Koromvokis.

1 cup brown rice
2 cups low-sodium chicken broth
1 tablespoon olive oil
1 medium onion, chopped
2 cups fresh tomatoes, chopped, or canned tomatoes, chopped with juice
1 9-ounce package frozen artichoke hearts
1½ teaspoons dried rosemary, crushed
Salt and freshly ground pepper to taste

In a 2-quart saucepan, cook the rice according to package directions, using chicken broth instead of water.

While the rice is cooking, put the olive oil in a large skillet and sauté the onion until soft and translucent. Add the tomatoes and bring to a boil. Add the artichokes, rosemary, salt, and pepper, reduce the heat, and simmer for about 10 minutes or until the artichokes are tender.

Add the tomato-artichoke mixture to the cooked rice, stir, and serve hot.

Per serving:

Calories	266
Total fat	6 g
Saturated fat	1 g
Cholesterol	0
Sodium	68 mg

Bulgur Pilaf with Fruit and Nuts

Serves 8 to 10

You can feel virtuous eating this very dense, fruity bulgur pilaf because it is packed with apricots, full of beta-carotene, as well as other dried fruits that are rich in a variety of disease-fighting compounds. Also, recent studies by U.S. Department of Agriculture scientists find that people who eat fruits and nuts are more apt to get their quotient of boron, a mineral that helps keep the brain alert.

For a lighter, less dense version, add another cup or two of cooked bulgur wheat.

2 large onions, chopped
1 teaspoon ground cumin
1¼ teaspoons ground coriander
2 teaspoons butter or margarine
½ cup low-sodium chicken broth (more if needed)
6 ounces coarsely chopped mixed dried fruits
½ cup chopped dried apricots
1½ cups slivered almonds
½ cup currants
4 cups cooked bulgur
2 teaspoons ground cinnamon
½ teaspoon ground cloves
Salt and freshly ground pepper to taste

Sauté the onion, cumin, and coriander in butter and chicken broth until the onion is translucent and soft.

Add the fruits, almonds, and currants and cook until heated through. Add more chicken broth if needed.

Preheat the oven to 350 degrees. Place the cooked bulgur wheat in a large bowl. Add the cinnamon, cloves, salt, and pepper and mix well.

Add the fruit-nut mixture to the bulgur mixture and toss until mixed thoroughly.

Put in a casserole and bake for about 30 minutes, until heated through, or use as stuffing for a turkey.

Per serving:	
Calories	348
Total fat	15 g
Saturated fat	1.9 g
Cholesterol	2.6 mg
Sodium	28 mg

FOOD PHARMACY FACT

Fruit and Nut Alert!

Not eating enough fruit and nuts high in the trace mineral boron can make your brain sluggish, according to research at the U.S. Department of Agriculture. In tests James G. Penland, Ph.D., put fifteen people over age forty-five alternately on a low-boron and a high-boron diet for about four months. In both cases he monitored the electrical activity of their brains. When they ate scant boron, their brain waves produced more beta and delta waves, signs of drowsiness and reduced mental activity. On high-boron diets their brain waves picked up.

"It's an exciting finding," he says, "because it confirms that a good diet enhances brain functioning." Foods high in boron are nuts, legumes, leafy vegetables like broccoli, and fruits, especially apples, pears, peaches, and grapes.

Shiitake Mushroom Sage Stuffing

Serves 8

A scientist at the University of Michigan first discovered in 1960 that the Oriental shiitake mushroom possessed a strong antiviral substance that stimulated immunity. But it is only recently that the wonderful meaty mushroom has become widely available in American markets. If you are lucky enough to get the fresh type, grab them, but the dried variety when reconstituted in water is fine, too. Of three stuffings I made one holiday, this was the favorite among most of the family. You can use any stale bread, but for a very interesting flavor I once used half sourdough and half Italian bread. Oh yes, sage in the dressing helps relieve indigestion in case you overindulge.

6 cups dry bread cubes
1 large onion, chopped
1 cup thinly sliced celery with leaves (2 large stalks)
½ cup chopped fresh or dried and rehydrated shiitake mushrooms
2 tablespoons butter or margarine
1 cup low-sodium chicken broth
½ cup chopped parsley
3 tablespoons chopped fresh sage *or* 1 tablespoon dried
½ teaspoon dried thyme *or* 2 teaspoons fresh
Salt and freshly ground pepper to taste

Put the bread cubes in a large bowl. (If making your own, cut fresh bread into cubes, place on a large sheet, and toast in a 250-degree oven until dried out.)

Sauté the onion, celery, and mushrooms in the butter and ¼ cup of the chicken broth until the vegetables are soft.

Preheat the oven to 350 degrees. Add seasonings and onion mixture to the bread cubes. Add the remaining chicken broth and combine until the bread cubes are moistened. Add salt and freshly ground black pepper to taste.

Put the mixture in a casserole and bake for 30 minutes or until the top is brown and slightly crunchy.

Per serving:

Calories	102
Total fat	3.9 g
Saturated fat	2 g
Cholesterol	8.4 mg
Sodium	247 mg

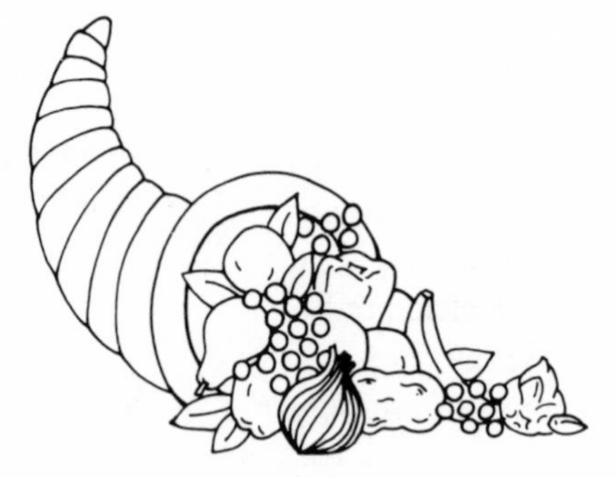

Seafood, Poultry, and Meat Main Dishes

Grilled Salmon with Fruit Salsa

Serves 6

Nothing is quite as wonderful for health or taste as fresh salmon on the grill. Of course it's delectable with just a few squirts of lemon juice. But for a spectacular presentation and taste treat you can accompany it with a mound of these fresh, diced tangy fruits. Need you be reminded that salmon is one of the highest of all fish in lifesaving omega-3-type oil?

1 medium-ripe but firm mango, peeled and cut into ½-inch cubes
1 cup diced fresh pineapple
1 cup diced honeydew melon
½ red bell pepper, diced
½ cup rice vinegar
¼ cup minced cilantro
½ teaspoon hot red pepper flakes
2 kiwifruit
6 salmon steaks or fillets (about 6 ounces each)

In a bowl, mix the mango, pineapple, melon, bell pepper, vinegar, cilantro, and hot pepper. (Can be made up to 2 days ahead to this point and refrigerated.)

Just before serving, peel the kiwifruit, cut into ¼-inch cubes, and gently stir into the fruit mixture.

Grill or broil the salmon until firm and opaque, about 10 minutes. To serve, put the salmon on each plate and top with 2 tablespoons of the fruit salsa. Pass the remaining salsa in a bowl.

Note: For variation, use other fish, including swordfish, shark, halibut, turbot, and snapper.

Per serving:

Calories	307
Total fat	11 g
Saturated fat	1.7 g
Cholesterol	94 mg
Sodium	84 mg

FOOD PHARMACY FACT

Fish Prolongs Life in Heart Attack Patients

A major British study found that eating oily fish like salmon, tuna, mackerel, and sardines cut the death rate by one third in middle-aged men who had already suffered a heart attack.

In the study of 2,033 men under age seventy, researchers told one group of men to eat fish high in omega-3-type oil at least twice a week; another group was told to cut down on high-fat foods; another to eat more fiber; and a fourth was given no dietary advice. After two years the odds of dying of heart disease dropped by 29 percent among the fish eaters compared with the other men in the study.

Peppered Tuna Steaks

Serves 4

This is the fisherman's steak au poivre—a quick, healthful way to get lots of omega-3s with little effort. How peppery the steaks are depends on the amount of pepper, but the steak surface should be well covered.

Cracked black pepper to taste
1½ pounds tuna steaks
1 teaspoon olive oil or olive oil spray to coat skillet
Lemon wedges for serving

Sprinkle the black pepper over each piece of tuna and press down until the pepper is slightly embedded. Repeat with the other side of the tuna.

Coat a nonstick heavy skillet with the olive oil and heat over medium-high heat.

Add the tuna steaks and sear until one side is nicely darkened and crusty. Turn the steaks and cook on the other side until the tuna is firm and opaque but still moist inside. Do not overcook or tuna will become dry and tough.

Serve with lemon wedges.

Per serving:

Calories	255
Total fat	9.5 g
Saturated fat	1.3 g
Cholesterol	65 mg
Sodium	66 mg

A THERAPEUTIC GUIDE TO SEAFOOD
OMEGA-3 PER 3½ OUNCES RAW SEAFOOD

	(Milligrams)
Roe, finfish, mixed species	2,346
Mackerel, Atlantic	2,299
Herring, Pacific	1,658
Herring, Atlantic	1,571
Mackerel, Pacific and jack	1,441
Sablefish	1,395
Salmon, chinook (king)	1,355
Mackerel, Spanish	1,341
Whitefish, mixed species	1,258
Tuna, bluefin	1,173
Salmon, sockeye (red)	1,172
Salmon, pink	1,005
Turbot, Greenland	919
Shark, mixed species	843
Salmon, coho (silver)	814
Bluefish	771
Bass, striped	754
Smelt, rainbow	693
Oysters, Pacific	688
Swordfish	639
Salmon, chum	627
Wolffish	623
Bass, freshwater, mixed species	595
Sea bass, mixed species	595
Trout, rainbow	568
Pompano, Florida	568
Squid, mixed species	488
Shrimp, mixed species	480
Mussels, blue	441
Oysters, eastern	439
Tilefish	430
Pollock, Atlantic	421
Catfish, channel	373
Halibut, Atlantic and Pacific	363
Carp	352
Rockfish, Pacific, mixed species	345

	(*Milligrams*)
Lobster, spiny, mixed species	373
Pollock, Alaska (walleye)	372
Crab, snow (queen)	372
Mullet	325
Crab, blue	320
Snapper, mixed species	311
Crab, Dungeness	307
Ocean perch, Atlantic	291
Tuna, skipjack	256
Grouper	247
Whiting, mixed species	224
Tuna, yellowfin	218
Cod, Pacific	215
Scallops, mixed species	198
Haddock	185
Cod, Atlantic	184
Crawfish	173
Eel, mixed species	147
Octopus	157
Clams	142
Omega-3 per 3½ Ounces Canned Fish	
Anchovies, canned in olive oil (drained)	2,055
Herring, Atlantic, pickled	1,389
Salmon, pink (including liquid and bones)	1,651
Sardines, Pacific, in tomato sauce (drained, without bones)	1,604
Salmon, sockeye (drained with bones)	1,156
Sardines, Atlantic in soybean oil (drained with bones)	982
Tuna (albacore), white in water (drained)	706
Tuna, light, in soybean oil (drained)	128
Tuna, light, in water (drained)	111

Source: U.S. Department of Agriculture

Three-Fish Teriyaki

Serves 4

Instead of grilling or broiling just one type of fish, try three different types, then cut them into chunks so eaters can try all three. It's fun and festive, and all three of these ocean fish are high in the magical omega-3 fatty acids that appear to suppress various disease processes from inflammation to blood clots to cancer. If you're on a very strict low-sodium diet, skip the soy sauce marinade and simply brush the steaks with a little olive oil before grilling.

- 1/4 cup reduced-sodium soy sauce
- 1 tablespoon olive or vegetable oil
- 2 tablespoons rice vinegar or lemon juice
- 1 tablespoon minced garlic
- 1 tablespoon minced fresh gingerroot
- 1 1/2 cups pineapple or orange juice
- About 1/2 pound each of 1-inch-thick salmon steak, tuna steak, and swordfish or shark steak

In a small bowl, combine the soy sauce, oil, vinegar, garlic, ginger, and pineapple juice.

Place the fish in shallow baking dish and pour on the marinade. Cover and marinate in the refrigerator for 2 hours, turning the fish twice.

Remove the fish from the marinade, reserving the marinade. Grill the fish for about 5 minutes on each side, or broil it for a total of 10 minutes.

In a small pan, bring the marinade to a boil; reduce the heat and simmer for 5 minutes. Serve with the fish.

Per serving:

Calories	278
Total fat	10.3 g
Saturated fat	2 g
Cholesterol	75 mg
Sodium	400 mg

Swordfish with Grapefruit and Brazil Nuts

Serves 4

Brimming with selenium and vitamins E and C, this dish fits the bill for lowering blood pressure, according to new research. Those three antioxidants have been linked to lower blood pressure. Swordfish and Brazil nuts are two of the most concentrated sources of selenium. If you can't get Brazil nuts, substitute walnuts, which are also high in omega-3 fatty acids, linked to lowering blood pressure. The spinach and grapefruit add a hefty shot of vitamin C and carotenoids to help protect lungs and arteries.

1¾ pounds swordfish steaks
Olive oil or olive oil spray
6 ounces fresh spinach, washed, stems removed, and leaves torn into bite-size pieces
1 grapefruit, peeled and divided into segments, cut in half
½ cup grapefruit juice
2 garlic cloves, minced or crushed
2 teaspoons balsamic vinegar
½ teaspoon reduced-sodium soy sauce
⅛ teaspoon grated fresh gingerroot (optional)
Freshly ground pepper to taste
½ cup coarsely chopped Brazil nuts

Preheat the broiler or a grill.

Spray or brush the fish steaks with a little olive oil. Broil or grill until firm and opaque (about 10 minutes per 1-inch of thickness).

In the meantime, place the spinach in a bowl and add the grapefruit segments.

In a separate bowl, mix the grapefruit juice, garlic, vinegar, soy sauce, and gingerroot. Add to the spinach and grapefruit and toss lightly.

Place a bed of spinach on each dinner plate and top with a piece of cooked swordfish. Be sure to arrange grapefruit sections around the fish. Grind on fresh pepper and sprinkle with Brazil nuts.

Per serving:

Calories	371
Total fat	18.9 g
Saturated fat	4.8 g
Cholesterol	69 mg
Sodium	236 mg

FOOD PHARMACY FACT

Fish, Nuts, and Greens May Keep High Blood Pressure Away

A large-scale Finnish study of 722 men aged fifty-four at the University of Kuopio found that those with low amounts of vitamin C and selenium in their blood and a low intake of linolenic acid were most apt to have high blood pressure. Seafood, especially swordfish, is rich in selenium and linolenic acid, as are some nuts, notably Brazil nuts.

FOOD PHARMACY FACT

Fish for Bad Genes

Here's another intriguing way that eating fish may help ward off heart disease. New research shows that many heart attack victims, especially younger men, have high blood levels of a peculiar type of cholesterol called *Lp(a)*. It's inherited, not very responsive to drugs or low-fat diets, and it's dangerous. Too much Lp(a) doubles the risk of heart attack, even in those with low levels of total cholesterol, and is estimated to trigger a quarter of all heart attacks in men under age sixty.

However, Dr. Jorn Dyerberg, a leading Danish scientist, found that fish oil lowered Lp(a) by a startling 15 percent in a group of otherwise healthy men with high levels of this dangerous type of cholesterol. Every day for nine months the men took four grams of fish oil—equal to eating seven ounces of mackerel a day.

Note: The fish oil does not seem to lower Lp(a) in those with normal levels.

Grilled Mackerel with Herbs and Spices

Mackerel is the king of fishes when it comes to omega-3—that wonderful type of oil that promises to save you from virtually everything. Mackerel, especially Atlantic mackerel, contains more omega-3 than any other species. Unfortunately this fish is not nearly as popular with Americans as it should be because it has a slightly stronger flavor than many fish. I stress "slightly," for once you taste mackerel you may be surprised, as I constantly am, by how pleasant it is. It is best cooked with spices and herbs. Here are three quick ways with mackerel—simply broiled or grilled with sage, garlic, or cumin.

There is virtually no fat added to the mackerel in these recipes. The fat comes entirely from the fish and is mostly from healthful omega-3. You can substitute bluefish, which is also high in omega-3.

MACKEREL WITH SAGE

Serves 4

4 mackerel fillets (about 2 pounds)
1/4 cup lemon juice
4 teaspoons dried sage
Salt and freshly ground pepper to taste

Brush both sides of the fish with lemon juice and sage. Sprinkle on salt and black pepper. Broil or grill fillets for a total of 7 to 10 minutes or until opaque and firm.

Per serving:

Calories	470
Total fat	32 g
Saturated fat	7 g
Cholesterol	160 mg
Sodium	207 mg

MACKEREL WITH GARLIC AND HERBS

Serves 4

4 garlic cloves, crushed
3 tablespoons chopped fresh herbs *or* 1 tablespoon dried (thyme, rosemary, parsley, basil, etc.), crushed
Salt and freshly ground pepper to taste
4 mackerel fillets (about 2 pounds)

Rub the garlic, herbs, salt, and pepper onto both sides of the fish. Broil or grill for a total of 7 to 10 minutes or until the fish is opaque and firm.

Per serving:

Calories	471
Total fat	31.5 g
Saturated fat	7 g
Cholesterol	159 mg
Sodium	206 mg

MACKEREL WITH CUMIN

Serves 4

3 tablespoons lemon juice
3 garlic cloves, crushed
1 teaspoon ground cumin
1/8 teaspoon cayenne pepper
1/3 cup plain nonfat yogurt
Salt and freshly ground pepper to taste
4 mackerel fillets (about 2 pounds)

In a small dish, combine the lemon juice, garlic, cumin, cayenne pepper, yogurt, salt, and pepper.

Place the fish in a dish. Cover with the yogurt mixture and marinate for 30 minutes.

Broil or grill the fish for a total of 7 to 10 minutes or until opaque and firm.

Per serving:

Calories	483
Total fat	31.7 g
Saturated fat	7 g
Cholesterol	159 mg
Sodium	222 mg

AN OUNCE (OR TWO) OF FISH A DAY KEEPS HEART DISEASE AWAY

Dutch investigators found that eating an ounce of fish each day on the average cut the risk of deadly heart attack by 50 percent.

British researchers found that telling men who had already had a heart attack to eat fatty fish twice a week cut their risk of death from a subsequent heart attack by 29 percent.

U.S. researcher Therese Dolecek found that American men who eat an average of 600 milligrams of omega-3 fish oil a day reduce their odds of heart attack by 36 percent. That 600 milligrams translates into one or two servings a week of a fatty fish or a small daily "dose" of the following.

1 ounce fresh Atlantic mackerel
1 ounce canned anchovies (1/2 small can)
1 3/4 ounces canned pickled herring
1 1/2 ounces canned pink salmon
1 1/2 ounces canned Pacific sardines
1 1/2 ounces fresh herring
1 3/4 ounces sablefish
1 1/2 ounces fresh Atlantic salmon
2 ounces fresh tuna
2 1/2 ounces Greenland turbot
3 ounces bluefish
3 ounces bass
3 ounces shark
3 1/2 ounces swordfish
3 1/2 ounces canned white albacore tuna
4 ounces rainbow trout

Baked Bluefish with Herbs

Serves 4 to 6

A marvelous choice for getting lots of health-promoting omega-3 fatty acids is this inexpensive, quick-to-fix, flavorful bluefish. It's great for a fast family dinner, but its slightly crunchy crust with herbs also gives it a dinner party touch, and my guests have loved it. Each serving has a whopping 1,500 milligrams of omega-3s that can infuse your cells with protection. That's more than twice the daily amount found to put a 36 percent dent in fatal heart attacks among American men.

2 pounds bluefish fillets
3 tablespoons reduced-calorie mayonnaise
3 tablespoons plain nonfat yogurt
1 cup dry bread crumbs made from cracked wheat or whole grain bread
1/2 teaspoon dried thyme, crumbled, or to taste
1/2 teaspoon dried rosemary, crumbled, or to taste
Salt and freshly ground pepper to taste
8 parsley sprigs

Preheat the oven to 350 degrees. Place the fish, skin side down, in a large, shallow baking pan.

In a small bowl, combine the mayonnaise and yogurt and spread over the top of the fish. Sprinkle on bread crumbs, then thyme, rosemary, salt, and pepper. Top with parsley sprigs.

Bake for about 10 to 15 minutes or until fish is firm and opaque.

Per serving:

Calories	352
Total fat	13 g
Saturated fat	3 g
Cholesterol	138 mg
Sodium	272 mg

Shark Steaks with Orange

Serves 6

Surprisingly, shark is a very good fish choice because it is extremely well endowed with omega-3-type oil. You get a whopping 4,600 milligrams of omega-3s from each serving of this recipe. And it's quick and easy to make in a microwave.

2 pounds shark steaks
3 tablespoons orange juice
2 tablespoons reduced-sodium soy sauce
1 tablespoon catsup
2 teaspoons olive oil
1 tablespoon chopped parsley
2 teaspoons lemon juice
1/2 teaspoon dried oregano
1 garlic clove, minced
1 large orange, peeled, seeded, and sectioned
1/4 cup sliced water chestnuts

Place the shark steaks in a single layer in a shallow 2-quart baking dish. Combine the remaining ingredients except the orange and water chestnuts. Pour the sauce over the steaks and marinate in the refrigerator for 30 minutes, turning once.

Cover the dish with plastic wrap, turning back one corner to vent. Microwave on HIGH for 6 to 8 minutes, rotating the dish every 3 minutes.

Top the steaks with orange sections and water chestnuts. Return to the microwave and cook on HIGH for 1 to 2 minutes. Let stand, covered, for 2 minutes.

Per serving:

Calories	236
Total fat	8.4 g
Saturated fat	1.6 g
Cholesterol	22 mg
Sodium	350 mg

COOK'S ADVICE

The only way to ruin fresh fish is to overcook it, drying it out. You're repeatedly told to cook fish until it flakes easily. But as Julia Child says, "If it flakes easily, it's overdone." It's done when it's opaque, she says. The rule of thumb: Cook fish about ten minutes for every inch of thickness at the thickest point. To check for doneness, break into the flesh at the thickest point with a fork. It should appear slightly opaque, not flaky like canned fish. Microwaved fish, of course, takes less time—and depends on the quantity in the oven. A six-ounce fish steak can take a couple of minutes or less to microwave, says Jane Morimoto, director of the test kitchen for the Alaska Seafood Marketing Institute.

Cajun Cod

Serves 4

"A spicy twist for a mild-mannered fish" is how well-known nutritionist Ann Louise Gittleman describes this fare in her book Beyond Pritikin. *Cod is a "lean" fish, but about half of its fat is made up of disease-fighting omega-3 fatty acids—more than any other popular fish, which makes it a favorite for the health-conscious. It is also very low in omega-6 fatty acids (3 percent of total fat), which is desirable because omega-6 can help destroy the benefits of eating the omega-3s.*

1 medium onion, chopped
1 green bell pepper, chopped
1 garlic clove, minced
1 teaspoon butter
2 tomatoes, seeded and chopped
1/2 cup dry red wine
1/4 teaspoon dried thyme
1/2 teaspoon cayenne pepper
4 5-ounce cod fillets
2 tablespoons lemon juice

Sauté the onion, green pepper, and garlic in butter until tender. Add the tomatoes, wine, thyme, and cayenne. Bring to a boil.

Add the cod, reduce the heat, cover, and simmer for about 10 minutes or until the fish flakes.

Add the lemon juice before serving.

Per serving:

Calories	154
Total fat	2.2 g
Saturated fat	.8 g
Cholesterol	64 mg
Sodium	94 mg

Halibut with Tarragon and Sesame Seeds

Serves 4

Such a mild, lean, and popular fish, halibut has an excellent balance of the wonderful omega-3-type fat and the less desirable omega-6-type fat. Also, there's evidence that all types of fish, even lean fish, help prevent cardiovascular disease. Another plus: low-fat, low-calorie fish gives you just as much protein as higher-fat meat.

1½ pounds halibut, cod, haddock, or other whitefish
1 teaspoon olive oil or cooking spray
1 tablespoon lemon juice
1 teaspoon dried tarragon leaves
Salt and freshly ground pepper to taste
1 tablespoon sesame seeds
1 tablespoon chopped parsley

Preheat the broiler. Brush or spray the fish with oil. Mix the lemon juice, tarragon, salt, and pepper. Pour it over the fish. Sprinkle sesame seeds evenly over the fish.

Broil the fish for 10 minutes, until the fish is opaque, firm, and browned.

Per serving:

Calories	165
Total fat	3.4 g
Saturated fat	.5 g
Cholesterol	73 mg
Sodium	94 mg

Microwave Dilled Flounder

Serves 2

Nothing can be easier, quicker, or more satisfying than a simple microwaved fish sprinkled with the herb most associated with fish—dill. With this recipe there's no excuse for not having fish more often. You can substitute numerous other fish, such as any type of whitefish or salmon.

- 3/4 pound flounder fillet
- 3 tablespoons chopped fresh dill *or* 1 tablespoon dried
- 2 tablespoons lemon juice
- Salt and freshly ground pepper to taste
- 1 lemon, cut into wedges

Arrange the fillets in a microwave dish in a single layer if possible. Sprinkle with dill, lemon juice, salt, and pepper.

Cover tightly with plastic wrap and microwave on HIGH for about 4 to 5 minutes, depending on the size and thickness of the fillets. Serve at once, garnished with lemon wedges.

Per serving:

Calories	162
Total fat	2 g
Saturated fat	.5 g
Cholesterol	81 mg
Sodium	144 mg

Flounder Stuffed with Vegetables

Serves 4

Fish fillets can be a hearty course when wrapped around rice and vegetables. Rice is one of those "seed" foods that contain lots of protease inhibitors, thought to help keep cancer at bay. You can make the rice and vegetable mixture the night before. Stuff flounder just before you put the fillets in to bake.

3/4 cup cooked rice
1/3 cup diced cooked carrots
1/3 cup diced red and/or green bell peppers
1/3 cup slivered almonds
1 tablespoon chopped parsley
Salt and freshly ground pepper to taste
1 teaspoon butter or margarine, melted
Vegetable oil cooking spray
1 1/2 pounds flounder fillets

Preheat the oven to 350 degrees. Combine the rice, carrots, bell peppers, almonds, parsley, salt, pepper, and butter and mix well.

Spoon 3 tablespoons of the rice mixture onto each fillet. Roll and secure with toothpicks or skewers.

Coat a 12- by 8- by 2-inch baking pan with cooking spray. Place the fillets in the pan and bake, uncovered, for 20 to 25 minutes.

Per serving:

Calories	289
Total fat	9.2 g
Saturated fat	1.6 g
Cholesterol	84 mg
Sodium	159 mg

FISH, FAT, AND CHOLESTEROL

Is it really good to eat fatty fish? After all, fat makes you fat, and besides, we've been told to eat less fat, not more. And aren't some seafoods, especially shrimp, high in cholesterol, making them undesirable?

It's safe to say that very few Americans ever got fat eating fish. Compared with other sources of fat and protein—like red meat, poultry, and cheese—even the highest-fat seafood is still relatively low in fat and calories. The fat in fish is mostly unsaturated, and it's thought that saturated fat—as in meat and dairy products—is more likely than other fat to make you fat.

Further, the enormous benefit to the body in all kinds of ways from the omega-3 oils in fish outweighs any dangers from fat per se.

Seafood does have cholesterol, but eating fish does not raise blood cholesterol. Shellfish does not have nearly as much cholesterol as previously thought, according to new techniques of analysis. Moreover, shellfish contains sterols that actually discourage absorption of cholesterol. All told, the cholesterol in seafood is not worrisome, except in a few cases: Fish eggs are extremely high in cholesterol. Three-and-a-half ounces of roe from various species has 374 milligrams; the same amount of caviar has 588 milligrams. Three-and-a-half ounces of squid has 233 milligrams and shrimp 152. Fish generally has between 40 and 60 milligrams of cholesterol in three-and-a-half ounces.

The case for the benefits of fish, especially fatty fish, is overwhelming compared with any possible detrimental effects from fat and cholesterol.

Rainbow Trout with Orange-Rice Stuffing

Serves 6

Rainbow trout are readily available and surprisingly high in omega-3 for freshwater fish. The rice stuffing turns this dish into a one-course meal, and the fish are definitely dressed up and pretty enough for company. I've served this platter of trout at dinner parties to much acclaim.

2 cups dry white wine
1¾ cups orange juice
2 tablespoons lemon juice
6 whole rainbow trout, cleaned
1½ cups rice
2 cups water
3 cups chopped watercress
3 scallions, including the green parts, finely sliced
1 tablespoon grated orange zest
⅓ cup sliced almonds, toasted
12 large parsley sprigs, plus additional for garnish
1 orange, sliced
Salt and freshly ground pepper to taste

To make a marinade, combine 1 cup of the wine, ¾ cup of the orange juice, and the lemon juice. Place the fish in a large, shallow baking dish and add the marinade. Marinate the fish in the refrigerator for 1 hour, turning twice to be sure all trout are exposed to the marinade.

In the meantime, cook the rice in the water and remaining orange juice according to the package directions. When the rice is about 10 minutes from being done, mix in the watercress, scallions, and orange zest. Continue cooking the rice until the liquid is absorbed. Stir in the toasted almonds.

Drain the fish and generously stuff the cavity of each trout with the rice mixture. You will have some rice left over.

Preheat the oven to 350 degrees. Place the stuffed trout in a shallow baking dish. Cover each fish with 2 parsley sprigs and an orange slice. Sprinkle with salt and pepper. Add the remaining cup of white wine and bake until the fish are opaque and firm, about 15 to 20 minutes.

Lift the fish out of the liquid and put them on a large serving plate surrounded by fresh parsley sprigs. Serve the remaining rice in a separate bowl. Reheat the rice in a microwave oven if necessary.

Per serving:

Calories	430
Total fat	8.4 g
Saturated fat	1.3 g
Cholesterol	90 mg
Sodium	55 mg

FOOD PHARMACY FACT

Fish Eaters Have Less Breast Cancer

New evidence supports the theory that something in seafood—probably the oil—helps manipulate female hormones that in turn discourage breast cancer. Fish eaters around the world seem to have less breast cancer, according to investigators at the Ludwig Institute for Cancer Research in Toronto, who compared food consumption statistics with cancer rates in thirty-two countries. They noted that those countries where people ate the most calories from fish had the fewest new cases of and deaths from breast cancer. For example, in Japan, where fish consumption is high, breast cancer is low. Numerous animal studies find that omega-3 fatty acids in the fat of fish may block the development of various cancers, in particular breast cancer.

Sweet and Sour Fish Curry

Serves 3

An easy yogurt-based curry, this recipe gives you an opportunity to use a variety of whitefish in a piquant sauce full of health-preserving onions and spices. Serve it with brown rice, raisins that have been plumped in hot water, and mango chutney.

- 2 medium onions, finely chopped
- 1 tablespoon olive oil
- 1 teaspoon finely chopped fresh gingerroot
- 1½ tablespoons good-quality curry powder
- 3 tablespoons lemon juice
- 2 to 3 teaspoons brown sugar or to taste
- 1 cup plain nonfat yogurt
- Salt to taste
- 1 pound fish fillets (rockfish, bass, cod, haddock, halibut), skin and bones removed, cut into serving pieces
- 3 tablespoons chopped parsley

In a large skillet, cook the onion in the oil until golden. Add the ginger and curry powder and fry for 2 or 3 minutes, stirring several times.

Stir in the lemon juice, brown sugar, yogurt, and salt.

Pat the fish pieces dry and place them in the sauce. Simmer until done, stirring gently from time to time. Sprinkle the parsley over the fish and sauce and serve.

Per serving:

Calories	272
Total fat	7.6 g
Saturated fat	1.2 g
Cholesterol	54 mg
Sodium	153 mg

Judy's Old-Fashioned Salmon Loaf

Serves 4

Since my sister Judy became concerned about her blood cholesterol she has started serving and eating more fish. Here is one of her ways to use inexpensive canned salmon, which has so much heart-protective omega-3-type fat. The paprika deepens the pinkness of the pale fish. It's also a good way to use potassium-rich leftover mashed potatoes.

1 15½-ounce can pink or red salmon
1 tablespoon lemon juice
1 large egg or ¼ cup egg substitute
1 large egg white
1 cup fresh bread crumbs
1 cup mashed potatoes made with skim milk
1 teaspoon celery seed
1¼ teaspoons paprika
1 teaspoon yellow mustard
1 teaspoon crushed fennel seeds (optional)
½ teaspoon prepared horseradish or to taste (optional)
Salt and freshly ground pepper to taste
Vegetable oil cooking spray

Remove as much skin from the salmon as possible. Mix together all ingredients except cooking spray until well combined. Preheat the oven to 350 degrees.

Spray a small loaf pan with cooking oil. Spoon the salmon mixture into the pan and bake, uncovered, for about 45 minutes.

Per serving:

Calories	226
Total fat	7 g
Saturated fat	1.9 g
Cholesterol	89 mg
Sodium	554 mg

FOOD PHARMACY FACT

Fish Can Help Save Bones

Eating seafood may help protect older women from bone fractures. The reason: seafood is one of the best sources of vitamin D, and without enough vitamin D older women lose calcium from bones, rendering them more fragile and apt to break. So notes Dr. Elizabeth A. Krall at the U.S. Department of Agriculture's research center at Tufts University.

In her study of 333 postmenopausal women Dr. Krall found women need about twice as much vitamin D to prevent calcium loss as they typically get. Most women take in only 112 international units (IUs) of vitamin D, when they need at least 220 IUs, says Dr. Krall. Worse, the ability to absorb vitamin D decreases with age. An excellent source of vitamin D is seafood. Eel has the most—three-and-a-half ounces of eel contains a whopping 6,400 IUs. The same amount of canned salmon has 500 IUs and canned sardines 300 IUs. A cup of milk fortified with vitamin D has 100 IUs.

Basque Tuna Stew

Serves 4

This seafood stew, a longtime tradition among fishermen, is a treasure of health-promoting ingredients and is a wonderful way to use fresh or frozen tuna with its high content of omega-3-type oil. It's brimming with vitamin C and vitamin A, both cancer fighters. And it contains a powerhouse of potassium, linked to preventing strokes.

1 to 2 tablespoons olive oil
1 medium onion, chopped
2 small green bell peppers, chopped
2 medium tomatoes, chopped, *or* 1 cup drained canned tomatoes, chopped
1¾ pounds potatoes (3 large), peeled and cut into medium chunks
2 cups tomato juice
4 garlic cloves, chopped
½ teaspoon dried rosemary, crushed
½ teaspoon dried thyme
3 tablespoons chopped parsley
Pinch of hot red pepper flakes or to taste
Salt and freshly ground pepper to taste
1½ pounds fresh or frozen tuna, cut into large chunks
¼ cup Pernod or other anise-flavored liqueur (optional)

In a large pot, heat the oil and sauté the onion and peppers until soft. Add the tomatoes, potatoes, tomato juice, garlic, rosemary, thyme, parsley, red pepper flakes, salt, pepper, and enough water to come about an inch above the potatoes. Simmer gently until the potatoes are tender. Smash three or four potato chunks against the side of the pan to thicken the stew.

Add the tuna chunks and cook for about 10 minutes, until the fish is opaque and firm.

Add the optional Pernod and stir. Or pass a small pitcher of anise-flavored liqueur and let diners add their own.

Per serving:

Calories	445
Total fat	12.2 g
Saturated fat	2.7 g
Cholesterol	65 mg
Sodium	95 mg

COOK'S ADVICE

Use potatoes as a low-fat thickener for soups, stews, and sauces. When potatoes are already present in a stew, simply smash a few chunks of potato against the side of the pot and stir. Add mashed potatoes (made without butter or other fat) to soups or stews five to ten minutes before other ingredients are cooked. To thicken soups, remove some liquid and puree it in the blender with a leftover baked or boiled potato. Mix the puree into the soup.

Caribbean-Style Mackerel by George

Serves 6

Here's another way to prepare this marvelous fish with lots of vegetables, herbs, and spices. It's the allspice that gives it a Caribbean flavor, says its creator, George Jacobs, who also is the creator of two cookbooks, including Light-Hearted Cooking by George! *I was fortunate enough to have George come to my own kitchen to make this dish. Its festive Spanish colors also make this dish a delight to present to a table of family or friends. Note: the fat in this recipe comes almost entirely from the fish itself and is what makes this fish so good for you—so high in omega-3 oils.*

1 large onion, thinly sliced
1 large green bell pepper, cut into spears
3 garlic cloves, chopped
Cooking spray
3 pounds mackerel fillets
2 cups sliced fresh mushrooms
1 fresh tomato, cut into chunks
1 28-ounce can whole tomatoes, juice reserved
1/2 teaspoon ground allspice
1/4 teaspoon dried thyme
1/8 teaspoon cayenne pepper or to taste
1/2 cup parsley sprigs
1 cup dry white wine

Put onions, green pepper, and garlic in a microwave-safe bowl, cover, and microwave on HIGH for 5 minutes to soften them.

Spray oil on the bottom of a large baking pan. Lay the fillets, skin side down, in rows in the bottom of the pan.

Preheat the oven to 375 degrees. Over the top of the fish, sprinkle the mushrooms, fresh and canned tomatoes—arranging whole tomatoes over and around the fish—allspice, thyme, cayenne pepper, and parsley. Add the reserved tomato juice and wine.

Bake for about 10 minutes or until the fish is opaque. Remove and place the pan under the broiler for a couple of minutes, until the top vegetables are browned and the sauce is bubbly.

Put each fillet covered with vegetables and sauce on a plate or in a shallow soup bowl. Serve with crusty bread for mopping up the sauce.

Per serving:

Calories	523
Total fat	32 g
Saturated fat	7.5 g
Cholesterol	159 mg
Sodium	429 mg

FISH BEATS FISH OIL CAPSULES

If fish is good for you, why not simply take fish oil capsules, available at health food stores? Most experts discourage such use without medical supervision, warning that the supplements may be ineffective and even dangerous in some cases.

Experts' greatest fear is that people will overdose on fish oil capsules, perhaps causing excessive bleeding and other problems. Although the amount of fish oil in a capsule a day "would do wonders for Americans," as William Lands, University of Illinois, says, he advises eating fish instead of taking capsules because "there is much less chance of overdosing."

Fish oil capsules may also ironically deliver an unintended effect. They may raise cholesterol instead of lowering it. In studies they have actually promoted migraine headaches, impaired blood sugar metabolism, and worsened psoriasis and blood pressure in certain individuals.

Also, fish oil supplements may not be as effective as eating the fish itself. Recently Dr. Paul Nestel, chief of Human Nutrition, Commonwealth Scientific & Industrial Research Organization in Australia, gave thirty-one men with moderately high cholesterol either fish oil capsules or a small fish serving a day (one-and-a-half pounds a week), usually salmon or sardines. The capsules and the fish had equal amounts of protective omega-3 fatty acids.

But after five weeks blood tests showed that the "fish outperformed the fish oil capsules." The fish eaters had less bad-type LDL blood cholesterol, less of a blood-clotting factor (fibrinogen), "thinner blood," and depressed production of a hormonelike agent (thromboxane) that promotes blood clotting.

"Is there something else beneficial in the fish?" asks Dr. Nestel. Possibly, he speculates, it's because the fish was richer in a type of omega-3 called *DHA*, and the fish oil supplements were made up of omega-3 EPA, with different effects on blood.

Additionally, other factors in seafood, such as the trace mineral selenium, may help protect against cardiovascular and other diseases. Dutch researchers raised this possibility when they noted that eaters of lean fish (low in omega-3) as well as fatty fish (high in omega-3) had lower rates of fatal heart attack.

Garlic Smoked Mussels with Tomatoes

Serves 4

Those mighty mollusks, including mussels, do very good things for your cardiovascular system, according to research. They lower your blood cholesterol, improve the ratio of your good cholesterol to bad cholesterol, and even promote absorption and metabolism of damaging cholesterol molecules so they do not get a chance to clog your arteries. I like this recipe also because it includes lots of therapeutic garlic and is an imaginative way to do mussels on the grill. This recipe comes from Chef Frank Terranova, one of the winners in a competition for seafood chefs sponsored by the National Fish and Seafood Promotional Council on behalf of the seafood industry.

8 large elephant garlic cloves, peeled
3 dozen mussels, well scrubbed
Fresh Tomato Concasse (recipe follows)

Place the garlic on a grill, 4 to 5 inches above the hot coals.

Quickly place the mussels in a single layer on the grill and cover with the lid or foil to seal in the smoke. Cook until the shells open, 8 to 10 minutes for large and 4 minutes for small mussels. Break off and discard the top shells.

Arrange the mussels on a hot tray or serving platter. Spoon a little fresh tomato concasse on each mussel and serve immediately.

Per serving:

Calories	98
Total fat	1.7 g
Saturated fat	.3 g
Cholesterol	20 mg
Sodium	210 mg

FRESH TOMATO CONCASSE

About 1½ cups

1 pound plum tomatoes
2 tablespoons olive oil
4 teaspoons white wine vinegar or balsamic vinegar
1 tablespoon chopped fresh basil *or* 1 teaspoon dried
1 tablespoon chopped fresh oregano *or* 1 teaspoon dried
¼ teaspoon freshly ground pepper

Place the tomatoes on the grill, 4 to 5 inches above the hot coals. Grill, turning frequently, until the skins pop and the tomatoes are slightly charred, about 10 minutes.

Core, cut in half, and squeeze to expel the seeds. Coarsely chop the tomatoes and place them in a bowl with the oil, vinegar, herbs, and pepper. Serve at room temperature.

Note: You can put the tomatoes under the broiler instead.

Per 1-tablespoon serving:

Calories	14
Total fat	1 g
Saturated fat	.2 g
Cholesterol	0
Sodium	1 mg

Stir-Fried Scallops with Walnuts and Snow Peas

Serves 4

Scallops are extraordinarily low in fat, but what fat they do have is virtually all from omega-3—which makes them particularly attractive for health. Walnuts are one of my favorite nuts because they too have omega-3 as well as other identified disease-fighting compounds. Combined, they also taste terrific as this quick stir-fry illustrates. Note: most of the fat in this stir-fry comes from the walnuts and is unsaturated.

1 tablespoon cornstarch
1/2 cup low-sodium chicken broth
2 tablespoons dry sherry
2 tablespoons reduced-sodium soy sauce
1 teaspoon grated fresh gingerroot
1/4 teaspoon hot red pepper flakes or to taste
1 cup walnut halves
1 1/2 tablespoons vegetable oil
1 tablespoon minced garlic
8 scallions, including some of the green, sliced into 1-inch lengths on a diagonal
1 1/2 cups snow peas
1 1/4 pounds sea scallops, halved or quartered and dried with paper towels

In a small bowl, combine the cornstarch and chicken broth. Whisk in the sherry, soy sauce, gingerroot, and red pepper flakes. Set aside.

Spread the walnut halves on a baking sheet and toast in a 350-degree oven until they are slightly browned—about 10 minutes.

Put 3/4 tablespoon of the oil in a wok or skillet over high heat. When the oil is hot, add the garlic, scallions, and snow peas and stir-fry for 2 minutes, until they are crisp-tender. Remove from the wok.

Add the remaining oil and the scallops and stir-fry for 1 minute. Stir in the chicken-broth-soy mixture and cook until slightly thickened, about 1 minute. Add the scallions, snow peas, and toasted walnuts. Cook for 1 more minute (do not overcook scallops). Serve at once.

Per serving:

Calories	385
Total fat	21.9 g
Saturated fat	2.2 g
Cholesterol	46.8 mg
Sodium	542 mg

Chef Kenneth's Crab Cakes

Serves 6

Chef Kenneth Juran, executive chef at the Washington, D.C., Park Hyatt Hotel is famous for these crab cakes, full of luscious Chesapeake Bay crabmeat. Eating crab instead of high-saturated-fat foods like meat can lower your cholesterol and triglycerides, according to studies. Although crab has some cholesterol, it's not enough to be worrisome. Crab also contains cell-protecting omega-3 fatty acids. Two crab cakes contain about 500 milligrams of omega-3s, nearly the daily dose needed to cut fatal heart attack risk by 30 to 40 percent, according to studies. Chef Kenneth often serves the crab cakes with a red pepper sauce, but I find them delectable plain or sprinkled lightly with fresh lemon juice.

2 pounds fresh crabmeat, preferably backfin
2 eggs
1 tablespoon Dijon mustard
2 drops Tabasco sauce
2½ tablespoons chopped parsley
1 teaspoon Worcestershire sauce
Salt and freshly ground pepper to taste
½ cup fresh white bread crumbs
1 tablespoon butter
1 teaspoon olive or canola oil

Pick over the crab, removing all shells and foreign material.

In a small bowl, combine the eggs, mustard, Tabasco, parsley, Worcestershire sauce, salt, and pepper and mix well.

Add the egg mixture to the crabmeat. Mix well. Then fold in the bread crumbs to bind.

Form 12 crab cakes. Preheat the oven to 375 degrees.

Put half the butter and half the oil in a large nonstick skillet. Sauté half the crab cakes over medium heat until lightly browned on both sides. Remove the crab cakes to a shallow ovenproof dish and repeat the process with the remaining six crab cakes. Bake the crab cakes for 8 to 10 minutes.

Per serving:

Calories	217
Total fat	7.3 g
Saturated fat	2.2 g
Cholesterol	227 mg
Sodium	566 mg

Seafood Chili with Red Beans

Serves 10

Chili has never been like this—a remarkable blending of the Mexican tradition of beans and hot peppers with, yes, the most popular food pharmacy lifesaver—seafood—substituting for the traditional beef. This does take a little time to make, but it is worth it—and beautiful with its burnt sienna base flecked with green and red. The chili is wonderfully flavorful even without the seafood. More thanks to my friend Chef Kenneth Juran for this remarkable health-promoting recipe.

- 2 quarts chicken stock, preferably homemade or low-sodium canned chicken broth
- 2 cups (1 pound) dried red beans, soaked overnight
- 2 tablespoons olive oil
- 2 tablespoons chopped garlic
- 4 small onions, finely diced
- 2 red bell peppers, finely diced
- 2 poblano peppers, finely diced, *or* 2 green bell peppers, finely diced, plus 1 teaspoon Tabasco sauce
- 1/2 cup tomato paste
- 10 very ripe plum tomatoes, finely chopped, *or* 10 canned plum tomatoes, drained and chopped
- 1 teaspoon ground cumin
- 1/3 cup chili powder
- 1 tablespoon chopped fresh oregano
- 1 tablespoon chopped fresh thyme
- 1 tablespoon chopped cilantro
- 2 cups dry white wine
- 1 1/2 pounds fresh seafood (shrimp, lobster, swordfish, scallops), cut into bite-size pieces

Bring the chicken stock and beans to a simmer and cook for about 30 minutes.

In a separate pan, heat the oil and sauté the garlic over medium heat for 1 minute (do not let garlic brown). Add the onions and continue cooking, stirring constantly, for 3 minutes more. Now add all the chopped peppers, tomato paste, and tomatoes. Cook for 10 minutes over medium heat, continuing to stir so it does not scorch on the bottom. Add the cumin and chili powder.

When the beans are done, remove half the beans and chicken stock and puree in a blender or food processor fitted with the steel blade. Return the puree to the whole beans and stock. Then add the bean mixture to the pepper mixture. Add all the fresh herbs.

Put the wine and seafood in a pot and cook slowly over medium heat until cooked all the way through; cooking time will vary with type of seafood. Shrimp and scallops take only a couple of minutes; swordfish, about 10 minutes. With a slotted spoon, remove the seafood and add to the pot of chili. Bring the mixture just to a simmer. Turn off the heat and serve immediately.

Per serving:

Calories	327
Total fat	6.9 g
Saturated fat	1.1 g
Cholesterol	51 mg
Sodium	283 mg

FOOD PHARMACY FACT

Want Good Cholesterol? Eat Vitamin C Foods

At least that's what government research suggests after studying 238 elderly Chinese-Americans, who eat more high-vitamin-C foods than most Americans. Researchers at Agriculture's Human Nutrition Research Center on Aging at Tufts found that among the Chinese-Americans those with the highest blood levels of vitamin C also had the highest levels of good-type HDL cholesterol, which whisks the bad-type LDL cholesterol out of the system. Previously scientists had discovered the same thing among a group of 700 mostly Caucasian men and women over sixty. But it does not hold true for smokers, who consistently had lower levels of C in their blood. The presumption is that eating more vitamin C somehow drives up the HDLs, thus lessening the danger of cardiovascular disease.

Puerto Rican Sardine Pie

Serves 6

Ah, sardine lovers, here is a dish literally to please your heart, plus your bones, joints, skin, and cells in general. The recipe also calls for that too infrequently used Swiss chard, a dark green vegetable also chockful of cell-protecting compounds. In addition, this pie tastes terrific, like a deep-dish pizza. It's one of my favorites. However, if you're on a low-sodium diet, you may want to pass it up. Many thanks to Phyllis Richman, The Washington Post, *for this hearty taste sensation.*

1 bunch Swiss chard (or spinach), cut into 1-inch pieces
1 large tomato (1/2 pound), chopped
2 medium onions (1/2 pound), chopped
1 small green bell pepper (1/4 pound), chopped
Salt to taste
1 tablespoon olive oil
1 pie shell made from bread dough (recipe follows) or frozen bread dough
8 to 10 canned sardines (about 2 4.34-ounce tins)
2 pimientos or canned roasted red peppers, cut into strips

Sauté all the vegetables in the olive oil until softened, about 10 minutes. Preheat the oven to 350 degrees.

Drain excess liquid and spread the vegetables over the pie shell. Arrange the sardines in spokes over the vegetables and decorate with pimiento strips. Bake for 25 minutes. Serve hot or at room temperature.

PIE SHELL

1 teaspoon sugar
1/2 cup lukewarm water
1 1/4-ounce package active dry yeast
1/2 teaspoon salt
3 tablespoons butter or margarine, melted
1 egg, beaten
2 cups flour

Add 1 teaspoon sugar to the lukewarm water, then add the yeast slowly and let stand for 10 minutes. Add the salt, butter, and egg and mix well.

Add the flour slowly to form a smooth dough. Knead lightly and place in a greased bowl. Let rise until double in bulk, about an hour.

Roll half of the dough into a circle about 10 inches in diameter and 1/4 inch thick. Place the dough in a 9-inch pie tin and build up the 1-inch overhang to form a ridge. Reserve the remaining dough for another use or double the filling and make 2 pies.

Per serving:

Calories	357
Total fat	13.8 g
Saturated fat	4.6 g
Cholesterol	101 mg
Sodium	602 mg

HOW TO CHOOSE THE SAFEST FISH

Some fish can be contaminated by environmental pollutants, like PCBs and pesticides, which tend to concentrate in fatty fish. Thus some ask: Could eating fish be more harmful than healthful? "Generally no," say even the most dedicated environmental experts. However, decidedly the government should tighten regulations to ensure safe fish; although the hazard is slight (92 percent of the fish consumed in the U.S. is caught three miles from shore, where pollution is less likely), it makes good sense to be cautious. Some facts and advice:

- Open-ocean fish are less likely to be contaminated than freshwater fish.
- The greatest threats are sport fish caught by recreational fishermen.
- Most endangered by pollutants in fish are nursing mothers, pregnant women, and children. For example, Michigan authorities have advised these groups to shun lake trout from Lake Huron.
- Always heed local and state warnings from health authorities about contamination dangers in special waters.
- It's best to shop for fish in large commercial markets.
- Eat a variety of fish to protect against contamination from one source.

According to Dr. David Rall, former director of the National Institute of Environmental and Health Sciences, "The nasty stuff is mainly in the skin and liver of the fish. If you avoid that—as most people do—there does not seem to be any problem. We think the danger of eating the flesh of fish is about zero."

Carol Mason's White Chili

Serves 6

Fans of Carol Mason, a chef and cooking instructor in Washington, D.C., have been raving about her white chili made with white beans and chunks of chicken for as long as I can remember. After trying it, you'll undoubtedly agree it's one of the best chilies you've ever had. I like it especially because the low-fat chicken is a welcome change from traditional beef, and I've lessened the amount of oil a bit to make it even lower in fat.

- 1 pound dried Great Northern beans, soaked overnight and drained, *or* 5 to 6 cups canned white beans with liquid
- 6 to 8 cups homemade chicken broth or canned low-sodium chicken broth diluted 50-50 with water
- 1 tablespoon minced garlic
- 2 cups chopped onions
- 1 tablespoon olive oil
- 1 4-ounce can chopped green chilies *or* 1 cup seeded and chopped fresh Anaheim chilies
- 1 poblano chili, seeded and chopped
- 2 teaspoons ground cumin
- 2 teaspoons dried oregano
- 1/4 teaspoon ground cloves
- 1/4 teaspoon cayenne pepper
- Dash of Tabasco sauce (more if desired)
- 4 cups cubed poached skinless chicken breast meat
- Shredded Monterey Jack cheese, chopped scallions, chopped tomatoes, chopped cilantro, or Salsa Cruda (page 385) for garnish (optional)

In a 4-quart casserole combine the drained dried beans with 6 cups of the chicken broth. Add the garlic and 1 cup of the onions.

Bring the beans to a boil, reduce the heat, partially cover, and simmer until the beans are tender but not mushy—about 2 to 3 hours. Add more chicken broth if necessary.

In a small saucepan sauté the remaining onions in the oil until translucent and soft.

Add the chilies and seasonings and mix thoroughly. Add the onion-chilies mixture to the beans.

Add the chicken cubes and cook over low heat for about 5 minutes or until the chicken is heated through. Add more chicken broth if needed and heat through.

Serve with a compatible mixture of some of the suggested garnishes.

Note: If you use canned beans, you will need only 1 to 2 cups chicken broth, which you can add as needed to maintain the desired amount of liquid in the chili. Also, if you're using canned beans, sauté all of the onions and garlic together in the oil, then combine with the spices, chillies, and beans and cook no longer than 15 minutes before adding the chicken.

Per serving:

Calories	485
Total fat	7.7 g
Saturated fat	1.7 g
Cholesterol	80 mg
Sodium	231 mg

FOOD PHARMACY FACT

Chicken Surprise

When you eat poultry, you take in some omega-3 fatty acids of the type found in fish that is so beneficial to health. The reason: since 1960 some farmers have included fish meal in chicken feed. The fish meal helps create omega-3s in the flesh of the chickens. It's estimated that we may be getting up to 20 percent of all our omega-3s from poultry. "Since Americans eat so little fish, this may be what's saving us from even more heart disease," quipped one expert on fish oil.

Ellen Brown's Jambalaya

Serves 8

For a gourmet party dish that's really good for your health, you can hardly beat this jambalaya created by Ellen Brown, a food writer and recipe originator par excellence. Just putting those colorful heaps of chopped onions, celery, peppers, scallions, and garlic into the pot makes you feel healthier already. Although the recipe calls for chicken, I've also made it with chunks of uncooked turkey breast and found it equally delicious. The recipe is reprinted from Brown's The Gourmet Gazelle Cookbook, *which contains many other low-fat, health-promoting recipes.*

2 tablespoons vegetable oil
1/2 cup reduced-sodium ham
2 large onions, peeled and coarsely chopped
2 celery stalks, washed and coarsely chopped
1 green bell pepper, coarsely chopped
6 scallions, including 3 inches of the green, chopped
3 garlic cloves, minced
1 cup brown rice
1 pound boneless, skinless chicken breasts, trimmed and cut into 2-inch cubes
2 bay leaves
1/2 to 1 teaspoon cayenne pepper (to taste)
1 tablespoon chopped fresh oregano *or* 1 teaspoon dried
2 teaspoons chopped fresh thyme *or* 1/2 teaspoon dried
1/2 teaspoon salt
1 cup salt-free tomato sauce
1 14-ounce can tomatoes, drained and chopped
1 cup fish stock or clam juice
1/2 pound medium shrimp, peeled and deveined

Preheat the oven to 350 degrees. Heat the vegetable oil over medium-high heat in a 4-quart ovenproof casserole. Add the ham and sauté for 1 minute. Add the fresh vegetables and garlic. Sauté for 5 minutes, stirring often, until the onion is translucent. Add the brown rice and sauté for 3 more minutes, stirring constantly.

Add the chicken, bay leaves, cayenne pepper, oregano, thyme, and salt. Cook for 2 minutes.

Add the tomato sauce, tomatoes, and fish stock. Bring to a boil, cover the casserole, and place in the center of the oven. Cook for 20 minutes. Stir the casserole, add the shrimp, and return to the oven for 10 to 15 minutes or until the liquid has been absorbed and the rice is tender. Serve immediately.

Note: You can make this dish up to two days in advance; however, remove it from the oven after the initial 20 minutes. It will still be slightly liquid. Before serving, place it in a 350-degree oven for 30 minutes, then add the shrimp and continue to bake for 10 minutes.

Per serving:

Calories	261
Total fat	6 g
Saturated fat	.1 g
Cholesterol	73 mg
Sodium	440 mg

Navajo Stew with Sweet Potatoes and Black Beans

Serves 6 to 8

Sweet potatoes, chili spices, and beans . . . this is an inspired combination, from both the health and taste standpoints. The sweet potatoes give you a huge shot of beta-carotene and vitamin A—about 38,000 international units—enough to last you for a week, and one-and-a-half times the daily dose of beta-carotene being used in the government's human studies to test the compound's powers to prevent cancer. The beans are full of anticancer compounds also. And combined with the chili spices, they taste so great that my friend Jim ate two huge servings—an unusual event. I thank Gourmet *magazine for the inspiration, although I have modified many of the ingredients.*

2 medium *or* 4 small onions, chopped
4 teaspoons chili powder
1/2 cup orange juice
2 pounds boneless turkey breast, cut into 1-inch cubes
1/2 cup water
2 teaspoons honey
Salt to taste
3 large sweet potatoes (about 3 pounds), peeled and cut into 1-inch cubes
2 teaspoons butter or margarine, softened
2 teaspoons flour
2 10-ounce cans black beans, drained and rinsed

Put the onions, chili powder, and 1/4 cup of the orange juice in a large bowl. Cover and microwave on HIGH for 3 minutes. Stir and microwave on HIGH for 3 minutes more or until the onions are limp.

Add the turkey cubes, remaining 1/4 cup orange juice, water, honey, salt, and sweet potatoes. Stir to combine all ingredients. Cover and microwave on HIGH for about 30 minutes or until the sweet potatoes are done but still hold their shape and are not mushy. Test and stir after 15 to 20 minutes.

Blend the butter and flour.

Add the beans along with the butter-flour mixture and microwave on HIGH for 4 minutes, until the stew has thickened slightly.

Per serving:

Calories	475
Total fat	4.7 g
Saturated fat	1.7 g
Cholesterol	97 mg
Sodium	516 mg

Pineapple Ginger Chicken

Serves 6

Search no further for an excellent ginger chicken, high in flavor and low in fat and calories. I especially like the combination of ginger and chicken because in tests ginger actually destroys bacteria called salmonella *that frequently contaminate chickens. It's as if the Oriental creators of this combination long ago were privy to some modern scientific wisdom. The pineapple juice is also a powerhouse of manganese, needed to protect bones. This recipe was created by Tracy Ritter, chef at the Golden Door Spa in California.*

2 cups unsweetened pineapple juice
1 cup dry white wine
2 tablespoons finely chopped fresh gingerroot
1/3 cup grainy mustard
2 tablespoons reduced-sodium soy sauce
2 teaspoons dark sesame oil
2 scallions, chopped
1 garlic clove, minced
6 whole boneless, skinless chicken breasts, cut in half

Combine the pineapple juice, wine, ginger, mustard, soy sauce, sesame oil, scallions, and garlic in blender. Blend until creamy.

Reserve half the marinade for the sauce. Arrange the chicken in a shallow pan large enough to hold the pieces in a single layer. Pour the marinade over them and cover. Refrigerate for 2 to 3 hours or overnight.

Preheat the broiler. Remove the chicken from the marinade and arrange on broiler rack. Broil on lowest level of broiler, 6 to 8 minutes total, or until the chicken is tender and brown. Baste once after turning.

To make the sauce, bring the reserved marinade to a boil and cook over high heat for about 10 minutes, until the sauce thickens slightly. Spoon the sauce over the chicken.

Per serving:

Calories	345
Total fat	8 g
Saturated fat	1.9 g
Cholesterol	146 mg
Sodium	380 mg

Barbecued Turkey with Garlic-Chili Sauce

Serves 4

This low-fat, spicy marinated turkey with its zingy barbecue sauce was the big winner at the great garlic cook-off held during the 1989 annual Garlic Festival in Gilroy, California. And small wonder. It combines all the best taste of health-promoting garlic and chili peppers with the lowest-fat animal protein around. Its originator, Chuck Dell'Ario of Oakland, was crowned with a garland of garlic.

4 dried ancho or pasilla chilies
1 cup water
1 tablespoon olive oil
1 onion, chopped
8 garlic cloves, minced
2 tomatillos, chopped
2 tablespoons Worcestershire sauce
1 tablespoon sugar
1 tablespoon chocolate chips
1 teaspoon ground cinnamon
1 teaspoon ground cumin
Salt and freshly ground pepper to taste
4 to 8 turkey tenderloins (fillets; 1½ to 2 pounds total)
1 cup chopped cilantro for garnish

Stem and seed the chilies. Heat the water, pour it over the chilies, and let stand for at least 30 minutes. Drain, reserving the water.

Heat the oil in a large saucepan. Sauté the onion and garlic until soft and translucent but not browned, about 5 minutes. Add the tomatillos, chilies, ½ cup chili soaking water, Worcestershire sauce, sugar, chocolate chips, cinnamon, and cumin. Simmer for 20 minutes. Add salt and pepper.

Transfer the mixture to a food processor fitted with the steel blade or a food mill and puree, then strain through a medium sieve. The sauce should be thick.

Trim the turkey tenderloins and place in a bowl. Cover with the sauce, then cover the bowl tightly and marinate in the refrigerator for at least 2 hours.

Drain the turkey, reserving the sauce.

Grill over hot coals or under a preheated broiler until just done, 4 to 5 minutes per side, basting with 1/2 cup sauce.

Heat the remaining sauce and pass with the cooked turkey. Garnish the turkey with the cilantro.

Note: the sauce may be made up to 2 days ahead.

Per serving:

Calories	354
Total fat	9.6 g
Saturated fat	1.8 g
Cholesterol	123 mg
Sodium	224 mg

FOOD PHARMACY FACT

It's Not the Meat; It's the Fat

You don't have to give up red meat, poultry, and eggs to lower your blood cholesterol and blood pressure. That's what Rita Dougherty of USDA's Western Human Nutrition Research Center in San Francisco found in a study of twelve men on low-fat diets. The men had an average blood cholesterol of 218 and average blood pressure of 135/85. They ordinarily ate 40 to 44 percent of their calories in fat, 21 percent from saturated fat.

During the test, for forty days they ate the same number of calories, but 25 percent of the calories came from fat, with 6 percent of those from saturated fat. They ate beef and pork from which the fat had been trimmed, poultry without skin, margarine instead of butter, skim milk instead of whole, vegetable oil instead of animal cooking fats.

In fact they ate as much meat, poultry, and dairy products as before and more total food than before. Still their cholesterol dropped on average 20 percent to 185 and their blood pressure 10 percent to 124/79. As Dougherty points out, the men ate red meat and eggs several times a week and milk and margarine daily, as much as they had previously. Obviously, she says, it's not these foods per se that are the villains, but the fat they carry as baggage. Get rid of that, and they are cholesterol-safe to eat.

Barley-Turkey Skillet Dinner

Serves 6

Here's a down-home way to eat barley, that often neglected grain that is high in both soluble and insoluble fiber, both known to be excellent for health. Barley, it's been shown, is just as effective as oats in lowering blood cholesterol. Using ground turkey also keeps down the fat content. Thanks to barley researcher Dr. Rosemary Newman, University of Montana, for this recipe.

1 pound ground turkey, chicken, or lean beef
1/2 cup chopped onion
1/2 cup chopped celery
1/4 cup diced green bell pepper
1 garlic clove, minced
2 tablespoons vegetable oil
3/4 cup pearl barley
1 16-ounce can tomatoes, chopped, with juice
1 1/2 cups water
1/2 cup chili sauce
1 teaspoon Worcestershire sauce
1/2 teaspoon dried marjoram
Salt and freshly ground pepper to taste

In a heavy skillet, sauté the turkey, onion, celery, green pepper, and garlic in the oil for 3 to 4 minutes.

Add the remaining ingredients, bring to a boil, reduce the heat to simmer, cover, and cook for about 1 hour or until the barley is tender and most of the liquid is absorbed. Adjust the seasonings.

Note: You may substitute 2 cups diced uncooked turkey or chicken in place of ground poultry.

Per serving:

Calories	283
Total fat	10.8 g
Saturated fat	2 g
Cholesterol	55 mg
Sodium	519 mg

Chinese Pepper Steak

Serves 3 to 4

Not only does this stir-fry have the typical peppers; it has the added appeal of Chinese black mushrooms known as tree-ear or wood-ear and mo-er. These are known in ancient Chinese medicine as "blood thinners" and "good for the heart." Indeed recent studies show the mushroom contains anticoagulantlike chemicals that do impede blood clotting; their effect is somewhat the same as that of aspirin, a well-proven "blood thinner" thought to help prevent heart attacks and strokes. Thus eating the small doses of mushrooms in this recipe will probably produce a "blood-thinning" effect.

1 pound lean sirloin steak, trimmed of fat and cut into 1/4-inch-wide strips
6 dried Chinese black tree-ear mushrooms
2 to 3 tablespoons olive oil
1-inch piece of fresh gingerroot, minced
2 garlic cloves, minced
2 scallions, minced
1 green bell pepper, cut into 1-inch pieces
1 red bell pepper, cut into 1-inch pieces
1 yellow bell pepper (or another red one), cut into 1-inch pieces

MARINADE

2 tablespoons reduced-sodium soy sauce
2 tablespoons rice wine or dry sherry
1 tablespoon dark sesame oil
1/2 teaspoon hot chili oil or Tabasco sauce
1 teaspoon sugar
2 teaspoons cornstarch

Combine the ingredients for the marinade and marinate the beef in it for 20 minutes.

Pour boiling water over the mushrooms and soak for 15 minutes. Remove the stems and cut the mushrooms into thin strips.

Just before serving, drain the meat, reserving the marinade. Heat 2 tablespoons of the oil almost to smoking in a wok or large skillet. Add the ginger, garlic, and scallions and stir-fry for 30 seconds or until fragrant. Add the beef and stir-fry for 1 to 2 minutes or until cooked to taste. Transfer the beef to a bowl and keep warm.

Add 1 tablespoon oil to the wok if necessary. Add the mushrooms and peppers and stir-fry for 1 minute. Return the meat to the wok and add the marinade. Stir-fry for 30 seconds or until all the ingredients are heated and the sauce is lightly thickened.

Per serving:

Calories	411
Total fat	23 g
Saturated fat	4.5 g
Cholesterol	92 mg
Sodium	501 mg

DOCTOR'S ADVICE

Eat Like the Chinese Do

"We're basically a vegetarian species and should be eating a wide variety of plant foods and minimizing our intake of animal foods." So says Dr. T. Colin Campbell, nutritional biochemist at Cornell University, after receiving preliminary data from China of the largest, most comprehensive study ever done of the relationship between diet and chronic disease.

Dr. Campbell's study of 6,500 Chinese, done in cooperation with Chinese doctors, clearly shows, he says, that the Chinese plant-food-oriented diet is healthier than our animal-dependent diet.

For example, the average Chinese eats but sixty-four grams of protein a day, 93 percent of it from plants. The average American eats one-third more protein (ninety-one grams), and a whopping 70 percent comes from animal products. Chinese who eat the most protein, particularly animal protein, also have the most heart disease, cancer, and diabetes.

The average Chinese eats a mere 15 percent of calories from fat compared with about 37 percent of calories from fat by the average American.

A typical Chinese, due to a high-plant diet, eats about three times as much dietary fiber as the typical American. Though most Chinese eat virtually no dairy calcium, they rarely suffer from osteoporosis. They eat only half as much calcium as Americans, and nearly all their calcium comes from plants.

Chinese women have extremely low rates of breast and reproductive-system cancers.

The average blood cholesterol among Chinese is 127 compared with 212 among those on a Western diet.

Nor is the iron in meat necessary to prevent anemia, says Dr. Campbell. Anemia is very rare among Chinese. They eat twice as much iron as Americans, but by far most of it comes from plants.

Dr. Campbell advises eating primarily a plant-based diet, with 80 percent of calories or more coming from plant foods, such as fresh or frozen fruits and vegetables and whole-grain foods.

Pork and Apple Stir-Fry

Serves 4

Many experts say we should eat more like Asians, as this recipe exemplifies, with small amounts of meat mixed with lots of vegetables and, in this case, apples. The apples not only add an interesting taste but, as Japanese studies show, may help reduce the risk of stroke. You can substitute chicken breast for the pork.

1 tablespoon vegetable oil
3 garlic cloves, crushed
1/2 pound lean boneless pork, thinly sliced (about 1/4 inch thick)
2 cups broccoli florets and sliced stalks (about 1/2 pound)
1 large red bell pepper, thinly sliced
4 cups sliced Napa cabbage (about 1 pound)
1 apple, such as Golden Delicious, cored and cut into 16 slices

SAUCE

2 tablespoons water
1 tablespoon reduced-sodium soy sauce
1 teaspoon cornstarch
1 teaspoon sugar
1 1/2 teaspoons grated fresh gingerroot
1/8 teaspoon hot red pepper flakes

Heat the oil in a large nonstick skillet over medium heat. Add the garlic and stir-fry until golden, then discard.

Add the sliced pork and stir-fry over medium-high heat until lightly browned; remove to a large serving bowl.

Add the broccoli and red pepper and stir-fry for about 2 minutes. Add the pork, sliced cabbage, and apple slices and stir-fry for about 2 minutes.

Combine the sauce ingredients, add them to the skillet, and stir-fry for about 3 minutes. Transfer to a serving bowl and serve immediately with rice or soft noodles.

Per serving:

Calories	199
Total fat	8 g
Saturated fat	1.9 g
Cholesterol	36 mg
Sodium	214 mg

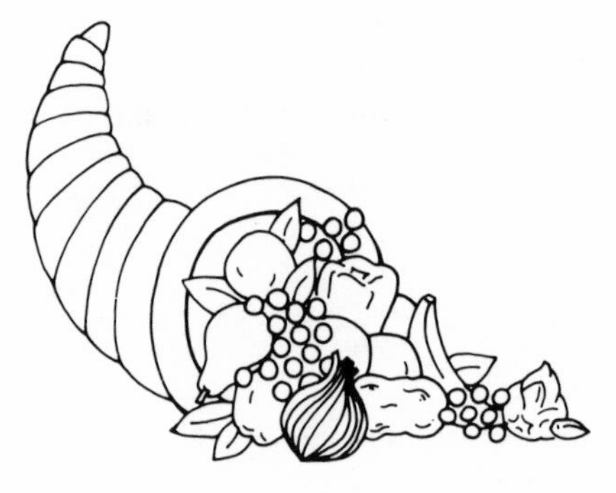

Oriental Hot Pot

Serves 6 to 8

The fondue parties of the sixties are being resurrected for the nineties—with one big change. Instead of high-fat cheese as the dipping sauce, it's now broths simmering with lean meat, seafood, and vegetables of all types. It's no longer high-calorie Swiss fondue; it's the Oriental hot pot. In this traditional Japanese recipe the cooking liquid is a delicate broth flavored with ginger and anise. Such one-pot dinners are fun, and the diners get to do the cooking and can pick and choose what they want—and certainly it's low in fat and a treasure of health-promoting vitamins, minerals, and other compounds.

5 to 6 cups chicken broth, preferably homemade or low-sodium canned chicken broth
1-inch piece of fresh gingerroot, thinly sliced
2 scallions
2 star anise, if available*
1/4 pound Chinese vermicelli (bean thread noodles)
1 small Napa cabbage, broken into leaves
3/4 pound boneless lamb loin
3/4 pound sea scallops
Sesame Dipping Sauce (recipe follows)
1 bunch watercress, washed and long stems removed
1/2 pound fresh spinach, washed and stemmed
1/2 pound mushrooms, cleaned and cut in half
3/4 pound boneless, skinless chicken breasts, trimmed of fat and sinew and cut into bite-size pieces
3/4 pound shrimp, peeled and deveined
1 pound firm tofu, cut into 1-inch cubes

Combine the chicken broth with the ginger, scallion, and star anise. Simmer for 10 minutes and strain.

Soak the vermicelli in cold water to cover for 15 minutes, then drain. Cut the cabbage leaves crosswise into 1-inch strips. Slice the lamb as

* Star anise is a star-shaped spice available in Asian markets. If it is unavailable, you can use a teaspoon of aniseeds, fennel seeds, or a splash of anisette liqueur, but the flavor will not be as pungent or distinct as from the spice.

thinly as possible (partial freezing ahead of time makes slicing easier). Remove the small half-moon-shaped membrane on the sides of the scallops.

Put the dipping sauce in a small bowl. Arrange the vermicelli, watercress, spinach, mushrooms, chicken, lamb, seafood on a large platter (ideally one with a swiveling base).

Fill a hot pot or fondue pot most of the way up with broth.

Let each person dip vegetables, noodles, tofu, meats, and seafoods into the simmering broth, cooking to taste, then into dipping sauce. Add broth as necessary.

Per serving:

Calories	457
Total fat	13.5 g
Saturated fat	2.9 g
Cholesterol	148 mg
Sodium	325 mg

SESAME DIPPING SAUCE

1 cup

½ cup tahini (sesame seed paste)
2 tablespoons reduced-sodium soy sauce
5 to 6 tablespoons low-fat milk or yogurt

Mix all the ingredients until well blended.

Per tablespoon:

Calories	48
Total fat	4.1 g
Saturated fat	.6 g
Cholesterol	.4 mg
Sodium	139 mg

Note: For other dipping sauces, see page 391–392.

Moroccan Lamb Stew with Fruit

Serves 6

The oranges and dried fruit are what attract me to this North African lamb dish. Even orange peel has been shown to have antioxidant cell-protecting properties. And the concentration of compounds in dried fruits undoubtedly helps account for their excellent showing in helping lower the risk of certain cancers. And prunes, it is true, are one of the highest-fiber foods.

3 pounds leg of lamb, cubed and trimmed of fat and gristle
½ cup flour
Salt and freshly ground pepper to taste
Olive oil for browning
1 tablespoon olive oil
1 cup chopped onions
4 garlic cloves, minced
Grated zest of 2 oranges
2 teaspoons dried thyme, crushed
1 teaspoon cumin seeds
2 teaspoons dried rosemary, crushed
2 bay leaves
2 cups low-sodium chicken broth
Juice of 2 oranges
12 pitted prunes, halved
8 dried figs, halved
½ cup slivered almonds, toasted
Chopped parsley for garnish

Pat the meat dry. Mix the flour with salt and pepper in a shallow bowl and dredge the lamb. Barely coat the bottom of a Dutch oven with olive oil and heat over medium-high heat. Brown a single layer of lamb on all sides, remove, and set aside; repeat until all the meat is browned. Wipe out the pan.

In the same pan, heat 1 tablespoon olive oil, add the onions, and cook until soft and lightly browned. Add the garlic, orange zest, thyme, cumin, rosemary, and bay leaves. Heat for about 1 minute, until fragrant, stirring constantly. Preheat the oven to 325 degrees.

Return the lamb to the Dutch oven, add the broth and orange juice, stir together, and bring to a gentle boil. Cover and bake for 1 hour. Stir in the prunes, figs, and almonds and bake for another 30 minutes. Remove the bay leaves. Garnish with parsley and serve with bulgur wheat or brown rice.

Per serving:

Calories	602
Total fat	24 g
Saturated fat	5 g
Cholesterol	145 mg
Sodium	166 mg

Desserts

Date-Wrapped Nuts

20 pieces

These simple tidbits are a delectable way to end a meal and to get the rich amounts of selenium and other health-protecting antioxidants and compounds in nuts, notably Brazil nuts. Dried fruits like dates are often found in the diets of those with lower rates of certain cancers.

20 pitted dates
20 Brazil nuts or almonds
¼ cup granulated sugar

Insert a nut into the pocket of each date. Roll in granulated sugar and arrange on a plate.

Per piece:

Calories	56
Total fat	2.4 g
Saturated fat	.6 g
Cholesterol	0
Sodium	.3 mg

DON'T POP A PILL—EAT A BRAZIL NUT

Brazil nuts are so high in the trace mineral selenium that eating but one nut a day is as protective as popping a selenium pill from a health food store, according to Dr. Donald J. Lisk, director of Cornell University's Toxic Chemical Laboratory. The Brazil nut (which is actually a seed inside a hard brown crescent) is highest of all nuts in selenium, a powerful antioxidant that scientists believe helps protect against toxins and a number of chronic diseases, including cancer and cardiovascular disease.

It's well known, for example, that people with low levels of selenium in their blood are more apt to have heart attacks, strokes, and in particular cancer. Lab studies also show that selenium at fairly low levels can block the development of cancer in animals.

Selenium has another amazing protective ability, particularly intriguing in an age of high environmental pollution. Selenium "dramatically protects against toxicity from heavy metals, such as mercury, lead, and cadmium," says Dr. Lisk. When animals are fed these dangerous heavy metals and also given selenium, they do not experience the expected symptoms of poisoning. The selenium somehow has the ability to wipe out or detoxify the metals' awful consequences to a large extent. This means that selenium may be a partial antidote to some of our modern environmental hazards by helping neutralize the danger of mercury contamination from certain fish, for example, or high lead levels in water or in lead paint, which may damage brain cells.

When Dr. Lisk and colleagues recently measured Brazil nuts for selenium content, they were amazed to find that on average Brazil nuts contain up to 2,500 more units of selenium than any other nut. In fact, says Dr. Lisk, eating a single Brazil nut daily would easily correct or ward off any fears of selenium deficiency. Eating only half a dozen nuts rapidly boosts blood selenium levels by 100 to 350 percent. The reason: the nuts come from trees growing in a section of Brazil where the soil is extremely rich in selenium.

A warning: in excess, selenium can become poisonous. So don't go overboard, cautions Dr. Lisk. Though the studies are not conclusive, you probably would not want to eat more than half a dozen a day on the average.

Other foods high in selenium: seafood, notably swordfish, salmon, tuna, lobster, shrimp, oysters, and haddock; cereals, grains, and sunflower seeds; pasta, and beef liver.

Strawberries with a Meringue Cloud

Serves 8

So quick and simple to make, but so luscious is this baked strawberry dessert. It also makes a stunning presentation, resembling baked Alaska, with heaps of fluffy white surrounded by a moat of deep red. Strawberries, like other red berries and vegetables, are full of lycopene and ellagic acid, both anticancer agents.

8 cups strawberries, sliced
1/3 cup Grand Marnier
3/4 cup sugar or to taste
4 egg whites
Pinch of salt
Pinch of cream of tartar
1/4 cup slivered almonds, toasted
1 tablespoon powdered sugar or to taste

Preheat the oven to 450 degrees.

Mix the strawberries with the Grand Marnier and sugar, reserving 4 tablespoons of sugar. Pour into a shallow, heatproof serving dish. The dessert can be prepared ahead to this point.

Beat the egg whites slowly with the salt and cream of tartar until frothy. Increase the speed to high and, when the whites form soft peaks, beat in the reserved 4 tablespoons sugar. Continue to beat the whites until stiff peaks are formed.

Mound the mixture over the center of the strawberries, leaving an inch or two of the outer edge of strawberries uncovered. Sprinkle with the nuts and then dust with the powdered sugar.

Bake for about 5 minutes or until the top is just golden. Serve immediately.

Per serving:

Calories	174
Total fat	2 g
Saturated fat	.2 g
Cholesterol	0
Sodium	46 mg

FOOD PHARMACY FACT

The Seeds of Berry Power

Strawberries, blackberries, raspberries, and to a lesser extent blueberries, cranberries, grapes, apples, Brazil nuts, walnuts, and cashews all contain the anticancer compound ellagic acid, says Dr. Gary D. Stoner, a pathologist at the Medical College of Ohio.

Ellagic acid is an antioxidant that helps detoxify cancer-causing agents in several different ways. It may block the activation of carcinogens, inhibit the carcinogen itself, or keep the DNA in cells from undergoing mutation.

For example, in one test, ellagic acid blocked damage in human and mouse lung cells dosed with cancer-causing agents. The strawberry acid stopped from 45 to 70 percent of the genetic damage to the cells.

Strawberries are particularly rich in ellagic acid. It's high in both the pulp and the seeds. So if you strain the berries, tossing out the seeds, you also throw away some of the berry's anticancer capabilities.

Ginger Baked Apples with Vanilla Topping

Serves 4

Speaking of rich-tasting desserts, you would never guess this is virtually lacking in fat, it is so satisfying. Many baked apples are made with cinnamon, but these use candied ginger, which provides a flavor surprise. You can also blend a tablespoon or two of amaretto liqueur (if using almonds) or orange-flavored liqueur (if using walnuts) into the yogurt topping. Sit back and enjoy what the apples are doing for your heart.

4 baking apples, cored, a 1-inch circle of peel removed at top
2 tablespoons chopped almonds or walnuts
1 tablespoon currants
3 teaspoons chopped candied ginger
1½ tablespoons lemon juice
⅔ cup maple syrup
1 cup vanilla nonfat yogurt, strained for at least 4 hours

Set the apples in a microwave-safe bowl large enough so they do not touch. In each cavity place equal amounts of nuts, currants, and candied ginger. Mix the lemon juice and maple syrup and pour into the cavities and around the apples.

Microwave, covered with plastic wrap, on HIGH for about 10 minutes or until the apples are soft when pierced with a knife. Let stand for 5 minutes.

Place each apple in a separate bowl, pour the maple sauce over the apples, and top with 2 tablespoons vanilla yogurt.

Per serving:

Calories	323
Total fat	2.7 g
Saturated fat	.3 g
Cholesterol	1.7 mg
Sodium	35 mg

Summer Berry Pudding

Serves 10 to 12

Once a peasant dish made with leftover bread, this makes a virtually nonfat dessert for those of elegant taste. There's never sufficient praise for the health benefits of berries and the beta-carotene-rich peach or mango. All of them contain various cell-protecting antioxidants as well as antiviral properties; berries are also rich in fiber. This lovely dessert is often made by Chef Kenneth Juran, Park Hyatt Hotel in Washington, D.C., who gave us this recipe.

18 to 20 slices country-style firm bread (remove crusts if too thick)
2 cups strawberries, washed, hulled, and quartered
2 cups raspberries, washed, *or* 2 10-ounce packages frozen berries, thawed and drained
1/4 cup sugar
1 cup blueberries, washed and picked over
1 pound ripe peaches or mangoes, peeled and sliced

Lay the bread slices out to dry on a sheet pan overnight at room temperature.

Puree 1 cup of the strawberries and 1 cup of the raspberries with the sugar in a food processor fitted with the steel blade or a blender. Mix the puree with the remaining strawberries, raspberries, and blueberries.

Line the bottom and sides of a 2-quart soufflé dish or glass casserole with some of the bread slices, cut to fit the dish. Cover the bread with about 1 cup berry mixture and some of the peach slices.

Layer the remaining bread and fruit, ending with bread. Cover the dish with plastic wrap. Set on a tray, then place a weight, such as heavy cans (about 5 pounds), on top of the covered bread to make the pudding firm. Refrigerate overnight.

Unmold the pudding onto a round serving platter and slice in wedges to serve.

Per serving:

Calories	155
Total fat	1.5 g
Saturated fat	.3 g
Cholesterol	1 mg
Sodium	193 mg

FOOD PHARMACY FACT

Blueberry Power

Add blueberries to the list of foods that might help your heart by lowering blood cholesterol. A study at Ohio State University found that blueberries have about the same amount of pectin as apples, pears, and peaches (but not as much as citrus fruits). Several studies find that pectin—a soluble fiber—in foods significantly lowers blood cholesterol.

New research also shows that blueberries, like cranberries, may help prevent urinary tract infections. Israeli scientists noted that blueberries contain unknown compounds that combat bacteria known to cause such infections. Blueberries work the same way cranberries do, said the scientists.

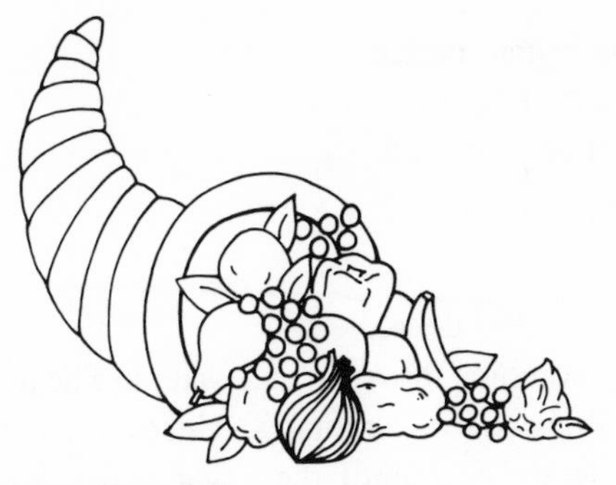

Coffee Crème Caramel

6 individual caramels or 1 8-inch flan

When cravings for this classic French dessert take over, it's nice to know there's a way to make it without all those egg yolks and fat. And I can vouch for the fact it still tastes good; some individuals I have served it to have eaten half the whole flan at one sitting. That's not recommended, however, when you are counting calories, because although the flan lacks fat, it still has sugar.

Caramel

2/3 cup sugar
1/4 cup water

Flan Mixture

3 tablespoons instant coffee
3 tablespoons boiling water
3 cups low-fat or skim milk
5 egg whites
1/2 cup sugar

Preheat the oven to 350 degrees.

For the caramel, combine the sugar and water in a heavy saucepan. Cook, covered, over high heat for 2 minutes. Uncover the pan and continue cooking over moderate heat until the sugar caramelizes—turns golden brown. Pour the caramel into 6 1/2-cup ramekins or one 8-inch cake pan and tilt to coat bottoms and sides. (Since molten sugar is extremely hot, you may wish to wear gloves to protect your hands.)

Meanwhile, in a small bowl dissolve the coffee in the boiling water. Scald the milk by heating it just until it is ready to boil.

In a large bowl, whisk together the egg whites and sugar. Whisk the hot milk, little by little, into the egg mixture. Whisk in the dissolved coffee.

Pour the coffee mixture into the ramekins or cake pan, filling to within 1/4 inch of the top.

Set the ramekins or cake pan in a roasting pan and pour boiling water into the roasting pan up to 1/2 inch deep. Bake the crème caramel for 40 to 60 minutes or until just set. (An inserted knife will come out clean when the crème caramel is done.) Add more boiling water to the pan if needed.

Let the crème caramel cool to room temperature, then refrigerate for at least 6 hours, preferably overnight. Just before serving, run the tip of a paring knife around the inside rim of each ramekin or the cake pan. Place a dessert plate over the ramekin or cake pan, invert, and give the ramekin or pan a firm shake. Lift the ramekin or pan; the crème caramel should slide right out.

Per serving:

Calories	219
Total fat	1.3 g
Saturated fat	.8 g
Cholesterol	4.9 mg
Sodium	108 mg

DOCTOR'S ADVICE

Sweet Tooth Better than Fat Tooth

If you have a sweet tooth, and fruit doesn't satisfy, eat a sugary food without the fat, advises Dr. George Blackburn, associate professor of surgery at Harvard Medical School. That means low-fat cake made with egg whites instead of cheesecake and ginger snaps instead of doughnuts. You'll still satisfy the sweet cravings without the added calories and hazards of fat. Plain old sugar, he says, is not as likely to put on weight or cause obesity or other medical problems as fat in foods.

Barley Cream Pudding

Serves 8

In parts of the Middle East barley is known as "good heart medicine." That's what Dr. Rosemary Newman, Montana State University, also found when she tested barley on volunteers. Their cholesterol went down, so she developed new recipes using barley and published them in a booklet, New Ways With Barley. *Her low-calorie barley pudding also contains apples, another known cholesterol lowerer.*

1/2 cup pearl barley
1 cup water
2 1/2 cups low-fat milk
1/4 cup raisins
1/4 cup chopped apples
1/4 cup brown sugar
1/4 teaspoon salt
3 tablespoons flour
1 teaspoon margarine or butter
1 teaspoon vanilla extract

Put the barley and water in a saucepan. Bring to a boil, cover, and simmer for 30 minutes. Add more water if necessary. Add the milk, raisins, and apples and bring to a boil again. Cover and reduce the heat to simmer for 15 minutes.

Stir in the sugar and the salt.

Remove 1 cup of the mixture and blend with the flour. Return to the pot and simmer for 5 minutes, stirring constantly. If the flour forms lumps, beat with a rotary beater for 1 minute. Cool slightly. Stir in the margarine and vanilla and serve warm or cold.

Per serving:

Calories	134
Total fat	1.5 g
Saturated fat	.6 g
Cholesterol	3 mg
Sodium	115 mg

Joan's Banana Bread Pudding

Serves 8

For a quick, easy, luscious low-fat dessert, here is my sister Joan's recommendation. It's fit for company because it looks gorgeous when it puffs up and browns. Yet you can put it together in a few minutes. And it's easy on the stomach. Bananas have been found to soothe the stomach, fighting dyspepsia and possibly helping ward off ulcers.

- 2 ripe bananas, sliced
- 10 slices baguette-size French bread with crust, about 1 inch thick
- 2 cups skim milk
- 2 eggs
- 1/2 cup maple syrup
- 1 tablespoon powdered sugar (optional)
- 1/4 teaspoon ground cinnamon (optional)

Preheat the oven to 375 degrees. Distribute the banana slices in the bottom of a 10-inch deep-dish pie plate. Cover the bananas with the bread slices.

Whip together the milk, eggs, and maple syrup. Pour over the bread and bananas, pushing the bread down to soak up the liquid.

Bake for about 30 minutes or until slightly browned and puffy and the liquid has been absorbed. For additional browning, run the pudding under the broiler for a couple of minutes.

Sprinkle the top with powdered sugar and cinnamon if desired.

Per serving:

Calories	243
Total fat	2.8 g
Saturated fat	.8 g
Cholesterol	56 mg
Sodium	304 mg

Egg White Chocolate Cake

Serves 8

For those who love chocolate but want to escape saturated fat and cholesterol, this cake is truly the answer. It is moist and dense with chocolate and as decadently satisfying as any cake I've ever had. The nuts, with their predominately monounsaturated fat, vegetable protein, fiber, and other compounds, have a variety of pharmacological benefits.

8 egg whites
1/2 teaspoon salt
1/2 cup unsweetened cocoa powder
1 cup sugar
3 tablespoons vegetable oil, preferably canola
1 cup coarsely chopped nuts (almonds, hazelnuts, walnuts, or a combination)
1/4 cup powdered sugar (optional)

Preheat the oven to 350 degrees.

Beat 6 of the egg whites with the salt until they hold firm peaks. Set aside.

Combine the cocoa with the sugar, oil, and remaining 2 egg whites in a large bowl. Add the nuts and mix well. Add one quarter of the beaten egg whites and mix to lighten. Fold in the remaining egg whites.

Oil a 9-inch cake pan. Cover the bottom of the pan with wax paper cut to fit. Lightly oil the top of the paper. Pour the batter into the cake pan.

Bake for approximately 30 minutes or until a knife inserted in the center comes out dry. Transfer to a wire rack to cool.

Invert on a cake plate to unmold. Remove wax paper. Reinvert and sprinkle the top with powdered sugar. Serve with fruit if desired.

Per serving:

Calories	282
Total fat	14.6 g
Saturated fat	2.1 g
Cholesterol	0
Sodium	194 mg

DOCTOR'S ADVICE

Don't deny sugar cravings if you suffer from premenstrual syndrome (PMS), says Judith Wurtman, Ph.D., a brain chemistry researcher at the Massachusetts Institute of Technology and a noted authority on carbohydrates and mood.

In recent tests she discovered that carbohydrates, including sugar, can dramatically relieve the symptoms of PMS. Women who were depressed, angry, hostile, fatigued, and weepy returned to normal moods within one hour after eating two cups of carbohydrate-rich cornflakes sweetened with glucose. "It was an amazing effect from a food," Wurtman says, "just like taking a Valium."

The theory is that eating carbohydrates leads to increased levels of a brain chemical called *serotonin*, which acts like a tranquilizer.

So, women with PMS mood swings should not deny a craving for carbohydrates, such as sweets, bread, potatoes, rice, pasta, and beans, says Dr. Wurtman. "That craving represents a cure for your PMS, not a cause."

Ginger Snaps

3 dozen cookies

Great-tasting and packed with high-fiber rice bran, these special ginger snaps were used experimentally as part of a diet to lower blood cholesterol by researcher Maren Hegsted and colleagues at Louisiana State University. They apparently worked. Average blood cholesterol dropped about 8 percent when a group of subjects ate these cookies as well as other rice bran foods. Each ginger snap contains 5 grams of bran and 1.2 grams of dietary fiber.

1 cup firmly packed brown sugar
3/4 cup vegetable oil
1/4 cup molasses
1 egg
1 1/2 cups all-purpose flour
1 1/2 cups rice bran
2 teaspoons baking soda
1 teaspoon ground cinnamon
1 teaspoon ground ginger
1/2 teaspoon ground cloves
3 tablespoons granulated sugar

Preheat the oven to 375 degrees. Combine the brown sugar, oil, molasses, and egg in a large mixer bowl. Beat until well mixed.

Combine the flour, bran, baking soda, cinnamon, ginger, and cloves. Add to the molasses mixture and mix on low speed for one minute or until thoroughly blended.

Form into 1-inch balls, roll in granulated sugar, and place on a greased cookie sheet. Bake for 6 to 8 minutes.

Per cookie:

Calories	105
Total fat	5.4 g
Saturated fat	.7 g
Cholesterol	6 mg
Sodium	50 mg

Lemony Garbanzo Bean Cake

Serves 8

Instead of traditional flour or grains, this cake uses garbanzo beans or chick-peas, one of the wealthiest beans in known health-protecting compounds. Yet it is moist and light-textured, and it comes from Mexico, according to the authors of The Brilliant Bean, *who gave us this brilliant recipe for what is truly a rich and wonderful-tasting cake.*

2 cups canned chick-peas, drained and rinsed, any loose skins discarded
4 eggs
1 cup sugar
1/2 teaspoon baking powder
Grated rind of 1 lemon
Juice of 1 lemon
Powdered sugar

Place the drained beans in a food processor fitted with the steel blade and puree. Add the eggs, sugar, baking powder, and lemon rind to the puree and pulse a few times just to combine the ingredients well.

Preheat the oven to 350 degrees. Butter a 9-inch cake pan. Cut a round of wax paper to fit the bottom of pan, set it in place, and butter the top side. Pour in the batter.

Bake on the center rack for 45 minutes or until a knife inserted in the center comes out dry.

Set on a wire rack to cool for 15 minutes, then remove the cake from the pan and allow to cool to room temperature.

Before serving, squeeze lemon juice over the cake and sprinkle generously with powdered sugar.

Per serving:

Calories	206
Total fat	3.2 g
Saturated fat	1 g
Cholesterol	106 mg
Sodium	238 mg

FOOD PHARMACY FACT

Bananas vs. Ulcers

Bananas have some mysterious substances that prevent ulcers in animals. A recent study by researchers at the University of New England in Australia noted that rats fed bananas and then fed high amounts of acid to induce ulcers had very little stomach damage. The bananas prevented 75 percent of the expected ulcers. Researchers believe the bananas somehow helped create a barrier between the stomach lining and the acid.

In other studies Indian physicians have successfully treated ulcers with powder made of unripe plantains, a larger member of the banana family.

Frozen Yogurts

The great advantage in making your own frozen yogurt is that you know for sure it has live, active cultures responsible for yogurt's multiple health benefits. Freezing does not destroy the cultures. However, some commercial frozen yogurts do not contain live cultures. You can also control the fat content when you make your own. It's easy to create frozen yogurt flavors; just use your imagination. Here are a couple of ideas to get you started.

FROZEN PEACH YOGURT

Serves 6

3 large fresh peaches (enough to make 2 cups peach puree)
2 cups plain nonfat or low-fat yogurt
2 tablespoons brown sugar
2 tablespoons Grand Marnier (optional)
1/2 teaspoon vanilla extract or to taste

Peel, pit, and slice the peaches and puree them in a blender.

Transfer the peach puree to a bowl and add the yogurt, brown sugar, and liqueur.

Blend thoroughly and freeze in an ice cream maker, such as a Donvier.

Per serving:

Calories	96
Total fat	.2 g
Saturated fat	.1 g
Cholesterol	1.5 mg
Sodium	59 mg

JILL'S FAVORITE PUMPKIN FROZEN YOGURT

Serves 6

This, of course, tastes a little like pumpkin pie and gives you an extra shot of pumpkin, which is chockful of beta-carotene, nature's antioxidant. This is the creation of my niece Jill.

2 cups plain nonfat yogurt
1 cup canned pumpkin puree
2 tablespoons sugar
6 tablespoons maple syrup
1 teaspoon ground cinnamon
1/2 teaspoon ground ginger
1/4 teaspoon ground cloves
Dash of salt

Mix together all ingredients and freeze, preferably in a Donvier ice cream maker.

Per serving:

Calories	124
Total fat	.3 g
Saturated fat	.2 g
Cholesterol	1.5 mg
Sodium	84 mg

Lemon Mousse

Serves 4

There's no better way to end a meal than with a cool, refreshing lemon mousse, and for years I have collected recipes for the same. Alas, I have given up the high-fat variety, and this low-fat recipe, made from thick, luscious yogurt, has become my new favorite. You can forgo the chocolate shavings if you wish, but chocolate and lemon do go together and this little bit is not likely to hurt you. This is a tart mousse; to make it sweeter, add more powdered sugar.

1 quart lemon nonfat or low-fat yogurt, strained overnight to make about 2 cups
1/3 cup powdered sugar
1/2 teaspoon grated lemon zest
1 tablespoon plain gelatin
2 1/2 tablespoons lemon juice
3 tablespoons semisweet chocolate shavings

Gently mix together the lemon yogurt, sugar, and lemon zest.

Dissolve the gelatin in the lemon juice and add to the yogurt mixture. Chill and serve topped by chocolate shavings.

Note: If gelatin has been added to the yogurt, it will not drain and become thick. Consult the label to be sure there's no gelatin.

Per serving:

Calories	213
Total fat	3.2 g
Saturated fat	2 g
Cholesterol	5 mg
Sodium	176 mg

Phyllis's Strawberry Sherbet

Serves 4

You can whip up this sherbet in a jiffy to end a dinner party, as my friend Phyllis Bonanno often does; it looks beautiful when mounded into a large glass bowl. The vanilla yogurt is already sweetened. If you wish more sweetness, you can simply add a little sugar or a tablespoon or two of frozen orange juice concentrate, says Phyllis. You can buy the strawberries already frozen or simply put fresh ones and the banana slices in separate plastic bags and pop them in the freezer.

1 pound frozen strawberries (about 3 cups)
1 banana, sliced and frozen
3 tablespoons vanilla nonfat yogurt

Put all the ingredients in a food processor fitted with the steel blade and process until smooth. Serve immediately.

Per serving:

Calories	75
Total fat	.2 g
Saturated fat	.1 g
Cholesterol	.3 mg
Sodium	10 mg

FOOD PHARMACY FACT

Pain-Killing Sugar

Scientists have long suspected that eating sugar and other carbohydrates affects brain chemistry through a complicated mechanism that boosts levels of a brain neurotransmitter called serotonin. Serotonin is known as a "calming" chemical.

But some researchers also think that sugar may have a more direct effect on the brain by activating natural painkillers. One bit of evidence: Researchers at Cornell University recently found that a few drops of sugar water virtually eliminated crying among a small group of newborn infants in a hospital nursery. Using a syringe, the researchers gave the crying infants a drop of either plain water or a water solution of 14 percent sugar once every minute for five minutes.

The babies who got the sugar water immediately stopped crying and remained quiet for about five minutes. The babies who got the unsweetened water cried on.

In another test the researchers found that a sugar solution was three to five times more effective at stopping the infant's crying than a pacifier was.

Psychologist Elliott Blass, who directed the study, suspects the sugar may activate natural "opioid" chemicals in the brain that reduce pain and distress.

FOOD PHARMACY FACT

Apples Suppress Blood Pressure and Stroke

For twenty years Japanese researcher Naosuke Sasaki, professor emeritus at the Hirosaki University School of Medicine in Hirosaki, Japan, has tracked the blood pressure in more than 2,400 villagers in two adjoining prefectures in northeast Japan. In the prefecture of Aomori farmers eat lots of apples. In Akita prefecture they do not, preferring rice instead. Dr. Sasaki has found that those eating less than one apple a day tend to develop typical high blood pressure as they age. But villagers eating one to two apples a day had only modest increases in blood pressure. And those eating three or more apples a day did not have the expected high blood pressure. Furthermore, apple eaters of Aomori had a much lower stroke rate. Dr. Sasaki theorizes that something in the apples—perhaps potassium—helped counteract the blood-pressure-raising effects of a high-sodium, liberal-soy-sauce diet.

Breads, Muffins, Biscuits, and Crackers

Squash Bread

1 loaf (16 slices)

This is a welcome and health-promoting change from carrot bread. Yellow summer squash, like carrot, has antioxidants, including beta-carotene and newly studied quercetin, linked to helping block numerous disease processes. This bread is also low-fat since the liquid comes from yogurt and egg whites.

1 cup whole wheat flour
1½ teaspoons baking powder
1 teaspoon baking soda
1 cup coarsely grated yellow (crookneck) squash (about ⅔ pound)
½ cup plain low-fat yogurt
2 teaspoons lemon juice
1½ teaspoons ground cinnamon
½ teaspoon ground nutmeg
½ teaspoon ground cardamom
½ teaspoon salt (optional)
2 tablespoons molasses
3 egg whites

Preheat the oven to 350 degrees. In a large bowl, stir together the flour, baking powder, and baking soda. Stir in the grated squash, yogurt, lemon juice, spices, salt, and molasses.

Beat the egg whites in a small bowl until foaming and stir them into the squash mixture. Pour the mixture into a nonstick 9- by 4-inch loaf pan.

Bake for 40 minutes. Cool on a rack for 15 minutes, then remove from pan.

Per slice:

Calories	44
Total fat	.3 g
Saturated fat	1.7 g
Cholesterol	.4 mg
Sodium	107 mg

Corn Bread

Serves 8

I'm always looking for the perfect corn bread recipe, and this may be it. It has come along just in time, considering that scientists are finding that the fiber in corn lowers blood cholesterol just about as well as other grain fibers, such as those found in oat and rice bran. It was an unexpected finding because the fiber in corn is largely insoluble, which scientists did not think could lower cholesterol. This recipe makes an old-fashioned-type grainy corn bread that crumbles just the way I like it. Don't make it in the microwave—it comes out the texture of soft cake.

1 cup skim milk
1 egg
2 tablespoons butter or margarine, melted
1 cup yellow cornmeal
1 cup flour
1 tablespoon baking powder
1 teaspoon salt (less if desired)
2 tablespoons maple syrup *or* 1 teaspoon sugar (omit sweeteners when using for stuffing)

Preheat the oven to 425 degrees.

In a large bowl, whisk together the milk, egg, and melted butter or margarine.

In another bowl, mix together the cornmeal, flour, baking powder, and salt.

Stir the wet ingredients into the dry ingredients just until the ingredients are combined.

Turn the batter into a greased 8-inch square cake pan and bake for about 25 minutes or until the top is lightly browned and a knife inserted in the corn bread comes out clean.

Per serving:

Calories	179
Total fat	4 g
Saturated fat	2 g
Cholesterol	35 mg
Sodium	489 mg

FOOD PHARMACY FACT

I Say Bananas, You Say Potatoes

When men with normal blood pressure were put on low-potassium diets for nine days, their blood pressure went up, according to Dr. G. Gopal Krishna and colleagues at Temple University in Philadelphia. Their blood pressure returned to normal when they ate normal amounts of potassium for another nine days. Interestingly, when they got little potassium, they retained sodium. That may be why their blood pressure went up, says Dr. Krishna. Thus he theorizes that potassium can help offset the risk of table salt. Both bananas and white potatoes are super sources of potassium. For others, see page 21.

Banana-Ginger Muffins

12 muffins

In case you need more reasons to make these muffins than the fact they taste so good (especially warm): Bananas are high in fiber and potassium; potassium seems to help control high blood pressure. And ginger, according to new tests, may help soothe the pain of arthritis.

1 cup whole wheat flour
1½ teaspoons baking powder
1 teaspoon baking soda
2 or 3 ripe bananas, mashed or pureed (1 cup)
2 tablespoons frozen unsweetened orange juice concentrate
½ cup low-fat or nonfat plain yogurt
1 teaspoon ground ginger
1 teaspoon ground nutmeg
1 tablespoon honey
3 egg whites, beaten until foamy and thick

Preheat the oven to 350 degrees.

Sift the flour, baking powder, and baking soda into a large bowl. Add the bananas, orange juice concentrate, yogurt, ginger, nutmeg, and honey. Mix well. Stir the beaten egg whites into the batter.

Pour the mixture into nonstick muffin pans or pans sprayed with oil. Bake for about 25 minutes.

Per serving:

Calories	73
Total fat	.5 g
Saturated fat	2.5 g
Cholesterol	.6 mg
Sodium	143 mg

Barbara Bush's Bran Muffins

4½ dozen muffins

Yes, this is what George and Barbara often eat for breakfast, according to The Washington Post, *and a good choice it is. The miller's or unprocessed wheat bran is the best natural laxative in existence. Additionally, there's compelling evidence the bran helps combat the early stages of colon cancer. The raisins also have anticancer properties. Just as the White House chef does for the Bushes, you can freeze these muffins and use as wanted.*

5 cups whole wheat flour
7½ cups miller's bran
2 tablespoons baking powder
1½ teaspoons salt
2 cups raisins
10 eggs
1½ cups honey
1 quart skim milk
⅔ cup vegetable oil
1½ teaspoons vanilla extract

Preheat the oven to 375 degrees.

In a bowl, mix the flour, bran, baking powder, salt, and raisins. Add the remaining ingredients and stir until blended.

Spoon the batter into lightly greased muffin tins and bake for 20 to 25 minutes.

Per muffin:

Calories	159
Total fat	4.8 g
Saturated fat	.8 g
Cholesterol	39.7 mg
Sodium	132 mg

FOOD PHARMACY FACT

New Cancer Fighters in Bran

Scientists have discovered a couple of specific agents in wheat bran that may help explain why it seems to protect against cancer, notably colon cancer. University of Maryland School of Medicine investigators found that phytic acid, a compound concentrated in wheat bran, reduced cancers in animals by 35 percent.

Norwegian scientists, in conditions simulating the human stomach, found that wheat bran (the amount found in two slices of whole wheat bread) reduced concentrations of nitrite, which reacts in the stomach with other substances to form cancer-causing nitrosamines. One wheat component that reduced nitrite was ferulic acid, shown in other studies to be anticancer.

Three-Grain Super-Fiber Muffins

12 muffins

Dr. Rosemary Newman, a barley researcher at Montana State University, came up with this super muffin to give you fiber from three different grains all in one muffin—soluble gum fiber, or beta-glucans in barley and oat bran to fight cholesterol and heart disease, and insoluble wheat fiber in whole grain flour and All-Bran to keep you regular and ward off colon cancer.

¾ cup barley flour
½ cup whole wheat flour
½ teaspoon baking powder
1 teaspoon baking soda
¼ teaspoon salt
¼ cup sugar
½ cup All-Bran cereal
½ cup oat bran cereal
1 cup buttermilk
1 egg
¼ cup molasses
¼ cup butter or margarine
½ cup raisins

Preheat the oven to 400 degrees.

Combine the barley flour, whole wheat flour, baking powder, baking soda, salt, and sugar. Set aside.

Combine the All-Bran, oat bran, and buttermilk. Let stand for 2 minutes or until the cereal is moistened.

Add the egg, molasses, and butter or margarine to the moistened cereal. Beat at medium speed until combined.

Stir the raisins into the cereal mixture. Then add the flour mixture. Beat at low speed just until moistened.

Put the batter into greased muffin cups and bake for 15 to 20 minutes or until lightly browned.

Per serving:

Calories	146
Total fat	5 g
Saturated fat	2.7 g
Cholesterol	29 mg
Sodium	232 mg

FOOD PHARMACY FACT

All-Bran vs. Colon Cancer

In an important first, researchers found that eating a high-fiber diet, including two bowls of Kellogg's All-Bran cereal a day, suppressed precancerous growths in the colon that can erupt into full-blown colon and rectal cancer. So discovered Dr. Jerome J. De Cosse, a surgeon at the New York Hospital–Cornell Medical Center in 1989. In his four-year study of fifty-eight patients at high risk for colon cancer because they were prone to developing precancerous growths or polyps, one group ate about twenty-two grams of fiber daily (most of it in All-Bran) and another, twelve grams—typical among Americans.

Within six months Dr. De Cosse observed that those on the high-fiber diet had fewer and smaller polyps. Within three years polyps had shrunk even more. Medical belief is that if you can keep polyps away, the bowel cancer cannot grow. Several surveys of dietary practices have found links between higher intakes of cereal fiber and lower rates of colon cancer. This is the first substantial proof that the cereal is indeed the active preventive agent.

Maxine's Apple-Bran Muffins

14 muffins

These muffins are made from the stuff that was found effective in shrinking the precancerous signs of colon cancer in a recent study. That's right—All-Bran. More than twenty studies done around the world show that people who eat more high-fiber wheat bran, like All-Bran and miller's bran, are less likely to develop colon cancer. Here's a wonderful-tasting high-fiber wheat bran muffin that includes spices and apples.

1 cup all-purpose flour
1/2 cup whole wheat flour
1 cup wheat bran cereal (such as All-Bran)
1/4 teaspoon salt
1 teaspoon ground cinnamon
1/4 teaspoon ground cloves
1 teaspoon baking soda
1 cup coarsely chopped Golden Delicious apple (or other sweet apple)
1 egg, lightly beaten
3/4 cup low-fat buttermilk
1 tablespoon molasses
1/4 cup golden raisins, plumped in 1/2 cup frozen and thawed apple juice concentrate for 15 minutes

Preheat the oven to 350 degrees. In a large bowl, stir together the flours, bran cereal, salt, spices, baking soda, and chopped apple.

Beat the egg in a small bowl and add the molasses, plumped raisins, and apple juice concentrate.

Stir the egg mixture into the dry ingredients.

Spoon the batter into a nonstick or paper-lined muffin pan. Fill about three-quarters full.

Bake for 20 minutes. Remove the muffins from the pan and cool on a rack.

Per muffin:

Calories	106
Total fat	.9 g
Saturated fat	.2 g
Cholesterol	16 mg
Sodium	175 mg

COOK'S ADVICE

Apples Are Good for You Cooked or Raw

It matters little whether you eat the apple raw or cooked as far as getting its fiber is concerned, says Ruth Matthews, an expert on food fiber at the U.S. Department of Agriculture. "Cooked apples should be as effective as raw apples in lowering cholesterol," she says. "If you eat the whole apple, either raw or cooked, baked or as applesauce or whatever, you still get the same amount of fiber."

Dr. Rosenthal's Blues-Fighting Muffins

1 dozen muffins

These muffins may put you in a good mood, literally, according to Dr. Norman Rosenthal, a depression expert at the National Institute of Mental Health and author of Seasons of the Mind: Why You Get the Winter Blues and What You Can Do About It. *One thing, he says, that may help if you are subject to light-deprivation-type winter depressions is to snack on high-carbohydrate foods. In Rosenthal's tests depressed patients who did that seemed to pep up, have more energy, and feel less fatigued and depressed. High in oat bran, which makes them dense and grainy like corn bread, these muffins are also likely to put a dent in your cholesterol.*

- 2 1/4 cups uncooked oat bran cereal
- 1/4 cup raisins
- 2 teaspoons baking powder
- 1/2 teaspoon salt (optional)
- 3/4 cup skim milk
- 1/3 cup honey
- 2 eggs, beaten
- 1 tablespoon vegetable oil, preferably canola oil

Preheat the oven to 425 degrees.

In a large bowl, combine the oat bran cereal, raisins, baking powder, and salt. Add the remaining ingredients and mix just until the dry ingredients are moistened.

Coat a muffin pan with nonstick spray or line with paper baking cups. Fill the prepared muffin cups almost full. Bake for 15 to 17 minutes or until golden brown.

Per muffin:

Calories	127
Total fat	3 g
Saturated fat	.5 g
Cholesterol	36 mg
Sodium	91 mg

FOOD PHARMACY FACT

Sweet Cure for the Winter Blues

Eating carbohydrates—sweets and starches—can help relieve a type of depression known as *seasonal affective disorder* (*SAD*), according to Dr. Norman Rosenthal, a psychiatrist at the National Institute of Mental Health.

Such depression, also called "the winter blues," strikes during dark winter days when sunlight is scarce, and it affects about thirty-five million Americans. In tests Dr. Rosenthal found that such depressed patients pepped up—had more energy and less fatigue and tension—within two hours of downing six cookies containing a hefty 105 grams of carbohydrate. In contrast, normal people eating the cookies felt more lethargic and drowsy.

Theory holds that victims of such depression have changes in brain chemistry that are somewhat reversed by eating foods high in carbohydrates. Dr. Rosenthal's advice: if you crave carbohydrates in winter, eat them; you'll feel better. And never go on a low-carbohydrate diet in the winter. Depression-alleviating high-carbohydrate foods include not only sugary sweets but also more nutritious starchy foods, like dried beans, pasta, cereal, bread, and crackers.

OAT BRAN DOES WORK!

If you're worried about high cholesterol, oat bran may make a dent. Fully eight out of nine studies on humans—and countless studies on animals—have documented that.

A much-quoted Northwestern University study found that oat bran lowered cholesterol about 3 percent over and above a low-fat diet. Other studies found much greater results. A study at the College of Medicine at the University of California in Irvine compared the effect of muffins made from oat bran, wheat bran, or mixed wheat and oat. In the double-blind study seventy-two medical student volunteers ate two muffins per day for twenty-eight days. Each oat bran muffin had five grams of dietary fiber, the amount in one rounded tablespoon of oat bran. Oat bran eaters saw their total cholesterol drop 5 percent, their bad-type LDL cholesterol sink 9 percent, and their triglycerides go down by 8 percent. Their good-type HDL cholesterol did not change. On the other hand the cholesterol of the wheat and wheat-oat muffin eaters stayed the same, and their triglycerides rose 6 percent.

Dr. James Anderson, University of Kentucky pioneer in oat bran studies, found that one-and-a-half ounces of oat bran daily depressed cholesterol by an average of 20 percent.

Then, in early 1990, along came a Harvard study claiming that oat bran was no better than a wheat cereal like cream of wheat in reducing cholesterol. Both reduced cholesterol about 7 percent, but researchers insisted it was because the oat bran and the cream of wheat both replaced fat in the diet that would ordinarily drive up cholesterol. However, a peculiarity of the study was that the subjects all had fairly low cholesterol—an average of 186—and there were only twenty-one subjects. What the study may prove is that oat bran does not further lower cholesterol when it is already that low—or, as one expert said, in people who don't really need to have it lowered.

Yet a subsequent study at the University of Syracuse did bring up another critical point: oat bran does not work equally well on everyone. In that study by Dr. Wendy Demark-Wahnefried of seventy-one men and women with high cholesterol, oat bran worked as well as a low-fat diet. Eating 1.7 ounces of ordinary oat bran or 1.5 ounces of Quaker's high-fiber oat bran cold cereal daily reduced cholesterol an average of 10 to 17 percent—about the same as cutting down on fatty foods. Still, for some oat bran was a health bonanza, driving down their cholesterol by eighty to one hundred points.

The bottom line: oat bran, especially in small amounts, is not a universal cholesterol cure-all. But it does work to varying degrees in many people. If it works for you, use it.

Oatmeal Biscuits

About 16 biscuits

In the Midwest, where I grew up, biscuits were made more healthful and crunchier by adding oats. Here is the recipe my sister Judy uses.

- 1½ cups sifted flour
- 1 tablespoon baking powder
- 1 teaspoon salt (less if desired)
- ⅓ cup shortening
- ½ cup uncooked quick or old-fashioned oats
- ⅔ cup skim milk

Preheat the oven to 450 degrees.

Sift the flour, baking powder, and salt together into a large bowl. Cut in the shortening until the mixture looks like large crumbs. Stir in the oats. Add the milk and combine with a fork to make a soft dough.

Put the dough on a lightly floured surface and knead with your fingertips about 10 times. With a rolling pin, roll the dough to a ½-inch thickness. Using a floured 2-inch round cutter, cut biscuits. Place them on an ungreased cookie sheet and bake for 8 to 10 minutes or until lightly browned.

Per biscuit:

Calories	90
Total fat	4.5 g
Saturated fat	1 g
Cholesterol	.2 mg
Sodium	223 mg

Oat Bran–Oatmeal Crackers

About 40 crackers

Here's a quick, pleasant, unusual way to get your quota of oat bran and oatmeal, both of which are good for your heart. These crackers are surprisingly easy to make, even if you've never thought of making crackers before. And they have received raves from friends who are not even worried about high cholesterol. For flavor you can use the seeds of your choice. In an informal test a group of friends preferred the caraway seeds. I like the flavor from the aniseeds best. You can serve them with soup, with dips, or as just plain good "eating crackers."

1 cup oat bran
1½ cups old-fashioned rolled oats
2 teaspoons aniseeds or caraway, dill, or fennel seeds
1 tablespoon vegetable oil
½ cup water
Coarse salt to taste

Preheat the oven to 325 degrees.

In a bowl, mix the oat bran and 1 cup of the rolled oats. Add the aniseeds, oil, and water and stir into a dough.

Sprinkle ¼ cup of the remaining oats on a counter or pastry sheet. Place the dough on top of the oats. Pat the dough out slightly and top with the remaining oats. Roll out the dough until ⅛ inch thick. Sprinkle with coarse salt to taste. (Note: The oats on the bottom and top of the dough make it easier to roll out, and are especially important on top because when baked they turn a nice golden brown.)

Using a 2-inch cutter, cut out rounds. Put the rounds on an ungreased baking sheet and bake in the middle of the oven for about 35 minutes. Remove the crackers from the baking sheet and let them cool.

Per cracker:

Calories	21
Total fat	.7 g
Saturated fat	.1 g
Cholesterol	0
Sodium	.2 mg

FOOD PHARMACY FACT

Oatmeal Equals Oat Bran

An amazing, often overlooked fact is that in a prominent study proclaiming the cholesterol-lowering powers of oat bran, plain oatmeal actually worked as well. The study was done by Linda V. Van Horn and colleagues at the Northwestern University Medical School with 200 middle-aged subjects averaging blood cholesterol of 208. All were on a low-fat diet; additionally, some ate oat bran or oatmeal.

In both cases cholesterol dropped an additional 3 percent. Yet the amount of fiber in the oat bran was more than double that of the oatmeal. The researchers were at a loss to explain the mystery of why oat bran then did not pack twice the cholesterol-lowering punch. Perhaps it's not all in the fiber.

FOOD PHARMACY FACT

Here Comes Rice Bran!

Rice bran—the stuff that is removed from the kernel when brown rice is converted to white rice—can reduce blood cholesterol about as well as oat bran, according to animal and human studies. That also helps confirm that brown rice does more for your heart than white rice.

First researchers at the U.S. Department of Agriculture in California discovered that rice bran depressed blood cholesterol in hamsters. Then tests at the University of California at Davis found that cholesterol fell an average of 8 percent in a group of men and women with high cholesterol (230 to 310) who ate three ounces of rice bran daily for six weeks. Most important, the reduction was due entirely to a drop in harmful-type LDL cholesterol. Rice bran also pushed down another blood component, apolipoprotein-B, which has been linked to heart disease. In the study rice bran rivaled oat bran in effectiveness; however, rice bran, unlike oat bran, raised triglycerides, another blood fat linked to heart disease, especially in older women.

Rice Bran Rolls

6 rolls

Take the outer coating off a grain of brown rice and you have rice bran. That's what these rolls are made with. Rice bran, like oat bran and barley, is rich in soluble fiber and has been shown to help lower blood cholesterol. Each roll in this recipe contains 10 grams of bran and 5.1 grams of dietary fiber. Thanks to researchers at Louisiana State University for the recipe used in cholesterol-lowering studies.

1 1/4-ounce package active dry yeast
1 1/4 cups warm water (about 110 degrees)
1 tablespoon sugar
3 tablespoons nonfat dry milk
1 teaspoon salt (less if desired)
1 tablespoon vegetable shortening
3/4 cup rice bran
2 1/2 to 3 1/2 cups bread flour

Dissolve the yeast in the warm water and let stand for 10 minutes.

Combine the sugar, dry milk, salt, and shortening. Add the softened yeast and mix until blended. Add the bran and then the flour; mix until the dough is smooth and elastic.

Let the dough rise in a warm place for approximately 1 hour or until double in bulk. Punch the dough down and shape it into 6 rolls. Place on greased baking sheets. Let rise again for approximately 1 1/2 hours or until double in bulk.

Preheat the oven to 400 degrees and bake the rolls for 30 to 40 minutes or until the rolls are golden brown and sound hollow when tapped on the bottom.

Per roll:

Calories	276
Total fat	5.2 g
Saturated fat	1 g
Cholesterol	.4 mg
Sodium	381 mg

Beverages

Orange-Banana Frappé

2 8-ounce servings

This shake—morning, noon, or night—gives your body a jolt of potassium to help ward off high blood pressure and strokes.

1 cup orange juice
1 banana, peeled and cut into chunks
4 dried apricots (8 halves)
½ cup plain nonfat or low-fat yogurt

Put all the ingredients in a blender and whirl until smooth.

Per serving:

Calories	173
Total fat	.5 g
Saturated fat	.2 g
Cholesterol	1 mg
Sodium	46 mg

Cool Yogurt Drinks

In India they call it lassi, in Turkey ayran (eyé-ran). In any language it is delicious and so good for you—yogurt whipped together with water or juices into a cool drink. After returning from Turkey, where ayran is a popular drink, I kept right on drinking it. Here are some of my favorite combinations.

PLAIN AYRAN

1 8-ounce serving

½ cup plain nonfat or low-fat yogurt
½ cup cold water

Whip the yogurt and water together in a blender.

Per serving:

Calories	64
Total fat	.2 g
Saturated fat	.2 g
Cholesterol	2.3 mg
Sodium	86 mg

FRUIT YOGURT DRINK

1 8-ounce serving

½ cup plain nonfat or low-fat yogurt
½ banana *or* ½ cup of any of the following:

- fresh or frozen strawberries, raspberries, blueberries, or peaches
- fresh papaya or cantaloupe
- fresh or canned pineapple chunks
- orange juice
- pineapple juice

- guava juice
- prune juice
- any other juice or fruit that strikes your fancy alone or in combination

Whip the yogurt and fruit together in a blender.

Per serving:

Calories	115
Total fat	.5 g
Saturated fat	.3 g
Cholesterol	2.3 mg
Sodium	87 mg

Fruit Fizzes

Real carbonated juices—what a treat, and what a difference from the fruit-deficient soft drinks. When mixing fruit and fruit juices to make healthful drinks, there is no end to what you can create. To launch your experimentation, here are five samples that my guests have liked. You can serve them with or without ice. For celebratory occasions you can also mix them with champagne instead of seltzer water.

MELON-CITRUS FIZZ

About 4 8-ounce servings

1 medium honeydew melon, very ripe
1 cup orange juice
2 tablespoons lime juice
2 teaspoons honey
Seltzer water

Halve the melon, discard the seeds, and scoop the flesh into a food processor fitted with the steel blade. Puree until smooth.

Add the orange juice, lime juice, and honey and blend. Pour into a container and chill.

To serve, mix 2 parts juice with 1 part seltzer water.

Per serving:

Calories	100
Total fat	.2 g
Saturated fat	0
Cholesterol	0
Sodium	18 mg

FOOD PHARMACY FACT

Fruit Zaps Appetite

Dieters, you may be better off drinking a 100-calorie fruit juice than a zero-calorie diet soft drink. That's because the sugar in fruit—fructose—stifles appetite. In a test Dr. Judith Rodin, Yale University, had two dozen men and women drink a lemonade-flavored drink with different sweeteners, including fructose and aspartame, used in diet sodas. About forty minutes later the subjects were offered a buffet and told to eat until "comfortably full."

The fructose drinkers generally ate 20 to 40 percent fewer calories than those who consumed aspartame. And that more than compensated for the 200 calories in the fructose drink itself, said Dr. Rodin. Most important, after drinking fruit fructose the subjects chose fewer ultra-fattening foods like ham, cheese, and cookies.

PINEAPPLE-GRAPEFRUIT FIZZ

3 8-ounce servings

1 16-ounce can pineapple tidbits in natural juice, drained and juice reserved
1 cup grapefruit juice
1/4 teaspoon ground allspice (more if desired)
1/2 cup pineapple juice
Seltzer water

Finely chop the pineapple in a food processor fitted with the steel blade. Add 1/2 cup of the grapefruit juice and the allspice and puree.

Add the remaining grapefruit juice and the pineapple juice, blend, and chill.

To serve, mix 2 parts juice with 1 part seltzer.

Per serving:

Calories	122
Total fat	.2 g
Saturated fat	0
Cholesterol	0
Sodium	2.4 mg

SPICED PEACH FIZZ

4 8-ounce servings

1 cup water
2 tablespoons sugar
6 peppercorns
6 cloves
6 allspice berries
3 cups sliced peeled very ripe peaches *or* 1 16-ounce bag frozen sliced peaches, thawed
Seltzer water

Bring the water, sugar, and spices to a boil in a small saucepan. Reduce the heat and simmer for 20 minutes. Strain the syrup and cool.

Put the peaches and cooled syrup in a food processor fitted with the steel blade and blend until smooth. Chill.

To serve, mix equal parts juice and seltzer water.

Per serving:

Calories	80
Total fat	.1 g
Saturated fat	0
Cholesterol	0
Sodium	.5 mg

CRANBERRY-CHERRY FIZZ

About 5 8-ounce servings

1 16-ounce bag frozen pitted cherries, thawed (do not drain)
1 cup cranberry juice cocktail
½ tablespoon honey or sugar
¼ teaspoon ground cinnamon
¼ teaspoon ground allspice
Seltzer water

Put the cherries in a food processor fitted with the steel blade and blend until smooth. Add ½ cup of the cranberry juice, the honey, cinnamon, and allspice; blend. Add the remaining cranberry juice, blend, and chill.

To serve, mix equal parts of juice and seltzer water.

Per serving:

Calories	100
Total fat	.9 g
Saturated fat	.2 g
Cholesterol	0
Sodium	1.2 mg

CANTALOUPE-ORANGE FIZZ

6 8-ounce servings

1 very ripe medium cantaloupe
2 tablespoons frozen orange or other citrus juice concentrate
1 tablespoon honey
½ teaspoon ground cinnamon
¼ teaspoon ground cardamom
Seltzer water

Halve the cantaloupe, discard the seeds, and scoop the flesh into a food processor fitted with the steel blade. Blend until smooth. Add the juice concentrate, honey, cinnamon, and cardamom and blend. Pour into a container and chill.

To serve, mix equal parts juice and seltzer water.

Per serving:

Calories	52
Total fat	.3 g
Saturated fat	0
Cholesterol	0
Sodium	8.4 mg

Fruit Slushes

Here are two other ways that you can use fruit and fruit juices to make healthful beverages.

STRAWBERRY-PINEAPPLE SLUSH

4 4-ounce servings

1½ cups sliced strawberries
Juice of 1 lemon
2 tablespoons sugar
1 cup pineapple juice

BANANA-ORANGE SLUSH

4 4-ounce servings

1 ripe banana, sliced
Juice of 1 lemon
¼ cup sugar
1 cup orange juice

Orange slices, fresh mint leaves, pineapple wedges, or strawberries for garnish (optional)

Using a blender or a food processor fitted with the steel blade, combine the fruit, lemon juice, and sugar. Blend well. Slowly add the fruit juice, blending until smooth.

Pour the mixture into a bowl or large measuring cup, cover, and freeze for about 1 hour.

Just before serving, stir to break up the chunks and spoon into glasses or small cups. Garnish with orange slices, mint leaves, pineapple wedges, or strawberries.

Per serving (strawberry-pineapple):

Calories	75
Total fat	.2 g
Saturated fat	0
Cholesterol	0
Sodium	1 mg

Per serving (banana-orange):

Calories	104
Total fat	.2 g
Saturated fat	0
Cholesterol	0
Sodium	1 mg

Creamy Fruit Cooler

Serves 2

1 cup fruit (raspberries, peaches, strawberries, etc.)
1/4 cup sugar
1/2 teaspoon vanilla extract
1 cup skim milk
1/2 cup water
6 ice cubes
Ground nutmeg (preferably freshly grated) or ground cinnamon plus 2 slices of fruit for garnish (optional)

Place all the ingredients except ice cubes and garnishes in a blender and blend until smooth. Add the ice cubes, one at a time, and blend until smooth.

Sprinkle with nutmeg or cinnamon and garnish with a slice of fruit. Serve immediately.

Per serving:

Calories	204
Total fat	4.4 g
Saturated fat	2.5 g
Cholesterol	17 mg
Sodium	60 mg

Holiday Punch

2 quarts

1 cup fresh orange juice
Juice of 2 lemons
2 cups cranberry juice cocktail
1 cup superfine sugar
1 quart chilled club soda
Lemon and orange slices or other fresh fruit for garnish (optional)

In a large pitcher, combine the juices and the sugar. Stir to dissolve the sugar. Add ice and pour in the club soda. Garnish with fresh fruit.

Per ½-cup serving:

Calories	74
Total fat	.06 g
Saturated fat	0
Cholesterol	0
Sodium	13 mg

Sauces and Dressings

Fresh Cocktail Sauce

Serves 16

Dipping seafood into this cocktail sauce can help clear your sinuses and may help relieve the stuffed-up symptoms of a cold. The more horseradish you use, the better it works. Horseradish is a well-known cold remedy in the Soviet Union and Middle European countries.

2 medium onions, minced
1 large green bell pepper, minced
1 tablespoon vegetable oil
3 large tomatoes, peeled, seeded, and chopped
2 teaspoons sugar
Salt and freshly ground pepper to taste *or* 1 teaspoon each
2 tablespoons red wine vinegar
1 6-ounce can tomato paste
½ cup prepared horseradish

In a saucepan, sauté the onions and pepper in the oil for 5 minutes, or until the onions are translucent and the pepper is soft. Add the tomatoes and cover. Simmer for 5 to 10 minutes, until tender.

Uncover and add the sugar, salt, pepper, vinegar, and tomato paste. Boil, uncovered, stirring until the mixture has thickened, about 4 minutes.

Let cool in a nonaluminum bowl. If you're going to serve it immediately, stir in the horseradish. (It's best to add it at the last minute so it doesn't lose any of its oomph!)

In a blender or a food processor fitted with the steel blade, blend the mixture until it is the consistency you like, either chunky or smooth.

Per serving:

Calories	32
Total fat	1 g
Saturated fat	.1 g
Cholesterol	0
Sodium	94 mg

A HOT PEPPER PRIMER

Anaheim: Also called California green or chiles verdes and, when ripe, chili Colorado. Mildly hot. About seven inches long by on-and-a-half inches wide. Known as a stuffing pepper, often used for chiles rellenos.

Ancho: Moderately hot, from three to four inches long and two to three inches wide, dark red to almost black. Made by drying poblano chilies.

Arbol: Very hot. Dried bright red chili, small and slender like a green bean.

Cayenne: Also called finger chili, bird pepper, and ginnie pepper. Fiery, bright red, and slender. Can be used fresh or dried; it is the pepper ground into cayenne pepper, commonly used.

Cherry pepper: Also called Hungarian cherry pepper, bird cherry, and Creole cherry pepper. Medium to very hot. Cherry-shaped, about two inches in diameter. It is used both green and red-ripe.

Chipotle: Fiery, dried, smoked jalapeño, commonly canned in tomato sauce.

Guajillo: Moderately hot. Slender, about four to six inches long, dried reddish-brown chili.

Habanero: Also called Scotch bonnets. The hottest chili pepper in the world. It's walnut-size, yellow to light green, lantern-shaped, and is found in the Yucatan Peninsula of Mexico, where it is used in sauces. Also common cooked or raw in the cuisine of Cuba, Jamaica, Puerto Rico, and Haiti. When still green the habanero is up to five times more tongue-blistering than a jalapeño pepper; when ripe and red, the habanero's fire-power is magnified ten times.

Jalapeño: Fairly hot. An American favorite, about two inches long, dark green, used raw or cooked.

Mulato: Spicy, earthy flavor resembling chocolate. Triangle-shaped, three to four inches long, heavily wrinkled, dark brown to black skin. Used in Mexican mole poblano.

New Mexico red: Also known as wreath chilies because they are often tied in wreaths.

Poblano: Large—about five inches long—dark green, mildly hot, the pepper of choice for chiles rellenos.

Serrano: Also called chili verde. Slightly hotter than jalapeño, with a delayed action bite. Bright green, smaller than a jalapeño. Can be substituted for jalapeños.

Spices from Chili Peppers: **Ancho**, dark maroon, used in most commercial chili powders; **cayenne**, red, extra hot; **paprika**, usually mild; **chipotle**, smoked dried jalapeño, brick red, very hot.

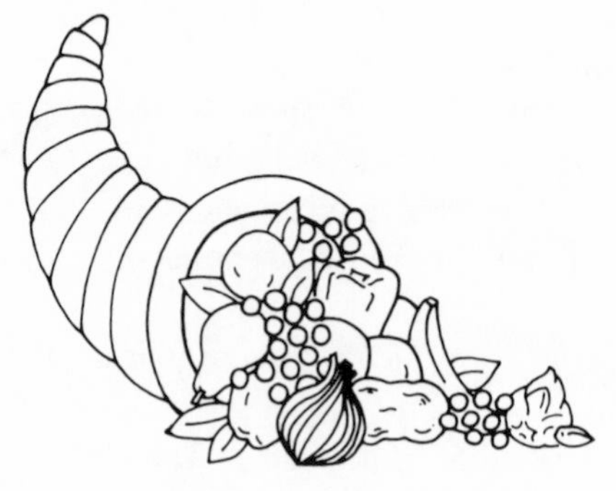

Salsa Cruda (Mexican Hot Sauce)

Serves 4

This simple sauce is a staple of Mexico and is served in Mexican restaurants everywhere. It's great as a dip for chips or served with fajitas, tacos, or burritos. You can make it as hot as you wish.

2 tomatoes, peeled, seeded, and diced
1 small red onion, finely chopped
1 or 2 jalapeño peppers, minced, seeds removed
½ cup coarsely chopped cilantro
Juice of 1 or 2 limes
Salt and freshly ground pepper to taste

In a bowl, gently mix together all the ingredients. For the freshest taste, serve within 20 minutes.

Note: If you like a really hot salsa, leave the seeds in the jalapeño peppers. Otherwise, remove them.

Per serving:

Calories	20
Total fat	.2 g
Saturated fat	0
Cholesterol	0
Sodium	6.2 mg

Berber Sauce (For Grilled Meat, Poultry, or Fish)

About 7/8 cup

Umm, luscious is this unusual spicy barbecue sauce or marinade that originated with the Berbers, a nomad people in North Africa. The roasted spices promise to help clear out your sinuses and help bring your lungs up to peak performance. It is wonderful on center-cut lamb chops or lamb tenderloin or lean steak, and I have also used it on grilled swordfish with great success.

1 small onion, finely chopped
1 clove garlic, minced
1 jalapeño pepper or other hot chili, minced
1-inch piece of fresh gingerroot, minced
2 teaspoons cracked black peppercorns
1 teaspoon coriander seeds
1 teaspoon cardamom grains
1/8 teaspoon ground cinnamon
1/8 teaspoon ground allspice
1 clove
1 1/2 teaspoons salt or to taste
1/3 cup paprika
1/2 cup olive oil
Juice of 1 lemon

Place the onions, garlic, jalapeño pepper, ginger, and all spices in a dry skillet and cook over medium heat for 1 to 2 minutes or until the spices are fragrant and lightly toasted.

Combine the roasted spices and seasonings with the olive oil and lemon juice in a blender or food processor fitted with the steel blade and blend to a smooth paste.

Spread the paste on meat, poultry, or seafood. Let it marinate in the refrigerator for 6 to 8 hours for meat, 2 to 3 hours for poultry, and 1 hour for seafood. Grill, broil, or bake the marinated food.

Per tablespoon:

Calories	80
Total fat	8 g
Saturated fat	1 g
Cholesterol	0
Sodium	237 mg

COOK'S ADVICE

Generally, the smaller the pepper, the hotter. The fieriest parts are the veins and seeds. To reduce the heat, remove the veins and seeds. When handling hot chili peppers, wear protective plastic or rubber gloves. And don't touch your eyes or face after handling chilies with bare hands; the residue can last for several hours and sting.

Quick Marinara Sauce (For Pasta or Pizza)

Serves 8

When juicy fresh summer tomatoes are not available, or when you just don't have time to bother, you can still get loads of health protection in tomatoes by cooking up this Italian tomato sauce in a jiffy.

1 medium white onion, finely chopped
1 garlic clove, minced
2 tablespoons olive oil
1 28-ounce can Italian-style crushed tomatoes
1 tablespoon minced parsley
1 tablespoon minced fresh basil *or* 1/4 teaspoon dried
Salt and freshly ground pepper to taste

In a large saucepan, sauté the onion and garlic in the oil until translucent and soft. Add the tomatoes, herbs, salt, and pepper. Cover partially and simmer, for 30 minutes.

Note: If the sauce becomes too thick, add 1/4 to 1/2 cup boiling water.

Per serving:

Calories	54
Total fat	3.6 g
Saturated fat	.5 g
Cholesterol	0
Sodium	162 mg

Yogurt Dressings

Yogurt is an excellent substitute for sour cream, oils, and mayonnaise in salad dressings and at only a fraction of the fat and calories. Additionally, yogurt contains natural antibiotics that help fight infections. Here are some ways to make yogurt dressings interesting.

MANGO-YOGURT SALAD DRESSING

About 3/4 cup

1/2 cup peeled and chopped mango
1 1/2 tablespoons reduced-calorie mayonnaise
1/4 cup vanilla nonfat yogurt

Place all the ingredients in a blender and puree.

Per 1-tablespoon serving:

Calories	13
Total fat	.5 g
Saturated fat	.1 g
Cholesterol	.7 mg
Sodium	14 mg

ORANGE-YOGURT SALAD DRESSING

2/3 cup

1/2 cup plain nonfat yogurt
1/4 teaspoon vanilla extract
1 teaspoon honey
2 tablespoons frozen orange juice concentrate

Place all ingredients in a small bowl and stir until combined.

Per 1-tablespoon serving:

Calories	14
Total fat	0
Saturated fat	0
Cholesterol	.2 mg
Sodium	9 mg

MUSTARD-YOGURT SAUCE

½ cup

½ cup plain low-fat yogurt
1 teaspoon Dijon mustard
Salt and freshly ground pepper to taste

Combine all the ingredients and chill until ready to use.

Per 1-tablespoon serving:

Calories	10
Total fat	.3 g
Saturated fat	.1 g
Cholesterol	.8 mg
Sodium	29 mg

MOCK SOUR CREAM

2 cups

1 cup low-fat cottage cheese
1 cup plain nonfat or low-fat yogurt
2 teaspoons cider vinegar

Place all the ingredients in a blender and process on high until the mixture is smooth and thick. Refrigerate.

Per 1-tablespoon serving:

Calories	9
Total fat	.1 g
Saturated fat	0
Cholesterol	.4 mg
Sodium	34 mg

Dipping Sauces

Here are some sauces for dipping seafood or cooked meats.

HORSERADISH SAUCE

3/4 cup

1/2 cup plain low-fat yogurt
1 tablespoon Dijon mustard
1 to 2 tablespoons prepared horseradish
1 tablespoon fresh lemon or orange juice
Salt and freshly ground pepper to taste

Combine all the ingredients in a bowl and whisk to blend.

Per 1-tablespoon serving:

Calories	8
Total fat	.2 g
Saturated fat	.1 g
Cholesterol	.6 mg
Sodium	46 mg

CHILI SAUCE

1/2 cup

1/2 cup plain low-fat yogurt
2 to 3 teaspoons chili powder
1 pickled jalapeño pepper, minced
Salt and freshly ground pepper to taste

Combine the ingredients in a bowl and whisk until smooth.

Per 1-tablespoon serving:

Calories	12
Total fat	.4 g
Saturated fat	.1 g
Cholesterol	.8 mg
Sodium	45 mg

GINGER SAUCE

3/4 cup

2 tablespoons minced fresh gingerroot
2 garlic cloves, minced
2 scallions, minced
1 serrano or other hot chili, minced
3 tablespoons reduced-sodium soy sauce
3 tablespoons water or chicken stock
2 tablespoons rice wine or mirin (sweet rice wine)
1 tablespoon dark sesame oil
1 teaspoon sugar or maple syrup

Combine the ingredients in a bowl and whisk to mix.

Per 1-tablespoon serving:

Calories	20
Total fat	1 g
Saturated fat	.2 g
Cholesterol	0
Sodium	150 mg

Recipe Credits

Appetizers

Quick Mexican Bean Dip: Jean Carper
Guacamole: Jean Carper
Tzatziki: Mary Koromvokis and Lee Koromvokis
Chick-Pea Dip (Hummus): adapted from a recipe by Howard Solganik
Rena's Syrian Baba Ghanouj: Rena Dweck
Radicchio with Garlic: Jean Carper
Bruschetta: Kathleen Drew
I Matti's Beans and Onions: I Matti Restaurant, Washington, D.C., Roberto Donna, owner
Dr. David's Caponata (Eggplant Appetizer): Dr. David Rall
Gazpacho Vegetable Pâté: reprinted from *Enjoy! Make-Ahead Dinner Party Menus* by Nina Graybill and Maxine Rapoport, Farragut Publishing Company, Washington, D.C.
Yogurt-Roquefort-Walnut Dip: Jean Carper
Yogurt Cheese and Lox: Jean Carper
Herbed Yogurt Cheese: Jean Carper
Steamed Clams Portuguese: Steven Raichlen
Cucumber Rounds with Anchovy Topping: Steven Raichlen
Mackerel Salad Spread: adapted from a recipe by Howard Solganik
Molly's Chopped Herring: Molly Schuchat
Salmon Pâté: adapted from *Beyond Pritikin* by Ann Louise Gittleman, Bantam Books, New York
Oriental Tuna-Stuffed Mushrooms: adapted from a recipe by Howard Solganik
Sardine-Avocado Sandwich: Lynn Fischer

Soups

Easy Pumpkin Applesauce Soup: adapted from *Cold Soups* by Maxine Rapoport and Nina Graybill, Farragut Publishing Company, Washington, D.C.

Spiced Carrot Soup: Adapted from a recipe provided by Gravetye Manor Restaurant, London

Curried Broccoli Soup: Jean Carper

Potato and Kale Soup: Steven Raichlen

Minted Pea Soup: Jean Carper

Tomato Basil Soup: adapted from a recipe by Howard Solganik

My Favorite Lentil Soup: Jean Carper

Mariana's Salmon Corn Soup: Mariana Gosnell

Oyster Chowder: Steven Raichlen

Seafood Minestrone: reprinted from *The Gourmet Gazelle Cookbook* by Ellen Brown, Bantam Books, New York

Dr. Ziment's Garlic Chicken Soup for Colds and Coughs: Dr. Irwin Ziment, adapted from *The Food Pharmacy* by Jean Carper, Bantam Books, New York

Dr. Weil's Miso Soup: reprinted from *Natural Health, Natural Medicine* by Andrew Weil, M.D., Houghton-Mifflin Company, New York

Chicken or Turkey Broth: Patricia Krause, adapted from *The Revolutionary Seven-Unit Low Fat Diet* by Audrey Eyton and Jean Carper, Bantam Books, New York

Vegetable Broth: Patricia Krause, adapted from *The Revolutionary Seven-Unit Low Fat Diet* by Audrey Eyton and Jean Carper, Bantam Books, New York

Lottie's Grapefruit-Vegetable Gazpacho: reprinted from *Cold Soups* by Nina Graybill and Maxine Rapoport, Farragut Publishing Company, Washington, D.C.

Grape Gazpacho (Ajo Branco): Steven Raichlen

Avocado Ceviche: adapted from a recipe by Pascal Vignau, executive chef, Four Seasons Hotel, Beverly Hills, California

Peachy Ginger Soup: adapted from a recipe by Howard Solganik

Chilled Cantaloupe Soup: adapted from *Cold Soups* by Nina Graybill and Maxine Rapoport, Farragut Publishing Company, Washington, D.C.

Cranberry Soup: Patricia Krause, adapted from *The Revolutionary Seven-*

Unit Low Fat Diet by Audrey Eyton and Jean Carper, Bantam Books, New York

Salads, Relishes, and Chutneys

Cabbage-Pepper Coleslaw: Jean Carper
Apple Coleslaw with Peanuts: Jean Carper
Dr. Duke's Anticancer Slaw: Dr. James Duke and Sara Benum, adapted from *Medical Nutrition*, Summer 1990
Turnip Slaw with Banana Dressing: Patricia Krause, adapted from *The Revolutionary Seven-Unit Low Fat Diet* by Audrey Eyton and Jean Carper, Bantam Books, New York
Carrots with Pineapple, Raisins, and Walnuts: Jean Carper
Carrots with a Touch of Cumin: Jean Carper
Minted Carrots with Lime Juice: Jean Carper
Tomatoes and Onions with Fresh Basil: Jean Carper
Red and Yellow Onion Rings: Jean Carper
Peach, Onion, and Bell Pepper Salsa: Carol Mason
Cantaloupe and Pear Salsa: Carol Mason
Tomato-Onion Salsa: Carol Mason
Confetti Jicama Salsa: Carol Mason
Onion-Rhubarb Salsa: Carol Mason
Chopped Broccoli-Pepper Salad: Maxine Rapoport
Broccoli-Cauliflower Garlic Salad: Jean Carper
Lynn's Caesar Salad: Lynn Fischer
Spinach with Strawberries and Honey Dressing: Jean Carper
Bitter Greens Salad with Tangy Avocado Dressing: Jean Carper
Greens with Apples and Blue Cheese Dressing: Jean Carper
Hashed Brussels Sprouts with Dates: Maxine Rapoport
Dilled Potato Salad: adapted from *Hearty Salads* by Nina Graybill and Maxine Rapoport, Farragut Publishing Company, Washington, D.C.
Black Bean Salad with Feta Cheese and Mint: Steven Raichlen
Three-Bean Salad with Poppy Seed Dressing: Jean Carper
Waldorf Salad with Sardines: Jean Carper
Herring Salad with Potatoes and Beets: Joan Nathan
Orange-Sangria Salad: adapted from a recipe by Elaine Hailgarten, *London Daily Mail*
Mango, Banana, and Blueberry Salad: Jean Carper

Joanna's Cranberry Fantasy: Joanna Simon
Spicy Indian-Style Fruit Salad: adapted from a recipe by Howard Solganik
Banana Raita: Jean Carper
Mint Raita: Carol Mason
Green Pepper and Watercress Raita: Carol Mason

Vegetables and Legumes

Whole Roasted Garlic: adapted from a recipe by Howard Solganik
Italian Baked Onions: adapted from a recipe by Howard Solganik
Carrot Puree: Maxine Rapoport
Honey-Lemon Carrots and Apples: Maxine Rapoport, adapted from a recipe by Phyllis Richman
Squash Puree with Apricot: adapted from a recipe by Howard Solganik
Spinach with Soy and Sesame Seeds: Jean Carper
New Southern-Style Collard Greens: Steven Raichlen
Stir-Fried Kale: Steven Raichlen
Mustard Greens: Jean Carper
Gingered Green Beans: Carol Mason
Sweet and Sour Cabbage: Jean Carper
Cabbage and Beans with Ham: adapted from a recipe by Carol Mason
Mapled Brussels Sprouts: Jane Stevens
Spicy Curried Cauliflower: Jean Carper
Roasted Potatoes with Garlic and Rosemary: Jean Carper
Phyllis Richman's Garlic-Stuffed Potatoes: Phyllis Richman
Genevieve's Italian Potatoes and Peppers: Genevieve Trezza Hill
Shepherd's Pie with Curried Eggplant: Jean Carper
Sweet Potatoes Amandine: Jean Carper
Slow-Baked Plantains: Jean Carper
Scalloped Corn with Peppers: Jean Carper
Turnips with Nutmeg: Joan Claybrook
Mexican "Refried" Beans: Patricia Krause, adapted from *The Revolutionary Seven-Unit Low Fat Diet* by Audrey Eyton and Jean Carper, Bantam Books, New York
Microwave Bean Burritos: Jean Carper
Boston Baked Soybeans: Maxine Rapoport
Dr. Jenkins's Greek Bean Stew: Dr. David Jenkins and Alexandra Jenkins
David Taylor's Hoppin' John: David Taylor

Lima Beans with Apple and Cinnamon: Jean Carper
L & N's Bean Casserole: Lisa Berger and Nina Graybill
Cuban Black Beans and Rice: adapted from *The Brilliant Bean* by Sally and Martin Stone, Bantam Books, New York
Spicy Tofu Stir-Fry with Vegetables: Steven Raichlen

Pizza, Pasta, and Grains

Pissaladière (Onion Pizza): reprinted from *Mediterranean Light* by Martha Rose Shulman, Bantam Books, New York
Pasta Salad with Tuna and Grapes: U.S. Department of Agriculture
Vegetable Confetti Pasta Salad: reprinted from *The Pasta Salad Book* by Nina Graybill and Maxine Rapoport, Farragut Publishing Company, Washington, D.C.
Spaghetti with Broccoli, Pine Nuts, and Parmesan: reprinted from *Mediterranean Light* by Martha Rose Shulman, Bantam Books, New York
Pasta with Asparagus and Salmon: Jean Carper
Pasta with Tuna-Tomato Sauce: Patricia Krause, adapted from *The Revolutionary Seven-Unit Low Fat Diet* by Audrey Eyton and Jean Carper, Bantam Books, New York
Linguine with Clams and Black Pepper: Kenneth Juran, executive chef, Park Hyatt Hotel, Washington, D.C.
Rotelle with Judy's Fresh Tomato Sauce: Judy Carper
Jean's Marco Polo Pasta: Jean Carper
Tabbouleh: Jean Carper
Bulgur with Chick-Peas: Jean Carper
Nutty Brown Rice: adapted from a recipe by Howard Solganik
Curried Apricot Rice: adapted from a recipe by Howard Solganik
Greek Rice with Artichokes: adapted from a recipe by Mary Koromvokis
Bulgur Pilaf with Fruit and Nuts: Jean Carper
Shiitake Mushroom Sage Stuffing: Jean Carper

Seafood, Poultry, and Meat Main Dishes

Grilled Salmon with Fruit Salsa: Carol Mason
Peppered Tuna Steaks: Jean Carper
Three-Fish Teryaki: Jean Carper

Swordfish with Grapefruit and Brazil Nuts: Jean Carper
Mackerel with Sage: Jean Carper
Mackerel with Garlic and Herbs: Jean Carper
Mackerel with Cumin: Jean Carper
Baked Bluefish with Herbs: Jean Carper
Shark Steaks with Orange: U.S. Department of Commerce
Cajun Cod: reprinted from *Beyond Pritikin* by Ann Louise Gittleman, Bantam Books, New York
Halibut with Tarragon and Sesame Seeds: U.S. Department of Commerce
Microwave Dilled Flounder: Jean Carper
Flounder Stuffed with Vegetables: adapted from a recipe by Howard Solganik
Rainbow Trout with Orange-Rice Stuffing: Jean Carper
Sweet and Sour Fish Curry: adapted from a recipe by Carol Mason
Judy's Old-Fashioned Salmon Loaf: Judy Stevens
Basque Tuna Stew: Jean Carper
Caribbean-Style Mackerel by George: George Jacobs
Garlic Smoked Mussels with Tomatoes: Chef Frank Terranova for the National Fisheries Association
Stir-Fried Scallops with Walnuts and Snow Peas: Jean Carper
Chef Kenneth's Crab Cakes: Kenneth Juran, executive chef, Park Hyatt Hotel, Washington, D.C.
Seafood Chili with Red Beans: Kenneth Juran, executive chef, Park Hyatt Hotel, Washington, D.C.
Puerto Rican Sardine Pie: Phyllis Richman
Carol Mason's White Chili: Carol Mason
Ellen Brown's Jambalaya: reprinted from *The Gourmet Gazelle Cookbook* by Ellen Brown, Bantam Books, New York
Navajo Stew with Sweet Potatoes and Black Beans: Jean Carper
Barbecued Turkey with Garlic-Chili Sauce: Chuck Dell'Ario for the Gilroy Garlic Festival
Barley-Turkey Skillet Dinner: Dr. Rosemary Newman
Chinese Pepper Steak: Steven Raichlen
Pork and Apple Stir-Fry: Maxine Rapoport, adapted from a recipe by the International Apple Institute
Oriental Hot Pot: Steven Raichlen
Moroccan Lamb Stew with Fruit: adapted from *Enjoy!* by Nina Graybill and Maxine Rapoport, Farragut Publishing Company, Washington, D.C.

Desserts

Date-Wrapped Nuts: Jean Carper
Strawberries with a Meringue Cloud: Carol Mason
Ginger Baked Apples with Vanilla Topping: Jean Carper
Summer Berry Pudding: Kenneth Juran, executive chef, Park Hyatt Hotel, Washington, D.C.
Coffee Crème Caramel: Steven Raichlen
Barley Cream Pudding: reprinted from *New Ways with Barley* by Dr. Rosemary Newman, Montana State University
Joan's Banana Bread Pudding: Joan Hickson
Lemony Garbanzo Bean Cake: reprinted from *The Brilliant Bean* by Sally and Martin Stone, Bantam Books, New York
Joan's Egg White Chocolate Cake: Carol Mason
Ginger Snaps: Louisiana State University
Frozen Peach Yogurt: Jean Carper
Jill's Favorite Pumpkin Frozen Yogurt: Jill Hickson
Lemon Mousse: Jean Carper
Phyllis's Strawberry Sherbet: Phyllis Bonanno

Breads, Muffins, Biscuits, and Crackers

Squash Bread: Maxine Rapoport
Corn Bread: Jean Carper
Banana-Ginger Muffins: Patricia Krause, adapted from *The Revolutionary Seven-Unit Low Fat Diet* by Audrey Eyton and Jean Carper, Bantam Books, New York
Barbara Bush's Bran Muffins: Phyllis Richman
Three-Grain Super-Fiber Muffins: Dr. Rosemary Newman
Maxine's Apple Bran Muffins: Maxine Rapoport
Dr. Rosenthal's Blues-Fighting Muffins: reprinted from *Seasons of the Mind* by Dr. Norman Rosenthal, Bantam Books, New York
Oatmeal Biscuits: Judy Stevens
Oat Bran–Oatmeal Crackers: Jean Carper
Rice Bran Rolls: Louisiana State University

Beverages

Orange-Banana Frappé: adapted from a recipe by Howard Solganik
Plain Ayran: Jean Carper
Fruit Yogurt Drink: Jean Carper
Melon Citrus Fizz: Maxine Rapoport
Pineapple-Grapefruit Fizz: Maxine Rapoport
Spiced Peach Fizz: Maxine Rapoport
Cranberry-Cherry Fizz: Maxine Rapoport
Cantaloupe-Orange Fizz: Maxine Rapoport
Fruit Slushes: adapted from a recipe by Howard Solganik
Creamy Fruit Cooler: adapted from a recipe by Howard Solganik
Holiday Punch: adapted from a recipe by Howard Solganik

Sauces and Dressings

Fresh Cocktail Sauce: adapted from a recipe by Howard Solganik
Salsa Cruda (Mexican Hot Sauce): Steven Raichlen
Berber Sauce: Steven Raichlen
Quick Marinara Sauce: Judy Carper
Mango-Yogurt Salad Dressing: Jean Carper
Orange-Yogurt Salad Dressing: Jean Carper
Mustard-Yogurt Sauce: Patricia Krause, reprinted from *The Revolutionary Seven-Unit Low Fat Diet* by Audrey Eyton and Jean Carper, Bantam Books, New York
Mock Sour Cream: Patricia Krause, reprinted from *The Revolutionary Seven-Unit Low Fat Diet* by Audrey Eyton and Jean Carper, Bantam Books, New York
Horseradish Sauce: Steven Raichlen
Chili Sauce: Steven Raichlen
Ginger Sauce: Steven Raichlen

Index